The Bare
ESSENTIALS
PLUS

The Bare ESSENTIALS PLUS

Sarah Norton
CENTENNIAL COLLEGE

Brian Green
NIAGARA COLLEGE

HARCOURT
BRACE
CANADA

Harcourt Brace & Company, Canada

Toronto Montreal Fort Worth New York Orlando
Philadelphia San Diego London Sydney Tokyo

Canadian Cataloguing in Publication Data

Norton, Sarah,
    The Bare Essentials Plus

Includes index.

ISBN 0-7747-3554-6

1. English language—Textbooks for second language learners.* 2. English language—Composition and exercises. I. Green, Brian. II. Title.

PE1128.N67 1996   808'.042   C96-9312318

Director of Product Development: Heather McWhinney
Acquisitions Editor: Kelly V. Cochrane
Projects Manager: Liz Radojkovic
Developmental Editor: Su Mei Ku
Director of Publishing Services: Jean Davies
Editorial Manager: Marcel Chiera
Supervising Editor: Semareh Al-Hillal
Production Editor: Louisa Schulz
Production Manager: Sue-Ann Becker
Production Co-ordinator: Sheila Barry
Copy Editor: Dallas Harrison
Cover Design: Sonya Thursby/Opus House
Typesetting and Assembly: MacTrix DTP
Technical Art: MacTrix DTP
Printing and Binding: Webcom Limited

This book was printed in Canada.
1 2 3 4 5   01 00 99 98 97

Preface

The Bare Essentials Plus is designed for Canadian college students who want to learn how to write clearly and correctly. In our increasingly multicultural environment, students and teachers need texts that reflect the requirements of both first- and second-language speakers. While the primary focus of *The Bare Essentials Plus* is on the skill-building needs of all college students, the book also addresses the special needs of second-language learners. We developed this text with three different audiences in mind: postsecondary students in a class comprised of both native speakers and second-language learners, high-functioning students in an ESL writing course, and students enrolled in individualized, self-paced learning programs.

The core of this text is essentially the same as *The Bare Essentials, Form A,* 4th edition, but *The Bare Essentials Plus* features additional instruction and exercises for advanced ESL learners. Unit Six, "Mastering Your New Language," is entirely new. This unit covers verbs, prepositions, articles, and idioms, all of which present problems for most second-language learners. It also includes more technical terms since students who have studied English as a foreign language tend to be more familiar with grammatical terminology than do native speakers. In Units One through Four, we have included new instruction and exercises on points that ESL students tend to find troublesome. Throughout the text, we have marked with a ☀ the material that has been designed primarily for ESL learners; however, we suggest that many native speakers would profit from a review of this material, too. For the convenience of both students and teachers, we have included definitions and illustrations of all grammatical terms used in the book in the "List of Grammatical Terms."

Like its predecessors, *The Bare Essentials Plus* addresses the points of grammar, usage, and mechanics that are indispensable to good writing: organization of ideas, paragraph development, syntax, grammar, spelling, and punctuation. Each "essential" is presented in a discrete unit, and the units may be covered in any order. The chapters within the units, however, should be presented in consecutive order since the exercises in later chapters sometimes include questions designed to reinforce material covered in earlier chapters.

We believe that students can learn to write clear, correct prose if they learn the principles involved, master them by doing appropriate exercises, and apply them in their own writing. We also recognize that instruction and practice alone are not enough. Students have to *want* to learn. We have tried to help motivate them by beginning most chapters within a few words about the practical significance of the material. A brief explanation of the writing principle appears next, followed by illustrative examples. Where the material is complex, we have broken it down into easy-to-follow steps.

Most of each chapter is devoted to exercises, and the student is directed to do as many as necessary to master the principle. We recognize that doing exercises can be mind-numbingly dull, so we have tried to forestall boredom by appealing to the interests of Canadian college students and by incorporating a little humour. Our level of diction is aimed at adult students, who, we believe, should be challenged but not frustrated in their efforts to learn more about the English language. We have tried neither to underestimate our students' abilities nor to condescend. We believe that students learn most and best when they are encouraged to reach a little beyond their grasp.

Several features make *The Bare Essentials Plus* easy to use. Students can do many of the exercises right in the text and can quickly find the answers in the back of the book. The first exercise in each chapter refers the student to the pages on which the answers for that chapter appear. Students are instructed to check their answers after completing each exercise. If they follow this instruction, they get immediate feedback on their grasp of the principle and can, if they need to, review the explanation and examples before moving on to the next exercise. We urge teachers to stress the importance of this instruction. If students ignore it and complete an entire set of exercises before checking their answers, they may reinforce rather than eliminate the error the exercises have been designed to correct. The final exercise in each chapter is a mastery test for which answers are provided in the Instructor's Manual.

On a fold-out page at the back of the book are "The Time Line" and a chart summarizing and illustrating the correct use of English verb tenses. Students can see at a glance what tense is appropriate in a particular context. On the inside front cover is a "Quick Revision Guide" for students to use in revising and editing their work.

Acknowledgments

We thank the teachers across Canada who kept using *The Bare Essentials* in ESL classes even though the book was not intended for that audience. Their persistence prompted us to adapt our original book to the needs of a multicultural student population. Carol Doughty, Sorel Friedman, Kay Lukes, Roberta Morris, Darcy Robb, Ann Rostrup, and Nathalie Sorenson helped confirm the additional support required by college-level ESL students. Clare Warwick created The Time Line and wrote much of the new material on tenses. Geri Dasgupta not only contributed to the text, but also checked and corrected our work. Ruth Colombo and Elizabeth Pearce helped us class-test the new exercises. The criticism and suggestions of our reviewers, Patricia Burke (Humber College), Charlotte Hoffman (Okanagan College), and David Southmayd (Vanier College), helped make this a more useful book.

We hope you and your students will enjoy using *The Bare Essentials Plus*, and we invite your comments, criticisms, and suggestions.

Sarah Norton

Brian Green

Contents

UNIT THREE
Grammar

UNIT FOUR
Punctuation

UNIT FIVE
Organizing Your Writing

UNIT SIX
Mastering Your New Language

Appendixes

Introduction

Why You Need This Book

Who needs to write anyway? If I get a general labour job, I won't ever need to write, and if I'm in management, a secretary will fix all my mistakes.

(college student)

We can train a person on the job to do the specific tasks we require in about two weeks . . . maximum. What we need you people at the colleges to do is teach them to communicate—with other workers, with their supervisors— orally and in memos, reports, and letters.

(president of a steel-fabricating firm
speaking to college faculty)

You look at the people who move up in this industry. They're the ones who can write intelligently and who can read and understand other peoples' writing. Hard work helps, and so does being the owner's nephew . . . but you've got to be able to read and write reasonably well to get a job and keep it these days— and those who can't know it better than anyone. Ask them.

(former employee in the Canadian mining industry)

To an employer, any employee is more valuable if he or she is able to write correctly and clearly. No one can advance very far in a career without the ability to construct understandable sentences. It's that simple. Fairly or unfairly, employers and others will judge your intelligence and ability on the basis of your use of English. If you want to communicate effectively and earn respect, both on and off the job, you need to be able to write well.

That's the bad news. The good news is that *anyone who wants to* can achieve the standards of written English that are acceptable anywhere. All that is needed from you, really, is caring. If you care enough about what others think of you and about career advancement, then you'll put out the effort necessary, whether that means looking up spelling, revising what you've written, or doing all the exercises in this book twice!

How to Use This Book

In each chapter, we do three things: explain a point, illustrate it with examples, and give exercises to help you master it. The exercises are arranged in sets that get more difficult as you go along. By the end of the last set in a chapter, you should have a good grasp of the skill.

Here's how to proceed.

1. Read the explanation. Do this even if you think you understand the point being discussed.
2. Study the examples carefully.
3. Now turn to the exercises. If you've found an explanation easy and feel you have no problems with the skill, try a set near the end of the group of exercises following the explanation. If you get all the sentences right, do one more set. If you get that one all right too, skip the rest and go on to the next point. Skip ahead only if you're really confident, though.

   If you don't feel confident, don't skip anything. Start with the first set and work through all the exercises until you're sure you understand the point.
4. ALWAYS CHECK YOUR ANSWERS TO ONE SET OF EXERCISES BEFORE GOING ON TO THE NEXT. If you ignore this instruction, this book can't help you. Only if you check your accuracy after every set can you avoid repeating your mistakes and possibly reinforcing your error.
5. When you discover a mistake, go back to the explanation and examples and study them again. Make up some examples of your own to illustrate the rule. When you're sure you understand, continue with the exercises.

On the inside of the front cover you'll find the Quick Revision Guide. Use it to check over your papers before handing them in. This book is meant to be a practical tool, not a theoretical reference. Apply the lessons in all the writing you do. Explanations can identify writing problems and show you how to solve them; exercises can give you practice in eliminating errors; but only writing and revising can bring real and lasting improvement.

A Note from the Publisher

Thank you for selecting *The Bare Essentials Plus* by Sarah Norton and Brian Green. The authors and publisher have devoted considerable time and care to the development of this book. We appreciate your recognition of this effort and accomplishment.

We want to hear what you think about *The Bare Essentials Plus*. Please take a few minutes to fill in the stamped reply card at the back of the book. Your comments and suggestions will be valuable to us as we prepare new editions and other books.

Spelling

CHAPTER 1

Three Suggestions for Quick Improvement

Of all the errors you might make in writing, spelling is the one that is noticed by everyone, not just English teachers. No piece of writing that is full of misspellings can be classified as good. Misspellings can cause misunderstanding, as when an English teacher promised his students a course with "a strong *vacational* emphasis." (Those students who weren't misled wondered what he was doing teaching English.)

Misspellings sometimes cause confusion. Take this sentence, for example:

Mouse is a desert with a base of wiped cream.

It takes a few seconds to "translate" the sentence into a definition of *mousse,* a *dessert* made with *whipped* cream.

Most often, though, misspellings are misleading; they spoil the image you want to present. You want, naturally, to be seen as intelligent, careful, and conscientious. But if your writing is riddled with spelling errors, your reader will think you are careless, uneducated, or even stupid. It is not true, by the way, that intelligence and the ability to spell go hand in hand.

It is true, though, that people generally think they do. So, to prevent both confusion and embarrassment, it is essential that you spell correctly.

There are three things you can do to improve your spelling almost instantly:

---

1. Buy and use a good dictionary.

A dictionary is a writer's best friend. You will need it every time you write, so if you don't already own a good dictionary, you need to buy one. A good dictionary is one that is reliable, current, and reasonably comprehensive. A convenient Canadian reference is the *Gage Canadian Dictionary,* which was last revised in 1983. It is the dictionary on which the examples and exercises in this chapter are based. Also recommended for Canadian writers are the *Funk & Wagnalls Canadian College Dictionary* (1986) and, for those whose native language is not English, the *Cobuild English Dictionary* (HarperCollins, 1995).

A good dictionary packs an astonishing amount of information into a small space. Thus, for each entry, you will find some or all of the following:

1. Spelling (if there are two or more acceptable spellings, the most common one is normally given first);
2. Syllables (to show you where hyphens can go, if you need to break a word at the end of a line);
3. Pronunciation (if there is more than one acceptable pronunciation, the most common one is listed first);
4. Grammatical form(s): e.g., noun *(n.),* verb *(v.),* adjective *(adj.);*
5. Any irregular forms of the word, such as the plural form of a noun, or the past tense and past participle of a verb;
6. Usage restrictions: e.g., slang, informal, archaic, offensive;
7. Definition(s) of the word (the most common meanings are given first, followed by the technical or specialized meanings), together with phrases or sentences illustrating how the word is used;
8. Idioms using the word;
9. Origins of the word (etymology);
10. Other helpful information: e.g., homonyms (words that sound the same as the entry word); synonyms (words that are similar in meaning to the entry word); antonyms (words opposite in meaning); and special variations in grammar, spelling, pronunciation, and usage.

Most of your doubts about spelling can be answered if you take the time to check your dictionary. The time you spend looking up words will not be wasted; your rewards will be the increased accuracy of your writing and the increased respect of your reader.

If you wonder how it's possible to look up a word you can't spell, look at the "Guide to the Dictionary," which you'll find in the front of your dictionary. In the Guide are a pronunciation key and a chart showing the common spellings for all the sounds in the English language. If you know how to pronounce a word, the chart will help you find its spelling. Another way to find a word you can't spell is to look up a synonym—a word with a meaning similar to that of the word you want. In the dictionary entry for the synonym, you'll probably find the word you're looking for.

The "Guide to the Dictionary" may not be the most entertaining reading you've ever done, but it will be among the most worthwhile. You will find a diagram of the kinds of information given for each word and an explanation of the abbreviations and symbols used. You will discover, for example, that you don't need to memorize long lists of irregular plurals: your dictionary gives the irregular plural for any word you look up. It also gives the irregular forms of verbs, adjectives, and adverbs. If you've forgotten how regular plurals, verbs, adjectives, and adverbs are formed, the Guide gives you that information, too. And it shows you how to read a dictionary entry so that you can see at a glance how to add various endings to a root word. Take half an hour to read the Guide in your dictionary; then do the following exercises. Be sure to check your answers to each set before you go on to the next. Answers begin on p. 340.

EXERCISE 1.1

1. What is a second way to spell the word *blond?* Are the two spellings interchangeable?
2. What is another spelling of the word *humour?* Which spelling must you use when you add an ending such as *-ous* or *-ist* to the root word?
3. Is *tatoo* spelled correctly? Is the word a noun or a verb?
4. How many correct spellings are there for the word *ketchup?* Which is the preferred spelling in Canada?
5. Find alternate spellings for the words *programme, theatre, centre, mediaeval,* and *judgement.* In each case, indicate the spelling most commonly used in Canada.

EXERCISE 1.2

Write the plural form of each word.

1. echo
2. ratio
3. criterion
4. ghetto
5. personnel
6. crisis
7. data
8. phenomenon
9. nucleus
10. appendix

EXERCISE 1.3

The following words are tricky to spell because they are not pronounced the way you might expect if you've had no previous experience with them. Look them up in your dictionary and, in the space beside each word, write out its pronunciation (the information given immediately after it in parentheses). Using your dictionary's pronunciation key to help you, practise sounding out each word, one syllable at a time. (No answers are given for this exercise.)

1. solder
2. epitome
3. impotent
4. phlegm
5. libido

6. eulogy
7. indict
8. colonel
9. maniacal
10. posthumous

In addition to your dictionary, a spell-check program is a useful tool, if you have access to a word processor. Spell-checkers aren't foolproof, though—as we'll see in the next chapter—so don't count on your computer to solve *all* your spelling problems.

---

2. Ask a good speller.

Some people seem to have been born with the ability to spell. Such people are more reliable than a computer program. Often, they are secretly proud of their talent and pleased to demonstrate it, so don't be afraid to ask. They probably aren't as good at something else as you are; you may have a talent they could use in exchange.

---

3. Learn three basic spelling rules.

English spelling is frustratingly irregular, and no rule holds true in all cases. But there are three simple rules that do hold for most words, and mastering these rules will help you avoid many common errors.

Before learning the three rules, you need to know the difference between **vowels** and **consonants.** The vowels are **a, e, i, o,** and **u** (and sometimes **y**). All the other letters are consonants.

Rule 1: Dropping the Final *e*

The first rule tells you when to drop the final, silent e when adding an ending to a word.

> Drop the final, silent *e* when adding an ending that begins
> with a vowel.
> Keep the final, silent *e* when adding an ending that begins
> with a consonant.

Keeping the rule in mind, look at these examples:

ENDINGS BEGINNING
WITH A VOWEL

-ing: amuse + ing = amusing
-ed: live + ed = lived
-able: like + able = likable
-ible: force + ible = forcible
-er: use + er = user

ENDINGS BEGINNING
WITH A CONSONANT

-ment: amuse + ment = amusement
-ly: live + ly = lively
-ness: like + ness = likeness
-ful: force + ful = forceful
-less: use + less = useless

In the following exercises, add *e* in the blank space wherever it's needed to complete the spelling. If no *e* is needed, leave the space blank.

EXERCISE 1.4

1. bor____ing
2. mov____ment
3. scarc____ly
4. unus____able
5. car____ful

6. advertis____ment
7. excus____able
8. provid____ing
9. sens____ible
10. improv____ment

EXERCISE 1.5

1. saf____ty
2. rang____ing
3. reduc____ible
4. balanc____ing
5. entir____ly

6. insur____ance
7. definit____ly
8. car____less
9. respons____ible
10. distanc____ing

Exceptions to Rule 1

Three common words do not follow the rule.

>   argue + ment = argument
>   nine + th = ninth
>   true + ly = truly

There is one more exception to rule 1: after soft *c* (as in *notice*) and soft *g* (as in *change*), keep the final, silent *e* when adding an ending beginning with *a* or *o*. Here are two examples:

>   notice + able = noticeable
>   outrage + ous = outrageous

Rule 2: Doubling the Final Consonant

The second rule tells you when you need to double the final consonant before adding an ending to a word.

> When adding an ending that begins with a vowel (such as
> *-able, -ing, -ed,* or *-er*), double the final consonant of the
> root word if the word
> 1. ends with a single consonant preceded by a single vowel
>   AND
> 2. is stressed on the last syllable.

Notice that a word must have *both* characteristics for the rule to apply. Let's look at a few examples:

begin + er   ends with a single consonant *(n)* preceded by a single vowel *(i)* and is stressed on the last syllable *(begín)*, so the rule applies, and we double the final consonant: **beginner**

control + ed   ends with a single consonant *(l)* preceded by a single vowel *(o)* and is stressed on the last syllable *(contról)*, so the rule applies: **controlled**

drop + **ing**   ends with a single consonant *(p)* preceded by a single vowel *(o)* and is stressed on the last syllable (there is only one: *dróp*), so the rule applies: **dropping**

appear + **ing**   ends with a single consonant *(r)* preceded by two vowels *(ea)*, so the rule does not apply, and we do not double the final consonant: **appearing**

turn + **ed**   ends with two consonants *(rn)*, so the rule does not apply: **turned**

open + **er**   ends with a single consonant *(n)* preceded by a single vowel *(e)* but is not stressed on the last syllable *(ópen)*, so the rule does not apply: **opener**

In words such as *equip, quit,* and *quiz,* the *u* should be considered part of the *q* and not a vowel. These words then follow the rule: *equipping, quitter,* and *quizzed.*

   Note: There is a group of words ending in *l, t,* or *s,* which, according to our rules, do not need a double consonant before the ending. Some examples are *label, counsel, focus,* and *format.* You will sometimes see this consonant doubled: *labelled, counselled, focussed,* and *formatting.* For these words, it doesn't matter which spelling you choose, but be consistent!

The following exercises require you to combine each word with the ending to form a new word. Check your answers to each set before going on.

EXERCISE 1.6

1. suffer + ing =
2. quiz + ed =
3. permit + ing =
4. strip + ed =
5. meet + ing =

6. compel + ing =
7. crop + ed =
8. tip + ing =
9. allot + ing =
10. quarter + ed =

EXERCISE 1.7

1. overlap + ed =
2. expel + ing =
3. bar + ed =
4. acquit + ed =
5. focus + ing =

6. excel + ing =
7. develop + ed =
8. transfer + ed =
9. parallel + ed =
10. rebel + ing =

EXERCISE 1.8

1. occur + ence =
2. exist + ence =
3. cohere + ence =
4. concur + ing =
5. interfere + ing =

6. subsist + ence =
7. differ + ence =
8. depend + ence =
9. recur + ence =
10. insist + ence =

When it comes to adding *-ence*, three words are especially troublesome. Prefer, refer, and confer all appear to require a doubled final consonant. But they don't, because, when you add *-ence*, the stress shifts to the first syllable of the word. So you write:

prefér	preférring	*but*	préference
refér	reférring	*but*	réference
confér	conférring	*but*	cónference

Rule 3: Words Containing *ie* or *ei*

There are almost a thousand common English words containing *ie* or *ei*, so remembering the rule that governs them is worthwhile. It helps to keep in mind that *ie* occurs approximately twice as often as *ei*.

The old rhyme tells you most of what you need to know to spell these words:

> Write *i* before *e*, except after *c*,
> Or when sounded like *a*, as in *neighbour* and *weigh*.

If you remember this rhyme, you'll have no difficulty in spelling words like *belief, piece, ceiling, receive,* and *freight*.

Unfortunately, the rhyme covers only two of the cases in which we write *e* before *i*: after *c*, and when the syllable is pronounced with a long *ā* sound. So we need an addition to the rule.

> If short *ě* or long *ī* is the sound that is right,
> Write *e* before *i*, as in *their* or in *height*.

This rule covers words such as *Fahrenheit, seismic, heir,* and *leisure* (pronounce it to rhyme with *pleasure*). *Either* and *neither* can be pronounced "eye-ther" and "nye-ther," so they too require *ei.*

There are, of course, exceptions. This silly sentence contains the most common ones:

A *weird species* of *sheik seized caffeine, codeine,* and *protein.*

These exercises will help you master *ie* versus *ei.* Fill in the blanks with *ie* or *ei.* After you finish each set, check your answers.

EXERCISE 1.9

1. I ordered chow m____n and a st____n of beer.

2. N____ther of us knows how to use a G____ger counter.

3. Our n____ghbour has offered to hire our n____ce.

4. Harry wore a b____ge l____sure suit to the graduation party for the Fashion Design students.

5. It is conc____vable that ____ther one could do the job.

EXERCISE 1.10

No answers are given for this exercise.

1. Each w____ner w____ghed 85 g.

2. It is the duty of a pr____st to comfort those who are gr____ving the loss of a fr____nd or relative.

3. That spec____s of ape grows to a h____ght of 2 m.

4. The front____r police s____zed my camera in the bel____f that I had entered a restricted zone.

5. Orin is so conc____ted he thinks he alone should rec____ve credit for conc____ving the idea for our hit song.

There are three or four more spelling rules we could explain here, but we won't—for two reasons. First, there are many exceptions to the remaining rules for English spelling. And second, you don't need to memorize more rules if you use your dictionary.

CHAPTER 2

Sound-Alikes, Look-Alikes, and Spoilers

Using a dictionary, asking a good speller for help, and applying the three spelling rules will make an immediate improvement in your spelling. By following two additional suggestions, you will further increase your spelling accuracy, but the skills involved will take longer to master. First, learn to tell apart words that are often confused because they sound or look alike. Second, learn to spell the words that most people find difficult— words we have called spelling spoilers. Don't try to master all of these words at once. Instead, memorize a few each week, and review them frequently. In two or three months, you could be one of the people poor spellers turn to for help!

Sound-Alikes and Look-Alikes

Some of your spelling troubles are probably caused by your using words that either sound or look like the words you really want. A spell-check cannot help you with these words because, if you're like most people, you don't misspell them. What makes the spelling "wrong" is the sense of the sentence in which you've used them. *Hear, our, meat,* and *have* are correctly spelled, as isolated words. But if you combine them into a "sentence"—

Meat me hear in have an our—you end up with a tangle of misspellings no computer can unravel.

Careful pronunciation sometimes helps to correct this problem. For example, if you pronounce the words *accept* and *except* differently, you'll be less likely to confuse them in your writing. It's also useful to make up memory aids to help yourself remember the difference between words that sound alike but have different meanings.

accept **except**	*Accept* means "t**a**ke." It is always a verb. *Except* means "**ex**cluding." Everyone *except* Mia *accepted* my explanation.
advice **advise**	The difference in pronunciation makes the difference in meaning clear. *Advise* (rhymes with *wise*) is a verb. *Advice* (rhymes with *nice*) is a noun. I *advise* you not to listen to free *advice*.
affect **effect**	*Affect* as a verb means "influence." As a noun, it means "a strong feeling." *Effect* is a noun meaning "result." If you can substitute *result*, then *effect* is the word you need. Occasionally, *effect* is used as a verb meaning "to bring about." Learning about the *effects* of caffeine *affected* my coffee-drinking habits. Depressed people often display inappropriate *affect*. Antidepressant medications can *effect* profound changes in mood.
a lot **allot**	*A lot* (often misspelled *alot*) should be avoided in writing. Use *many* or *much* instead. *Allot* means "distribute" or "assign." *many* *much* He still has ~~a lot of~~ problems, but he's coping ~~a lot~~ better. The teacher will *allot* the marks according to the difficulty of the questions.
are **our**	*Are* is a verb. *Our* shows ownership. Farley Mowat and Alice Munro *are* two of Canada's best-known writers. Canada is *our* home and native land.

choose
chose

Pronunciation gives the clue here. *Choose* rhymes with *booze* and means "select." *Chose* rhymes with *rose* and means "selected."

Please *choose* a topic.
I *chose* film making.

coarse
course

Coarse means "rough, unrefined." (Remember: the word **arse** is co**arse**.) For all other meanings, use *course*.

That sandpaper is too *coarse* to use on a lacquer finish.
You'll enjoy the photography *course*.
Of *course* you'll come with us.

complement
compliment

A *complement* compl**e**tes something. A *compliment* is a gift of praise.

A glass of wine would be the perfect *complement* to the meal.
Some people are embarrassed by *compliments*.

conscience
conscious

Your *conscience* is your sense of right and wrong. *Conscious* means "aware" or "awake"—able to feel and think.

After Ann cheated on the test, her *conscience* bothered her.
Ann was *conscious* of having done wrong.
The injured man was *unconscious*.

consul
council
counsel

A *consul* is a government official stationed in another country. A *council* is an assembly or official group. Members of a *council* are *councillors*. *Counsel* can be used to mean both "advice" and "to advise."

The Canadian *consul* in Venice was very helpful.
The Women's Advisory *Council* meets next month.
Maria gave me good *counsel*.
She *counselled* me to hire a lawyer.

desert
dessert

A *désert* is a dry, barren place. As a verb, *desért* means "leave behind." *Dessért* is the part of a meal you'd probably like two helpings of, so give it two *s*'s.

The tundra is Canada's only *desert* region.
As soon as our backs were turned, our lookout *deserted* his post.
Jell-O is the children's favourite *dessert*.

dining
dinning

You'll spell *dining* correctly if you remember the phrase "wining and dining." You'll probably never use *dinning*. It means "making a loud noise."

> The dog is not supposed to be in the *dining* room.
> We are *dining* out tonight.
> The sounds from the karaoke bar were *dinning* in my ears.

does
dose

Pronunciation provides the clue. *Does* rhymes with *buzz* and is a verb. *Dose* rhymes with *gross* and refers to a quantity of medicine.

> Josef *does* drive fast, *doesn't* he?
> My grandmother used to give me a *dose* of cod liver oil every spring.

forth
fourth

Forth means "**for**ward." *Fourth* contains the number **four,** which gives it its meaning.

> Please stop pacing back and *forth*.
> The Raptors lost their *fourth* game in a row.

hear
here

Hear is what you do with your **ear**s. *Here* is used for all other meanings.

> Now *hear* this!
> Ranjan isn't *here*.
> *Here* is your assignment.

it's
its

It's is a shortened form of *it is*. The apostrophe takes the place of the *i* in *is*. If you can substitute *it is*, then *it's* is the form you need. If you can't substitute *it is*, then *its* is the correct word.

> *It's* really not difficult. (*It is* really not difficult.)
> The book has lost *its* cover. ("The book has lost *it is* cover" makes no sense, so you need *its*.)

It's is also commonly used as the shortened form of *it has*. In this case, the apostrophe takes the place of the *h* and the *a*.

> *It's* been a bad month for software sales.

later
latter

Later refers to time and has the word **late** in it. *Latter* means "the second of two" and has two t's. It is the opposite of *former*.

> It is *later* than you think.
> You take the former, and I'll take the *latter*.

led
lead

The word **lead** is pronounced "led" only when it refers to the heavy, soft, grey metal used in items such as lead bullets or leaded windows. Otherwise, *lead* is pronounced to rhyme with "speed" and is used as the present tense of the verb *to lead*. (*Led* is the past tense of the same verb.)

> When I asked her to *lead* me to the person in charge, she *led* me to the secretary.
> Your suitcase is so heavy it must be filled with either gold or *lead*.

loose
lose

Pronunciation is the key to these words. *Loose* rhymes with *goose* and means "not tight." *Lose* rhymes with *ooze* and means "misplace" or "be defeated."

> A *loose* electrical connection is dangerous.
> Some are born to win, some to *lose*.

miner
minor

A **min**er works in a **mine**. *Minor* means "lesser" or "not important." For example, a *minor* is a person of less than legal age.

> Liquor can be served to *miners*, but not if they are *minors*.
> For some people, spelling is a *minor* problem.

moral
morale

Again, pronunciation provides the clue you need. *Mo'ral* refers to the understanding of what is right and wrong. *Mora'le* refers to the spirit or mental condition of a person or group.

> Parents are responsible for teaching their children *moral* behaviour.
> The low *morale* of our employees is the reason for their high absenteeism.

peace
piece

Peace is what we want on **ea**rth. *Piece* means a part or portion of something, as in "a **pie**ce of **pie**."

> Everyone hopes for *peace* in the Middle East.
> A *piece* of the puzzle is missing.

personal
personnel

Personal means "priv**a**te." *Personnel* refers to the group of people working for a particular employer or to the office responsible for maintaining employees' records.

> The letter was marked "*Personal* and Confidential."
> We are fortunate in having highly qualified *personnel*.
> Yasmin works in the *Personnel* Office.

principal **principle**	*Principal* means "m**a**in." A princi**ple** is a ru**le.** A *principal* is the main administrator of a school. The federal government is Summerside's *principal* employer. The *principal* and the interest totalled more than I could pay. (In this case, the principal is the main amount of money.) One of our instructor's *principles* is to refuse to accept late assignments.
quiet **quite**	If you pronounce these words carefully, you won't confuse them. *Quiet* has two syllables; *quite* has only one. The chairperson asked us to be *quiet*. We had not *quite* finished our assignment.
stationary **stationery**	*Stationary* means "fixed in pl**a**ce." *Stationery* is writing pap**er.** Did you want a laptop or *stationary* computer? Please order a new supply of *stationery*.
than **then**	*Than* is used in comp**a**risons. Pronounce it to rhyme with *can*. *Then* refers to time and rhymes with *when*. Karim is a better speller *than* I. He made his decision *then*. Tanya withdrew from the competition; *then* she realized the consequences.
their **there** **they're**	*Their* indicates ownership. **There** points out something or indicates place. It includes the word **here,** which also indicates place. *They're* is a shortened form of *they are*. (The apostrophe replaces the *a* in *are*.) It was *their* fault. *There* are two weeks left in the term. Let's walk over *there*. *They're* late, as usual.
too **two** **to**	The *too* with an extra *o* in it means "more than enough" or "also." *Two* is the number after one. For all other meanings, use *to*. She thinks she's been working *too* hard. He thinks so, *too*. There are *two* sides *to* every argument. The *two* women knew *too* much about each other *to* be friends.

were
where
we're

If you pronounce these three carefully, you won't confuse them. *Were* rhymes with *fur* and is a verb. *Where* is pronounced "hwear," includes the word **here**, and indicates place. *We're* is a shortened form of *we are* and is pronounced "weer."

> You *were* joking, *weren't* you?
> *Where* did you want to meet?
> *We're* on our way.

who's
whose

Who's is a shortened form of *who is* or *who has*. If you can substitute *who is* or *who has* for the *who's* in your sentence, then you are using the right spelling. Otherwise, use *whose*.

> *Who's* coming to dinner? (*Who is* coming to dinner?)
> *Who's* been sleeping in my bed? (*Who has* been sleeping in my bed?)
> *Whose* paper is this? ("*Who is* paper" makes no sense, so you need *whose*.)

woman
women

Confusing these two is guaranteed to irritate your women readers. *Woman* is the singular form; compare **man**. *Women* is the plural form; compare **men**.

> One *woman* responded to our ad.
> The affirmative action policy promotes equality between *women* and men.

you're
your

You're is a shortened form of *you are*. If you can substitute *you are* for the *you're* in your sentence, then you're using the correct form. If you can't substitute *you are*, use *your*.

> *You're* welcome. (*You are* welcome.)
> Unfortunately, *your* hamburger got burned. ("*You are* hamburger" makes no sense, so *your* is the word you want.)

In the exercises that follow, choose the correct word in each pair. If you don't know an answer, go back and reread the explanation. Check your answers after each set. Answers begin on p. 341.

EXERCISE 2.1

1. (Its It's) no longer unusual for (woman women) to be elected to public office.
2. The thieves came back (later latter) and took everything (accept except) my roller blades.

3. Let (their there they're) be (peace piece) in (are our) time.
4. Edmund Burke believed that manners are more important (than then) (morales morals).
5. (Were We're Where) do you think (were we're where) going to get the money for a vacation in Cabo San Lucas?
6. I (hear here) (your you're) sorry you (choose chose) this (coarse course).
7. Aline Chrétien is one person (whose who's) (advice advise) Jean takes seriously.
8. Following your (advice advise), I applied to the bank for a (personal personnel) loan, and (its it's) costing me a bundle.
9. I suggest that (their there they're) behaviour can hardly be described as (moral morale).
10. The deficit and unemployment are Canada's (principal principle) concerns; world (peace piece) is considered almost a (miner minor) problem in comparison.

EXERCISE 2.2

1. Do you think most Canadians (are our) (conscience conscious) of their national identity?
2. One's ability to learn is (affected effected) by one's (personal personnel) well-being.
3. I made the turn, (than then) saw the sign: "No left turn; buses (accepted excepted)."
4. If you let your dog run (loose lose), you must (accept except) the consequences.
5. Surely (its it's) a question of (principal principle).
6. Some (miners minors) have little difficulty convincing a bartender that (their there they're) of age, especially if (their there they're) using someone else's ID.
7. Last summer, Alla (choose chose) to work in the (dining dinning) room of the Banff Springs Hotel.
8. I'd rather write an essay (than then) do an oral report in front of (are our) class.
9. Sea salt is (to too two) (coarse course) (to too two) pass through the holes of a saltshaker.
10. Judging by the noise I (hear here), I'd say (your you're) car needs a tune-up.

EXERCISE 2.3

(Lead Led) by my desire to watch more television (than then) the six or seven hours a day I normally viewed, I decided to subscribe to satellite TV. The (affect effect) of this move was (later latter) to prove detrimental to my health and my wealth. First, I did not know that (their there they're) is a monthly subscription fee in addition to the initial purchase price of almost $1000 for the "unobtrusive pizza-sized (stationary stationery) dish antenna." Second, I was (quiet quite) surprised to find that I was able to get many "pay-per-view" programs in addition to the basic 40 available stations. I was even more surprised to discover how fast I was running up a bill by (choosing chosing) to view these optional programs. To restore my (peace piece) of mind, not to mention my bank balance, I telephoned the satellite service (personal personnel) to request that they limit my monthly spending for pay-per-view programs. Seven hockey games, four basketball games, (to too two) movies, six music specials, and an award ceremony (later latter), my TV screen informed me that I had reached my spending limit. I'm afraid I responded with a few (coarse course) expressions, since I was all set to see a new fine (dining dinning) show on exotic (deserts desserts) featuring papaya as the (principal principle) ingredient. Then my TV screen informed me I could override my limit simply by pressing "star." I did, and went on watching with a clear (conscience conscious) since, after all, I had limited my spending. In addition to (its it's) (affect effect) on my budget, satellite service caused me to (loose lose) what little muscle tone I had left, since the only times I left the couch were to go (forth fourth) to the kitchen for more food. The (moral morale) of my sad story is that (your you're) probably better off with less choice and poorer quality on (your you're) TV than in (your you're) life.

EXERCISE 2.4

Your own writing is the best test of your spelling accuracy. Write ten or more sentences using the sound-alikes and look-alikes that cause you the most difficulty.

Spelling Spoilers

Here is a list of words that are frequently misspelled. Have someone dictate the list to you. Circle the ones you misspell and memorize them, a few at a time. Try to learn ten each week. Review your list often, until you have mastered every word. Making up memory aids for especially troublesome words will help you conquer them. Here are some examples to get you started:

accommodate: It means "make room for," and the word itself makes room for two *c*'s and two *m*'s.

business: Bu*sin*ess is no *sin*.

environment: The word *environment*, like the earth, has ***iron*** in it.
friend: He is a fri***end*** to the ***end***.
grammar: Poor gram***mar*** will ***mar*** your writing.

absence
accommodate
achievement
acknowledge
acquire

across
address
adolescence
among
answer

apparent
argument
beginning
business
careful

category
clothes
committee
conscious
convenience

criticism
definitely
dependent
desperate
development

disappear
disappoint
discipline
dissatisfied
doesn't

eighth
embarrassed
environment
exercise
existence

explanation
extremely

familiar
February
finally

forty
friend

gauge
government
grammar

guarantee
guidance
height
hoping
hypocrisy

immediately
independent
indispensable
laboratory
library

license (or licence)
likely
loneliness
lonely
maintenance

marriage
mentally
necessary
ninety
ninth

occasion
occasionally
omission
opinion
opportunity

paid
parallel
perform
planned

possess

prejudice
privilege
procedure
proceed
professor

psychology
recommend
relevant
repetition
restaurant

rhythm
ridiculous
safety
schedule
secretary

separate
shining
similar
somewhat
speech

studying
succeed
surprise
technique
thorough

tragedy
truly
unnecessary
until
unusual

usually
vacuum
Wednesday
writing
written

EXERCISE 2.5

Make up sentences containing the words you misspelled when the list of spelling spoilers was dictated. Underline the spelling spoiler in each sentence. (If you do this exercise once a week, you will master the list very quickly.)

One final suggestion. Despite all your efforts, you may find that there are a few words you just cannot spell correctly. The solution? Either write them out on the inside cover of your dictionary or, even simpler, don't use them. Look in your dictionary or in a thesaurus to find synonyms (different words with the same or similar meanings), and use those instead. Two thesauruses that are available in inexpensive paperback editions are *Roget's Thesaurus* and Soule's *Dictionary of English Synonyms*.

Choose synonyms with caution. Inexperienced writers sometimes assume that long, obscure words are sure to impress the reader. In fact, the opposite is usually true. Most readers are irritated, if not confused, by unnecessarily "fancy" language. Why write "The children were enthralled by the antics of the prestidigitator" when what you mean is "The children loved the magician's act"?

CHAPTER 3

Capital Letters

Capital letters should be used in a few specific places and nowhere else. Some people seem to have "capitalitis": they put capital letters on words randomly, regardless of whether the words are nouns, verbs, or adjectives. Like "exclamatosis," "capitalitis" is a disease communicated by comic books, which capitalize every word.

Not many people have this problem. If you are in the majority who generally use capitals properly, skip this chapter and go on to something else. If you are puzzled about capital letters, though, or have readers who are puzzled by your use of them, read on.

Capitalize the first letters of words that fit these descriptions:

1. The first word in a sentence or in a direct quotation:
    > Please do not play games on this computer.
    > Our instructor inquired sweetly, "Now, who would like to go first?"

2. The names of specific persons:

Jean Chrétien	Neil Bissoondath

    The names of specific places:

Baffin Island	Robson Street
Saturn	South Africa
Marineland	Climax, Saskatchewan

    The names of specific things:

Pacific Ocean	North American Free Trade Act
Empress Hotel	Red Deer College
Mighty Morphin Power Rangers	Lake Superior

3. The days of the week, the months of the year, and specific holidays (but not the seasons or geographic directions):

Wednesday	June
Thanksgiving	Canada Day
winter	south

4. The titles of specific people (but not the names of their positions), books, films, television shows, newspapers, etc., and school courses (but not subject names, unless they are languages):

> Governor General Romeo LeBlanc (*but* the governor general)
> Bishop Terence Finley (*but* the bishop)
> Mr. Conrad Black, Ms. Barbara Amiel
> *The Bare Essentials; Schindler's List; Roseanne; The Winnipeg Free Press*
> Biology 101 (*but* the biology course)
> French 200; conversational Spanish; the English language; the study of Chinese history

5. The names of specific companies, products, businesses, organizations, and departments:

> Calona Winery   Kleenex, Tide, Kraft Dinner
> Reform Party   Human Resources Department
> Royal Trust   Kiwanis Club

Correct the capitalization in these sentences. Check your answers to each set before continuing. Answers begin on p. 342.

EXERCISE 3.1

1. diana always wanted to be a Princess when she grew up.
2. It amazes me that anyone could think *beavis and butthead* is funny.
3. Beatrix, queen of the netherlands, visited Canada last Winter.
4. The rotary club of Halifax sponsors a scholarship to dalhousie university.
5. Gina tries hard, but she'll never be as good at Data Processing as Ravi.
6. *Black robe* was a Canadian-made film that featured international stars as well as young canadian actors.
7. I should be looking for a sensible Sedan, but I'm tempted by the Sports Models every time I visit the GM, ford, or honda dealer.
8. I wonder how the College gets away with requiring us students to take english and mathematics in addition to our Major subjects.
9. We were late for professor Chan's lecture on Time Management.
10. Stock is running low, so if you need xerox paper or toner, you'd better see Carla in office supplies right away.

EXERCISE 3.2

1. My Mother and Father drive South each Fall to look at the leaves.
2. Ali went with his english class to the Calgary stampede and then to the West edmonton mall.
3. Alain took a greyhound bus to the Coast and then a ferry to Prince Edward island.

4. Her parents thought they were seeing Gina off to University, but in fact she spent the Winter in Mexico.
5. I've always wanted to be a Pope, but, unfortunately, I am not italian, catholic, or male.
6. Luc went to Paris last Summer to study french, art history, and gourmet cooking.
7. Although I am generally fairly Conservative, I consider myself a Liberal on matters such as abortion and gun control.
8. Clement works for bell canada, which has an office on Bayview avenue.
9. After the Baseball and Hockey seasons were cancelled, Sabina became a Basketball fan and now is devoted to the raptors.
10. A letter to the Editor in today's *Globe and mail* says Jean Chrétien's claim to fame is that "he is the only Canadian Prime Minister to have mastered neither of the country's two Official Languages."

EXERCISE 3.3

1. Since you have yet to pass a single Physics or Math course, I suggest you reconsider your decision to be an Engineer.
2. As the official representative of queen Elizabeth, Canada's Governor General opens each new session of Parliament.
3. During the Spring break, Saieed drove down to florida, where he toured walt disney world, the epcot center, and Busch gardens.
4. The Quebec Premier influences not only the policies of his own Province, but also those of the rest of Canada.
5. After Clive missed the meeting, the President told him angrily, "that, Young Man, was what is called a CLM: a career-limiting move."
6. Visitors to Canada are sometimes surprised to find they cannot see the rockies, Niagara falls, Newfoundland, and the arctic Tundra all in one week.
7. We stopped at safeway for the basics: spaghetti, milk, a box of kellogg's cornflakes, and a tube of crest.
8. Canada's immigration act sets out the policies that govern the conditions for entry into the Country by immigrants from all over the World.
9. We went to see Atom Egoyan's film *exotica,* which was playing at the capitol theatre.
10. Among Canada's great waterways, the St. Lawrence river, the Mackenzie river, the Fraser river, and the red river are the most interesting to me because of the role each played in developing our Nation.

EXERCISE 3.4

Correct the capitalization in this paragraph. No answers are provided for this exercise.

Rico went to france last Summer in the hope of tracing his Noble Ancestry. In a small Village just outside Lyons, he discovered an old family Bible containing a record of his family's births and deaths back to the Seventeenth Century. From this bible, he was able to conclude that his Father's ancestors came from Switzerland. Accordingly, he moved on to Geneva, where his fluent french and english were both put to the test in getting access to the information he needed. Finally, he appealed to the Mayor, and a clerk from the Municipal Office came to help him with his quest. It was with the help of this Clerk that Rico finally discovered the Truth: the founder of his family had been hanged in 1177 for stealing sheep. Far from being descended from the Nobility, as he had always assumed, rico was the descendant of a thief!

CHAPTER 4

The Apostrophe

We have chosen to deal with apostrophes as a spelling problem because, unlike other punctuation marks, apostrophes are not used to indicate the relationship between the parts of a sentence. An apostrophe indicates either a relationship between two elements of a single word, in a contraction, or a relationship between one word and the word immediately following it, in a possessive construction.

Apostrophes are often misused, causing readers to be confused or amused. Sometimes you need an apostrophe so that your reader can understand what you mean. For example, there's a world of difference between these two sentences:

> The instructor began the class by calling the students' names.
> The instructor began the class by calling the students names.

In most cases, however, a misused apostrophe just irritates an alert reader:

> Seasons Greetings from the Norton's.
> Give the baby it's soother.
> Fresh-picked apple's for sale.

It isn't difficult to avoid such embarrassing mistakes. Correctly used, the apostrophe indicates either **contraction** or **possession**. Learn the simple rules that govern these two uses, and you'll have no further trouble with apostrophes.[1]

---

[1] Note that we do NOT add an apostrophe to create a plural. See Chapter 29.

Contraction

You'll need to use contractions less often than possessives. Contractions lend a conversational tone to written English, and in most of the writing you do in college or on the job, you will avoid them. However, when you are writing informally, or when you are quoting someone's spoken words, you'll need to know how contractions are formed.

The rule about where to put an apostrophe in a contraction is one of the rare rules to which there are no exceptions. It *always* holds.

When two words are shortened into one, and a letter (or letters) is left out, the apostrophe goes in the place of the missing letter(s).

---

she is →	she's	they have →	they've
we are →	we're	there is →	there's
he had →	he'd	he will →	he'll
you would →	you'd	do not →	don't
it is, it has →	it's	will not →	won't (Note the slight
who is, who has →	who's		spelling variation here)

EXERCISE 4.1

Make these sets of words into contractions. Answers for this chapter begin on p. 343.

1. you are
2. we would
3. they will
4. can not
5. I will

6. did not
7. should not
8. could have
9. who had
10. everybody is

EXERCISE 4.2

Place apostrophes correctly in these words, which are intended to be contractions. Notice that when an apostrophe is missing, the word often means something completely different.

1. cant
2. shed
3. didnt
4. lets
5. shell

6. wouldnt
7. wed
8. theyre
9. wont
10. hell

EXERCISE 4.3

Correct these sentences by placing apostrophes where needed.

1. Well have to postpone the meeting because theyre still not here.
2. If Krystal finds out whats been going on, shell be furious.
3. Its been a long time since weve had a break, hasnt it?
4. Were still about 10 km away from where theyd planned to meet us.
5. Its a tough decision, but somebodys got to make it, or well never get out of here.
6. Hockey is Canada's most popular game, so Im surprised to learn its not our official national sport.
7. Everyones welcome, but if youre all coming, wed better buy another keg.
8. Hes offered to drive all those whore going to the game.
9. Lets first find out whos coming; then well know if weve bought enough to go around.
10. Youll have to wait until hes sure you havent brought along someone whos under age.

Possession

The apostrophe is also used to show ownership or possession. Here's the rule that applies in most cases:

> 1. Add *'s* to the word that indicates the *owner*.
> 2. If the resulting word ends in a double or triple *s*, erase the last one, leaving the apostrophe in place.

person + s = person's	man + s = man's
people + s = people's	men + s = men's
sisters + s = sisters'ș	mother-in-law + s = mother-in-law's
Socrates + s = Socrates'ș	goodness + s = goodness'ș

When you're forming possessives, you must first figure out whether the owner is singular or plural. For example:

the employee's duties (the duties belong to one *employee*)
the employees' duties (the duties belonging to two or more *employees*)

If you remember that possession indicates what belongs to whom, you can figure out where to put the apostrophe by "translating" your sentence, like this:

Incorrect:	The bartender asked Rudolf for his drivers license.
	1. Translation: the license belongs to one *driver*
	2. Add *'s:*
Correct:	The bartender asked Rudolf for his driver's license.

Incorrect:	The college finally met the students demands.
	1. Translation: the demands belonged to—the *student?* or the *students?*
	Here's where you have to decide whether *one* or *more than one* is involved.
	2. Add *s:*
Correct:	The college finally met the student's demands.
	(Only one student was involved.)
Also correct:	The college finally met the students' demands.
	(More than one student was involved.)

Possession does not have to be literal. The owner does not have to be a person or thing. Ideas or concepts can be "owners," too:

a life's work = the work of, or belonging to, a life
at arm's length = at length of, or belonging to, an arm
two cents' worth = the worth of, or belonging to, two cents

There is an alternative to part 2 of the possession rule given in the box at the start of this section. Many writers prefer to keep the final *s* when it represents a sound that is pronounced, as it does in the possessive form of one-syllable words (e.g., boss, class) and of some names (e.g., Harris, Brutus). The following examples illustrate this alternative usage:

boss's temper	Ms. Harris's promotion
class's decision	Brutus's betrayal

You should note that a few words, called **possessive pronouns**, are already possessive in form and so do not take an apostrophe:

you/yours	our/ours
her/hers	their/theirs
his, its	whose

Your decision is *yours* to make, not *his* or *hers.*

Whose turn is it next: *ours* or *theirs?*

Four of these possessive pronouns are often confused with the contractions that sound like them. When you need to decide which spelling to use, separate the contraction into its two root words and try them out in the sentence. If the sentence makes sense, then the contraction is the spelling you need. If not, use the possessive.

POSSESSIVE	CONTRACTION
its	it's = it is *or* it has
their	they're = they are
whose	who's = who is *or* who has
you	you're = you are

You'll understand the difference between these sound-alikes if you study the following examples carefully:

They're going to try their luck at cards. (They are going to try ~~they are~~ their luck.)

You're losing your hair. (You are losing ~~you are~~ your hair.)

It's obvious your car has a hole in its muffler. (It is obvious ~~you are~~ your car has a hole.)

Who's been sleeping in whose bed? (Who has been sleeping in ~~who is~~ whose bed?)

EXERCISE 4.4

Make the following words possessive.

1. woman
2. technicians
3. the Simpsons
4. management
5. workers
6. someone
7. Iguassu Falls
8. memo
9. babies
10. Dennis

In the following exercises, make the words in parentheses possessive.

EXERCISE 4.5

1. (Biff) favourite pastime is spending his (girlfriend) money.
2. (Who) fault is it that the (car) tank is empty?
3. After about one (second) hesitation, I accepted a (week) pay instead of time off.
4. (Bikers) equipment is on special at (Leather Larry).
5. Virtue may be (it) own reward, but I won't refuse (you) offer of cash.

6. Our college aims to meet its (students) social needs as well as (they) academic goals.
7. To (no one) surprise, the (children) scores were higher than ours on every game we tried.
8. The traditional male dominance in medicine and law is disappearing as (women) acceptance into these programs now exceeds (men).
9. The (college) climate survey revealed that most (students) opinion of their program is positive.
10. (The United States) vast wealth makes some Canadians wonder whether it is worth maintaining our (country) independence.

EXERCISE 4.6

1. (Mei-ling) paper got a better grade than (Louis).
2. (Gordie Howe) record may eventually fall, but his (career) achievements will never be surpassed.
3. Alicia gave one (month) notice before leaving her position as (children) wear buyer for (Eaton).
4. After the (union) strike threat, the (owners) solution was to lock out the players for the rest of the season.
5. One of (Toronto) landmarks is (Honest Ed) store at the corner of Bloor and Bathurst.
6. Canadian (authors) works are increasingly recommended by the (Ministry of Education) curriculum planners.
7. (Cassandra) fate was probably more miserable than (anyone), including (Achilles).
8. Our (group) presentation was on (Davies) *Fifth Business*, while (they) was on (Yeats) early poetry.
9. The (survey) results were not surprising: more than half the voters surveyed were unhappy with (they) (MP) performance.
10. (Dorothy Parker) solution to boredom was to hang a sign on her office door reading ("Men) Room."

EXERCISE 4.7

Correct these sentences by placing apostrophes where they are needed in contractions and possessives.

1. Todays popular music is returning to the sounds and themes of its roots in the sixties.
2. Our government is not serious about solving its financial problems; in fact, its getting deeper and deeper into debt.
3. Charles feelings about Dianas book are well-known, but who knows what Camillas thoughts are?

4. A patients fears can be eased by a sensitive nurses attention.
5. The girls won the cheaters money in Luisas fathers poker game.
6. The speakers topic was well beyond our classes ability to understand.
7. We were told to read Northrop Fryes essay, "Dont You Think Its Time to Start Thinking?" for tomorrows class.
8. In the paper today, theres a short article entitled, "Its Clear the Apostrophes Days are Numbered, Isnt It?"
9. At her wits end, the angry mother turned to her daughter and shouted, "Whore you to tell me what youll do and wont do?"
10. The Crash Test Dummies first major hit was the off-beat "Supermans Song"; in contrast, their award-winning *God Shuffled His Feet* features Brad Roberts songs, which are rich in symbolism and insight.

EXERCISE 4.8

This exercise will test your ability to use apostrophes correctly, both in contractions and in possessive constructions. Correct the errors in the following sentences. No answers are provided for this exercise.

1. Jodies roommates gerbil got loose last night and, after getting into Jodies stash of candy, it made a disgusting mess on her roommates essay.
2. The gerbils health was not permanently damaged by its chocolate feast, but it's appetite for healthy foods has been replaced by a passion for Reeses Pieces.
3. Ruths three-week visit with the Seths was great fun both for her and for the Seths daughter, Indira, who's social life was almost nonexistent before Ruth took her out to meet people who's interests they shared.
4. The casseroles pungent aroma comes from its forty cloves of garlic, but the taste of the dish is quite mild because the garlics strong flavour is moderated by its long, slow cooking in bouillon and wine.
5. Italys tourist appeal results partly from the countrys wonderful people, and partly from the local regions unforgettable foods and wines.
6. Im delighted to be able to tell you that the rumours about the Italians hair-raising driving habits are just that: rumours'. In fact, nowhere in Europe did I encounter drivers who's courtesy and kindness exceeded the Italians.
7. Leonard Cohens latest CD is, in the critics opinion, his best in years because its a combination of his greatest early songs, in updated versions, and some of his latest music.
8. Some members of the teachers union are concerned about our colleges interest in distance education and self-directed learning because they fear these methods of course delivery will reduce the number of faculty needed by the schools programs.

9. Krystals brother is thinking of touring with a friends band as soon as the school years over. The money wont be very good, but theres a chance that the tours outcome might be a recording session at a major labels studio.

10. Our departments computer graphics students combined Kevins chin with Keanus lips, Brads eyes, Robs nose, Toms ears, Arnolds forehead, and Seans hair to make a portrait of the ideal mans face. Id be happy with the bits they threw away.

Sentence Structure

CHAPTER 5

Cracking the Sentence Code

There is nothing really mysterious or difficult about sentences. You've been speaking them successfully since you were two. The difficulty arises when you go to write—not sentences, oddly enough, but paragraphs. Almost all college students, if asked to write ten sentences on ten different topics, could do so without an error. But if those same students were to write paragraphs, then fragments, run-ons, and other sentence faults would creep in. These errors confuse and annoy readers.

The solution to fragment and run-on problems has two parts:

Be sure every sentence you write
1. sounds right
AND
2. has a subject and a verb.

Your ear is the best instrument with which to test your sentences. If you read your sentences aloud, you'll probably be able to tell by the sound whether they are complete, clear, and satisfactory. A complete sentence is one that makes sense by itself.

Read these sentences aloud:

Ultimate is one of the world's newest sports.

Although Ultimate is still a young sport.

The second "sentence" doesn't sound right, does it? It does not make sense on its own and is in fact a sentence fragment.

Testing your sentences by reading them aloud won't work if you read your paragraphs straight through from beginning to end. The trick is to read from end to beginning. That is, read your last sentence aloud, and *listen* to it. If it sounds all right, then read aloud the next-to-last sentence, and so on, until you have worked your way back to the first sentence you wrote.

Now, what do you do with the ones that "sound funny"? Before you can fix them, you need to be able to decode each sentence, to discover whether it has a subject and a verb. The subject and verb are the bare essentials of a sentence. Every sentence you write must have both. (The only exception is a **command,** in which the subject is understood rather than expressed. Consider this command: "Do the following exercises." The subject *you* is understood.)

Finding Subjects and Verbs

A sentence is about *someone* or *something*. That someone or something is the **subject.** The word (or words) that tells what the subject *is* or *does* is the **verb.** The verb expresses some sort of action, or condition, or occurrence.

Find the verb first. One way is by finding the word whose form can be changed to indicate a change in time. In the sentence

The prime minister called an election.

called (in the past) can be changed to *calls* (present) or *will call* (future); so *called* is the verb.

Once you have found the verb, find the subject by asking *who* or *what* the verb is referring to.

Look at these examples. We have underlined the subjects once and the verbs twice.

Jean helps me.
(Helps expresses an action and is the verb.
Who or what helps? Jean helps, so Jean is the subject.)

Finding verbs is relatively easy.
(Is expresses a condition and is the verb.
Who or what is [easy]? Finding, which is the subject.)

Jacques Cartier <u>described</u> Canada as "the land God gave to Cain."
(<u>Described</u> expresses an occurrence and is the verb.
Who or what <u>described</u>? <u>Jacques Cartier</u>.)

This new accounting <u>program</u> <u>will save</u> me hours of time.
(<u>Will save</u> expresses an action and is the verb.
Who or what <u>will save</u>? The <u>program</u>.)

Hint: You can test whether you've identified the subject and verb correctly by saying them together to see whether or not they make sense. For example, "<u>Finding</u> <u>is</u>" makes sense; *"<u>verbs</u> <u>is</u>" does not. "<u>This program</u> <u>will save</u>" makes sense; *"<u>me</u> <u>will save</u>" does not.

EXERCISE 5.1

Find the subject and the verb in the following sentences. Underline the subject with one line and the verb with two. Check your answers (beginning on p. 345), and if you made even one mistake, carefully reread "Finding Subjects and Verbs." Be sure you understand this material thoroughly before you go on.

1. Algy met a bear.
2. A bear met Algy.
3. The bear was bulgy.
4. Sad to say, the bulge was Algy.
5. Grizzlies are famous for their unpredictability.
6. Meeting bears unexpectedly is clearly risky.
7. According to an old myth, bears never run downhill.
8. Take it from me. They do.
9. Females with cubs are known to be especially dangerous.
10. Defending oneself presents a real problem.

EXERCISE 5.2

1. Change is the only constant in life.
2. Information doubles every 18 months.
3. Our survival depends on our ability to adapt to change.
4. Today, effective planning means training for change.
5. Otherwise, we risk becoming roadkill on the highway of life.
6. Learning to adapt to change is, therefore, everyone's challenge.
7. Silicon, a form of sand, is a computer chip's main component.
8. To get ahead in the 90s, people need knowledge from many fields.
9. Soon, a single crystal will hold the entire Library of Congress catalogue.
10. Ironically, high technology is now our forests' best friend.

The subject usually comes before the verb in a sentence, but not always. Occasionally, we find it after the verb:

> Back to the refreshment stand for the fourth time <u>stumbled</u> the weary <u>father</u>.
> (Who or what <u>stumbled</u>? The <u>father</u>.)
>
> At the bottom of the page, in red ink, <u>was</u> my <u>grade</u>.
> (Who or what <u>was</u>? My <u>grade</u>.)

In sentences beginning with *There* + some form of the verb *to be,* or with *Here* + some form of the verb *to be,* the subject comes after the verb.

> There <u>are</u> three good <u>reasons</u> for learning to write well.
> (Who or what <u>are</u>? <u>Reasons</u>.)
>
> There <u>will be</u> a <u>test</u> next week.
> (Who or what <u>will be</u>? A <u>test</u>.)
>
> Here <u>are</u> the <u>solutions</u> to last week's problem set.
> (Who or what <u>are</u>? <u>Solutions</u>.)

In questions, the subject often follows the verb:

> <u>Are</u> <u>you</u> sure about this?   <u>Is</u> <u>he</u> late again?
> (Who or what <u>are</u>? <u>You</u>.)   (Who or what <u>is</u>? <u>He</u>.)

But notice that, in questions beginning with *who, whose, what,* or *which,* the subject and verb are in "normal" order:

> <u>Who</u> <u>met</u> the bear?   <u>What</u> <u>happened</u> to Algy?
> <u>Whose</u> <u>belly</u> <u>was</u> bulgy?   <u>Which</u> <u>grizzly</u> <u>ate</u> Algy?

In the following exercises, underline the subject in each sentence with one line and the verb with two. Check your answers to each set before you go on.

EXERCISE 5.3

1. Canada is a country with two official languages and no official culture.
2. The word "Ai!" means "hello" in Inuktitut.
3. Newfoundland is a piece of rock entirely surrounded by fog.
4. Are you from B.C.?
5. There is the CN Tower, the world's tallest freestanding structure.
6. Money, like manure, does good only when spread around.
7. Here are the steps to follow.
8. Flin Flon is named after the hero of a ten-cent novel published in 1905.

9. Whose idea was this, anyway?
10. Drive carefully.

EXERCISE 5.4

1. Doing grammar exercises is boring.
2. Were they happy with their choice?
3. In the playground were thirty-four screaming children.
4. Are you still angry with me?
5. In July each year, in Calgary, Alberta, the famous Stampede is held.
6. Please stop at the next corner.
7. Santa Claus's address is c/o The North Pole, Canada, HOH OHO.
8. Have you finished the lab yet?
9. Under our back porch lives a family of skunks.
10. Deep in the hills, over the winding river and beyond the shining desert, lived a tribe of gnomes.

More about Verbs

The verb in a sentence may be a single word, as in most of the exercises you've just done, or it may be a group of words. **Helping verbs**[1] are often added to main verbs so that an idea can be expressed precisely. The words *shall, should, may, might, can, could, must, ought, will, would, have, do,* and *be* are helping verbs.

> The complete verb in a sentence consists of the main verb + any helping verbs.

Here are a few of the forms of the verb *write*. Notice that in questions the subject may come between the helping verb and the main verb.

You <u>may write</u> now.

He certainly <u>can write</u>!

We <u>should write</u> home more often.

I <u>shall write</u> tomorrow.

He <u>could have written</u> yesterday.

She <u>is writing</u> her memoirs.

<u>Did</u> he <u>write</u> to you?

He <u>had written</u> his apology.

You <u>ought to write</u> to him.

We <u>will have written</u> by then.

I <u>will write</u> to the editor.

The proposal <u>has been written</u>.

Orders <u>should have been written</u>.

<u>Could</u> you <u>have written</u> it in French?

---

[1] Those who have studied grammatical terminology will know these verbs as auxiliary verbs. They include the modals (see Chapter 28).

One verb form *always* takes a helping verb. Here is the rule:

> A verb ending in *-ing* MUST have a helping verb (or verbs) before it.

Here are a few of the forms an *-ing* verb can take:

I <u>am writing</u> the report.
You <u>will be writing</u> a report.
He <u>should have been writing</u> it.
<u>Is</u> she <u>writing</u> the paper for him?
She <u>must have been writing</u> all night.
You <u>are writing</u> illegibly.
I <u>was writing</u> neatly.
<u>Have</u> you <u>been writing</u> on the wall?

Beware of certain words that are often confused with helping verbs:

> Words such as *not, only, always, sometimes, never, ever,* and *just* are NOT part of the verb.

These words sometimes appear in the middle of a complete verb, but they are modifiers, not verbs. Do not underline them:

I <u>have</u> just <u>won</u> a one-way ticket to Aklavik.
She <u>is</u> always <u>chosen</u> first.
Most people <u>do</u> not <u>welcome</u> unasked-for advice.

In the following exercise, underline the subject once and the complete verb twice. Correct each set of ten sentences before you go on to the next.

EXERCISE 5.5

1. Dwight is sleeping again, unfortunately.
2. You should have been paying attention.
3. Should we conclude the meeting now?
4. In Canada, fall arrives one month before winter.

5. What mark did you get?
6. We do not want to hear your band's demo tape.
7. Where and when are we meeting?
8. The old will always think young people foolish.
9. Their coach has just begun to suffer.
10. Back and forth, lazily but without stopping, swam the shark.

EXERCISE 5.6

1. The whole country is covered with hip-deep snow for several months.
2. Why would anyone want to go over the falls in a barrel?
3. Canadians should be more concerned about the national debt.
4. Never again will I agree to ride with you!
5. A person may forgive an injury, but not an insult.
6. There have been better players.
7. You can become addicted to coffee.
8. How long did you stay in Climax, Saskatchewan?
9. Have you ever been to the Gaspé?
10. Only recently has our track coach become interested in chemistry.

More about Subjects

Very often, groups of words called **prepositional phrases** come before the subject in a sentence, or between the subject and the verb. When you're looking for the subject in a sentence, prepositional phrases can trip you up unless you know this rule:

> The subject of a sentence is never in a prepositional phrase.

You must be able to identify prepositional phrases so that you will know where *not* to look for the subject. A prepositional phrase is a group of words that begins with a preposition and ends with the name of something or someone (a noun or a pronoun). Often, a prepositional phrase will indicate the direction or location of something. In the phrases below, the italicized words are prepositions:

about the book	*between* the desks	*near* the wall
above the book	*by* the book	*of* the program
according to the book	*concerning* the memo	*on* the desk
after the meeting	*despite* the order	*onto* the floor
against the wall	*down* the hall	*over* a door
along the hall	*except* the staff	*through* the window
among the books	*for* the manager	*to* the staff
among them	*from* the office	*under* the desk
around the office	*in* front *of* the desk	*until* the meeting
before lunch	*inside* the office	*up* the hall
behind the desk	*in* the book	*with* a book
below the window	*into* the elevator	*without* them
beside the computer	*like* the book	*without* the software

Before you look for the subject in a sentence, cross out all prepositional phrases. For example:

> The keyboard ~~of your computer~~ should be cleaned occasionally.
> What <u>should be cleaned</u>? The <u>keyboard</u> (not the computer).

> ~~In case~~ ~~of an emergency~~, a member ~~of the class~~ should go ~~to the nearest security office for help~~.

> Who <u>should go</u>? A <u>member</u> (not the class).

In the following exercises, first cross out the prepositional phrase(s) in each sentence. Then underline the subject once and the verb twice. Check your answers to each set of ten sentences before going on. If you get three sets entirely correct, skip ahead to exercise 5.9.

EXERCISE 5.7

1. A bird in the hand is worth two in the bush.
2. Only a few of us have done our homework.
3. Most of your answers are entertaining but wrong.
4. More than a dozen brands of video recorders are now on the market.
5. Meet me at six at the corner of Robson and Granville.
6. A couple of hamburgers should be enough for each of us.
7. Do you know anything about the latest rumours in the government?
8. There is a show about laser technology on television tonight.
9. After eight hours of classes, the thought of collapsing in front of the TV set is very appealing.
10. One episode of *Geraldo* was more than enough for me.

EXERCISE 5.8

1. The verb in this sentence is "is."
2. For many students, lack of money is probably the most serious problem.
3. In the middle of May, after the end of term, the Intercollegiate Arm-Wrestling Championships will be held.
4. One strand of fibre optics can carry both telephone and television signals.
5. During the second week of term, the class will be taken on a tour of the resource centre.
6. Contrary to your expectations and despite the rumours, your instructor does not bite.
7. On Callisto, one of Jupiter's thirteen moons, snow "falls" up, not down.
8. On the eastern shore of Vancouver Island, you can find both oysters and clams.
9. One of the most entertaining comedies of the 1990s was *Wayne's World.*
10. In similar circumstances, most of us would probably have taken the money.

EXERCISE 5.9

Write ten fairly long sentences of your own. In at least three of them, place the subject after the verb. Cross out all the prepositional phrases, and underline the subject once and the complete verb twice.

Multiple Subjects and Verbs

So far, you have been working with sentences containing only one complete subject and one complete verb. Sentences can, however, have more than one subject and verb. Here is a sentence with a multiple subject:

Southlands and West Point Grey are suburbs of Vancouver.

This sentence has a multiple verb:

He elbowed and wriggled his way along the aisle of the bus.

And this sentence has a multiple subject and a multiple verb:

The sergeant and the detective leaped from their car and seized the suspect.

The elements of a multiple subject or verb are usually joined by *and*. Multiple subjects and verbs may contain more than two elements, as in the following sentences:

> <u>Clarity</u>, <u>brevity</u>, and <u>simplicity</u> <u>are</u> the basic qualities of good writing.

> I <u>finished</u> my paper, <u>put</u> the cat outside, <u>took</u> the phone off the hook, and <u>crawled</u> into bed.

In the following exercises, underline the subjects once and the verbs twice. Be sure to underline all the elements in a multiple subject or verb. Check your answers to each set of ten sentences before continuing.

EXERCISE 5.10

1. Maple sugar and wild rice are native Canadian products.
2. Kim or Avi will go next.
3. Professor Singh handed out the tests and wished us luck.
4. I tried and tried but didn't succeed.
5. The two canoeists and their dog were missing for four days.
6. Point and Click, my nerdy brother's two cats, are sleeping peacefully on the sofa.
7. Point and Click killed two pigeons and slaughtered a squirrel before breakfast.
8. Timothy Findley farms, writes, and lectures—in that order.
9. Wait ten minutes and then call again.
10. Shooting often and scoring occasionally are not marketable talents.

EXERCISE 5.11

1. Misspellings can create misunderstandings and cause embarrassment.
2. Several years ago, the *Durham County Review* printed an article about a British military leader.
3. In the article, the old soldier was highly praised but unfortunately was described as "battle-scared."
4. Furious, the soldier called the paper and demanded an apology.
5. The writer and the editor soothed the old man and promised to publish a retraction.
6. In the retraction, the paper apologized for the error and explained, "What we really meant, of course, was 'bottle-scarred.'"
7. Drive slowly and see our city; drive fast and see our jail.
8. Good drivers obey all traffic regulations and never lose their heads.
9. Drink if you want, but don't drive if you do.
10. Come-by-Chance, Blow-Me-Down, Run-by-Guess, and Jerry's Nose are places in Newfoundland.

EXERCISE 5.12

This exercise will test your subject- and verb-finding ability. Underline the subjects with one line and the verbs with two lines. Be sure to underline all elements in a multiple subject or verb. No answers are given for this exercise.

1. Take only pictures. Leave only footprints. (Sign posted in Banff National Park)
2. Dwight and Rudolf studied for more than a week but failed the exam anyway.
3. In the tidal pool were two starfish, several sand dollars, and dozens of tiny crabs.
4. He worked and saved all his life and died miserable and alone.
5. Everybody but me went to camp or spent a few weeks at a cottage.
6. Among the many kinds of cheese made in Canada are Camembert, Fontina, and Quark.
7. Shoe companies, video companies, and exercise equipment manufacturers are all profiting from the fitness craze.
8. We took a train from Clarenville to Bonavista and then went by bus to St. John's.
9. The politicians of our time try in vain to change the world but seldom try to change themselves.
10. According to its campaign literature, the incoming government will provide jobs for all Canadians, eliminate the national debt, find a cure for cancer, land a Canadian on Pluto, and lower taxes, all in its first year of office.

CHAPTER 6

Solving Sentence-Fragment Problems

Any group of words that is punctuated as a sentence but does not have a subject or a complete verb is a **sentence fragment.** Fragments are appropriate in conversation and in some kinds of writing, but normally they are not acceptable in college, technical, and business writing. You've already learned how to spot a sentence fragment: read the words aloud, and check to see whether the subject or the verb (or both) is missing. Let's look at a few examples:

> Now, as always, is greatly influenced by her willful neighbour.
> (Who or what <u>is influenced</u>? The sentence doesn't tell you. The subject is missing.)

> The argument being over sharing responsibility for housework and child care.
> (The verb is missing.)

> The committee attempting to analyze Canada's participation in U.N. peacekeeping missions.
> (Part of the verb is missing. Remember that a verb ending in -*ing* must have a helping verb in front of it.)

To help students in every lab but this one.
(Subject and verb are both missing.)

Regarding the matter we discussed last week.
(Subject and verb are both missing.)

Now, what do you do with the fragments you've found?

> To change a sentence fragment into a complete sentence,
> add whatever is missing: a subject, a verb, or both.

You may need to add a subject:

Now, as always, <u>Canada</u> is greatly influenced by her willful neighbor.

You may need to add a verb:

The argument <u>was</u> over sharing responsibility for housework and child care.

You may need to add part of a verb:

The committee <u>is attempting</u> to analyze Canada's participation in U.N. peacekeeping missions.

You may need to add both a subject and a verb:

A <u>technician</u> <u>is</u> available to help students in every lab but this one.

And sometimes you need to add more than just a subject and a verb:

<u>I</u> <u>have written</u> to <u>the dean</u> regarding the matter we discussed last week.

Don't let the length of a fragment fool you. Students sometimes think that if a string of words is long, it must be a sentence. Not so. No matter how long the string of words is, if it doesn't contain both a subject and a verb, it is not a sentence. Consider this example, taken from "The Men of Moosomin," by Sara Jeannette Duncan:

Here and there a ruddy little pond, like a pocket looking glass dropped on the prairie, with a score or so of wild ducks swimming in it, or a slight round hollow where a pond used to be, with the wild ducks flying high.

Do you know what's missing? Can you change the fragment into a sentence?

In the following exercises, read each "sentence" aloud. Put S before each complete sentence and F before each sentence fragment. Make each fragment into a complete sentence by adding whatever is missing: a subject, a verb, or both. After you complete each set of ten sentences, check your answers. Answers begin on p. 347.

EXERCISE 6.1

1. ____ About sentence fragments.

2. ____ To go to the wall.

3. ____ Glad to do it for you.

4. ____ Falling asleep in class, after working all night.

5. ____ The Doom players meeting in the upper lounge.

6. ____ Look at the helicopter.

7. ____ Watching television a cheap form of entertainment.

8. ____ Hoping to hear from you soon.

9. ____ Saved by the bell.

10. ____ Thinking the class was over, I left.

EXERCISE 6.2

1. ____ To whom it may concern.

2. ____ Turtles being both cheap and easy to train.

3. ____ Never cared for them, frankly.

4. ____ Learning how to write a computer program.

5. ____ The reason being they love hockey.

6. ____ Jackie Burroughs, famous for her role in *Road to Avonlea*.

7. ____ Are you sure about that?

8. ____ Many of whom have seen the film dozens of times.

9. ____ Suddenly screeched to a stop.

10. ____ Never put off until tomorrow what you can put off until next week.

EXERCISE 6.3

____ The fact being that I have to hold down at least one part-time job to go to school. ____ The cost of tuition, books, rent, food, and other living expenses, not to mention clothing and a little money for entertainment. ____ I can't survive without working. ____ Getting the minimum wage for work that is heavy, dirty, and boring. ____ Jobs such as dishwasher, stock clerk, warehouser, cleaner, and short-order cook throughout my college years. ____ What I do find upsetting, though. ____ Some teachers not understanding that I work out of necessity, not out of choice. ____ I wish I did have the luxury of concentrating on nothing but school work. ____ Instead of dealing with problems such as class schedules that conflict with my work schedule. ____ Or assignments that are due with less than a week's notice. ____ The inescapable fact, however, being that I can't attend all my classes and hand in all my assignments on time because I'm too busy working to pay for the education I'm not getting!

Independent and Dependent Clauses

A group of words containing a subject and a verb is a clause. There are two kinds of clauses. An **independent clause** is one that makes complete sense on its own. It can stand alone, as a sentence. A **dependent clause,** as its name suggests, cannot stand alone as a sentence; it depends on another clause to make complete sense.

   Dependent clauses are easy to recognize, because they begin with words such as these:

DEPENDENT-CLAUSE CUES

after	so that
although	that
as, as if	though
as long as	unless
as soon as	until
because	what, whatever
before	when, whenever
even if, even though	where, wherever
if	whether
in order that	which, whichever
provided that	while
since	who, whom, whose

Whenever a clause begins with one of these words or phrases, it is dependent.

A dependent clause must be attached to an independent clause.
If it stands alone, it is a sentence fragment.

Here is an independent clause:

   I am a poor speller.

If we put one of the dependent clause cues in front of it, it can no longer stand alone:

   Because I am a poor speller

We can correct this kind of fragment by attaching it to an independent clause:

> Because I am a poor speller, I have chained my dictionary to my wrist.

In the following exercises, put an S before each clause that is independent and therefore a sentence. Put an F before each clause that is dependent and therefore a sentence fragment. Circle the dependent clause cue in each sentence fragment.

EXERCISE 6.4

1. ____ All those who are late coming back from lunch.

2. ____ The party that was in power being full of crooks and scoundrels.

3. ____ Although we're poor, we're happy.

4. ____ What we think doesn't seem to matter.

5. ____ Where you left them yesterday, I guess.

6. ____ Frequently, when she's away on business.

7. ____ Whether she believes him or not.

8. ____ In a situation like this, whichever decision you make.

9. ____ Despite our efforts to help you, until you decide you want to learn.

10. ____ In view of the fact that you lied about your age, education, and work experience.

EXERCISE 6.5

1. ____ She frowns because it gives people the impression she's thinking.

2. ____ Though most of us don't even know who the candidates are.

3. ____ A job that demands intelligence, physical fitness, and a genuine liking for people.

4. ____ Wherever you go, I'll follow.

5. ____ Whether or not you want me is irrelevant.

6. ____ Unless you conceal yourself, I'll be there.

7. ____ If I wrote his letters for him and typed his résumé.

8. ____ Because jargon is full of long words, uses more words than necessary, and contains long, awkward sentences.

9. ____ Until death do us part, or as long as we love each other, whichever comes first.

10. ____ When Kim approached the table where the five of us sat indulging in quantities of food that had been prepared by the students themselves.

Most sentence fragments are dependent clauses punctuated as sentences. Fortunately, this is the easiest kind of fragment to recognize and fix. All you need to do is join the dependent clause either to the sentence that comes before it or to the one that comes after it—whichever linkage makes better sense.

One final point. If you join your clause fragment to the independent clause that follows it, put a comma between the two clauses (see Chapter 17, p. 160).

Read the following example to yourself; then read it aloud, beginning with the last sentence and working back to the first.

> Montreal is a sequence of ghettos. Although I was born and brought up there. My experience of French was a pathetically limited and distorted one.

The second "sentence" sounds incomplete, and the dependent-clause cue at the beginning of it is the clue you need to identify it as a sentence fragment. You could join the fragment to the sentence before it, but then you would get "Montreal is a sequence of ghettos, although I was born and brought up there," which doesn't make sense. The fragment should be linked to the sentence that follows it, like this:

> Montreal is a sequence of ghettos. Although I was born and brought up there, my experience of French was a pathetically limited and distorted one. (Mordecai Richler, "Quebec Oui, Ottawa Non!")

EXERCISE 6.6

Correct the sentence fragments in exercises 6.4 and 6.5. Make each fragment into a complete sentence by adding an independent clause either before or after the dependent clause. Remember to punctuate correctly: if a dependent clause comes at the beginning of your sentence, put a comma after it. When you have completed this exercise, exchange with another student and check each other's work.

Identify the sentence fragments in the paragraph below. Circle the dependent clause cue in each fragment you find. Then correct each fragment by joining it to a complete sentence before or after it—whichever makes better sense. Check your answers on p. 348.

EXERCISE 6.7

Although spring is my favourite season and I look forward eagerly to its arrival after the long winter. There are some things about the season. That I could do without. When the warm weather begins. I am always tempted to buy new, fashionable shoes. Which are ruined in the wet muck. That is everywhere. Unless I act quickly. My dog also becomes a problem in the spring. She delights in tracking mud from the backyard into the house. After she creates a mess that Mr. Clean would need steroids to tackle. She will go back outside and find something sticky and smelly to roll in. Until the warm weather dries up the mud, and my dog loses the annual urge to coat herself with disgusting substances. My joy at the arrival of spring is always a little restrained.

EXERCISE 6.8

As a final test of your skill in correcting sentence fragments, try this exercise. Put an S before each item that contains only complete sentences. Put an F before each item that contains one or more sentence fragments. Then make each fragment into a complete sentence. No answers are provided for this exercise.

1. _____ In terms of both qualifications and experience, absolutely perfect for the job.

2. _____ On the few occasions that your timetable has you scheduled for two classes in a row. You can count on their being located in buildings at opposite ends of the campus.

3. ____ In the next decade will see more changes in methods of food production than have occurred in the last thousand years. Thanks to
advances in biotechnology.

4. ____ When I read a description of the computer game, *Doom*, I couldn't
believe what I was reading. Then discovering that my children
had been playing it happily for months.

5. ____ While in the Industrial Age, progress depended on physical
strength. In the Information Age, progress will depend on intellect and imagination.

6. ____ "Better never than late" is futurist Frank Ogden's motto.

7. ____ In the past ten years, science having learned more about how the
brain functions than in all of humankind's previous history.

8. ____ Although she reads the "Companions Wanted" column faithfully,
Drusilla has yet to find a man who fulfils her requirements. One
who is sensitive, well-educated, cuddly, and rich.

9. ____ One of George Orwell's most famous sentences from *Animal Farm*
being "All animals are created equal, but some animals are more
equal than others."

10. ____ As a general rule, it is best to avoid writing sentence fragments.
Until you are an experienced, skilful, and confident writer. Even
then, fragments appropriate only in informal writing.

CHAPTER 7

Solving Run-On Sentence Problems

Some sentences lack essential elements and thus are fragments. Other sentences contain too many elements, or elements that are incorrectly linked together. A sentence with too much in it or with inadequate punctuation between clauses is a **run-on.** Run-ons tend to occur when you write in a hurry, without taking time to organize your thoughts first. If you think about what you want to say and punctuate carefully, you shouldn't have any problems with run-ons.

Let's look at the three kinds of run-on sentences: the comma splice, the fused sentence, and the true run-on.

Comma Splices and Fused Sentences

As its name suggests, the **comma splice** occurs when two complete sentences (independent clauses) are joined together with only a comma between them. Here's an example:

Our dog is obedient, he has been well trained.

A **fused sentence** occurs when two complete sentences are joined together with no punctuation between them. For example:

> Our dog is obedient he has been well trained.

There are three ways you can fix a comma splice or fused sentence.

> 1. Use a semicolon to separate the independent clauses.

For example:

> Our dog is obedient; he has been well trained.

(If you are not sure how to use semicolons, see Chapter 18.)

> 2. Add an appropriate linking word between the two clauses.

Two types of linking words will work.

 1. You can add one of these words: *and, but, or, nor, for, so,* or *yet.* These words should be preceded by a comma. Here is an example:

> Our dog is obedient, for he has been well trained.

 2. You can add one of the dependent-clause cues listed on p. 52. For example:

> Our dog is obedient because he has been well trained.

> 3. Make the independent clauses into two separate sentences.

> Our dog is obedient. He has been well trained.

Note that all three solutions to comma splices and fused sentences require you to use a word or punctuation mark strong enough to come between two independent clauses. A comma by itself is too weak, and so is a dash.

The sentences in the following exercises will give you practice in fixing comma splices and fused sentences. Correct the sentences where necessary, then check your answers, beginning on p. 348. Since there are three ways to fix each sentence, your answers may differ from our suggestions. If you're confused about when to use a semicolon and when to use a period, be sure to read p. 164 before going on.

EXERCISE 7.1

1. I hate computers they're always making mistakes.
2. Snowboarding is lots of fun, but it isn't as fast as skiing.
3. Stop me if you've heard this one, there was this cab driver on her first day at work.
4. Rudolf is bone lazy, Dwight isn't much better.
5. Chocolate is Ninik's weakness she cannot resist a Toblerone bar.
6. I'll probably be going out tonight, Gretta offered to take me to a movie.
7. Efficiency is what most consumers look for in a new car, high performance isn't as important as it used to be.
8. I have a 3000-word assignment due tomorrow, if it weren't for that, I'd love to teach you to play solitaire.
9. It bothers me to see Krystal and Sparkle playing cards all the time they could easily fail the term.
10. Anand was transformed overnight he had changed from a normal-looking student into a fashion plate.

EXERCISE 7.2

1. A fine mess this is, I'll never forgive you for getting me into this situation.
2. Let's take the shortcut, we need to get there as quickly as possible.
3. No one in the department supports her, she's both arrogant and indolent.
4. I want to play the banjo, the only thing stopping me is a complete lack of musical talent.
5. Of course, it would also help if I owned a banjo.
6. I'd rather be lucky than good, on the other hand, I'd rather be good than unlucky.
7. Many environmentally aware people are heating their homes with woodstoves nowadays, the result is "ecologists' smog."
8. The snow is turning into freezing rain we'll be lucky to get home before dawn if these conditions persist.
9. When you are looking for a new car, there are many factors to consider, the most important is probably price.

10. Many good films are made in both Canada and the United States, I wish I could tell which ones they were before paying my admission to a movie theatre.

EXERCISE 7.3

1. The largest dog in the world is the Irish Wolfhound, the strongest dog in the world is the Newfoundland, the stupidest dog in the world is my Afghan.
2. Please go to the door and see who's there, I'm on the phone.
3. Early Canadian settlers saw the Americans as a constant menace, even Ottawa—miles from anywhere and hardly a threat to anyone—was not considered safe.
4. They can crawl on their knees and beg that's the only way they'll ever get any more money from me!
5. Think carefully before you answer, a great deal depends on what you decide.
6. Cooking is my favourite pastime, I don't enjoy it nearly so much when I have to do it as when I choose to do it.
7. There is a great deal to be said for woodcutting as a career, much of it bad.
8. My chiropractor has given me a sheet of exercises that he says will make my back stronger, he has convinced me that if I do these exercises daily, my pain will disappear.
9. Karin was given the choice of joining her father's firm as a driver or continuing her education at college, knowing Karin, I think she's sure to take the job.
10. There are two students in this class named Xan, one is from China, the other from Russia, the latter's name is a nickname it is a short form of Alexandra.

In the exercise that follows, correct the comma splices and fused sentences any way you choose. This would be a good time to review the three ways of fixing these errors. Your goal should be to produce paragraphs in which the sentences are correct and effective.

EXERCISE 7.4

An acquaintance of mine recently became a Canadian citizen when she

told me about her citizenship hearing, however, I couldn't bring myself to

offer her the congratulations she was obviously expecting. In preparation for the hearing, she had been told to study a small book containing basic facts about Canada, its government, history, and people, and she was told the judge who interviewed her would ask questions based on the information in this book, she neglected to study, or even to read the book.

At the hearing, the judge asked her to identify the name of the current governor general, to explain some of the advantages of being a Canadian citizen, and to tell him whether health care was a federal or a provincial responsibility. Unable to answer any of these questions, my friend just giggled and shrugged then she listened while the judge gave her the answers. She expected to be told to come back when she had learned more about her adopted country, she was astonished when the judge congratulated her for successfully completing the interview and set a date to confirm her citizenship.

I find the judge's decision appalling for three reasons, first, my friend's failure even to open the book she was given suggests she doesn't have much respect for Canadian citizenship, second, her low opinion of our citizenship process was reinforced when the judge passed her, third, I can't help but feel that she was passed because she is an attractive blonde woman, a university professor, and speaks with a polished, upper-class English accent. If she had been a man or woman of colour, or spoken little or no English, or had a less impressive job, I cannot help but think she would have been rejected, she deserved to be.

The True Run-On Sentence

In the true **run-on sentence,** too many words or too many clauses are crowded together into one sentence. There is no hard-and-fast rule about how many independent clauses you may have in a sentence, but more than two can result in a sentence that is hard to read and even harder to understand.

> There were still a dozen or so guests who remained at the party, not counting the host, but after Raoul and Su Mei left, we decided it was time to go, so we collected our coats and said goodbye to the others, and then, after driving home very cautiously at speeds not exceeding 50 km/h, we sat up drinking coffee until three o'clock in the morning discussing our host's terrible taste in friends.

Clearly, the writer who created this monster got carried away with enthusiasm and just scribbled down everything that came to mind without thinking of the reader's tolerance or patience. If you take your time and remember your readers, you probably won't make this error. If you do find run-on sentences in your writing, however, you can correct them by following these steps:

> 1. Cut out all unnecessary words.
> 2. Apply the three solutions to comma-splice and fused-sentence problems: semicolons, linking words, and sentence breaks.

To turn a monster sentence into a correct and civilized one, first read through your sentence and identify any words or phrases that are not essential to its meaning.

> *There were still* a dozen *or so* guests *who* remained at the party, *not counting the host,* but after Raoul and Su Mei left, we decided *it was time* to go, so we collected our coats and said goodbye *to the others,* and then, after driving home *very* cautiously at *speeds not exceeding* 50 km/h, we sat up drinking coffee until three o'clock *in the morning* discussing our host's terrible taste in friends.

Run-on sentences are often made worse by **wordiness**. In this example, the words in italics are unnecessary or redundant and should be eliminated. Here's how the sentence reads without them:

A dozen guests remained at the party, but after Raoul and Su Mei left, we decided to go, so we collected our coats and said goodbye, and then, after driving home cautiously at 50 km/h, we sat up drinking coffee until three o'clock discussing our host's terrible taste in friends.

This version is an improvement, but it is not as clear and concise as it could be. Let's move on to step 2:

A dozen guests remained at the party, but after Raoul and Su Mei left, we decided to go. We collected our coats and said goodbye. Then, after driving home cautiously at 50 km/h, we sat up until three o'clock drinking coffee and discussing our host's terrible taste in friends.

This version is both concise and clear.

In the following exercise, first eliminate all unnecessary words. Then use semicolons, linking words, or sentence breaks to correct what is left. There is more than one right way of fixing these sentences. Just make sure your corrections make sense and are easy to read. The answers we've provided, which begin on p. 350, are only suggestions.

EXERCISE 7.5

1. Special effects have been the focus of sci-fi movies since Stanley Kubrick made a computer and a space ship the stars of *2001: A Space Odyssey* and George Lucas continued the trend with the *Star Wars* trilogy, and movie makers ever since have been employing increasingly more powerful computers to generate increasingly more spectacular effects.
2. A great many films have been made about Count Dracula, from *Buffy the Vampire Slayer* to *Nosferatu*, Dracula has been portrayed as a completely depraved monster, a legendary warrior, and even a misunderstood social outcast and so many different versions of his story have been told that fact and fiction are now inseparable.
3. For more than thirty years, Clint Eastwood has held the Hollywood record for successful films and while others have had longer careers, and though Clint is still going, no one has nearly equalled his record in producing box-office winners, and furthermore, he is widely acclaimed internationally as a director as well as an actor.
4. Each year an annual poll is taken among film critics to determine the best movies ever made and every year one film ranks first on top of the poll and this movie didn't even win the Academy Award as best picture for its year. Shot in black and white, it is the story of a

newspaperman who is driven to succeed and it was made in 1941 and this film is *Citizen Kane*.

5. Some of the worst movies ever made have become big money-makers, thanks to the industry's practice of describing all movies as "the best," "the biggest," and "not-to-be-missed," no matter how mediocre or even downright bad they may be and a good example is the work of Edward D. Wood, Jr., the man known as the world's worst director, and if you want to see a couple of sensationally dreadful films, check your local video store for Wood's truly awful *Bride of the Monster* and *Plan 9 from Outer Space*.

EXERCISE 7.6

As a final test of your ability to identify and correct sentence errors, supply the appropriate sentence breaks to make this garble into a grammatically correct paragraph. No answers have been provided for this exercise.

Since cats can't read, I wonder why the companies that make cat food pay advertising agencies millions of dollars to create packages for their products the labels proclaim the box or can contains "irresistible morsels of delectable goodness" with a "rich, meaty taste" of course the answer is that people buy cat food, and people are apparently easily persuaded that what a package says on the outside is a reliable indicator of what is to be found inside, but the fallacy of this assumption is easily proved just open a can of cat food and examine the contents for any sign of the qualities advertised on the label I speak from experience I recently bought a case of cat food, or "premium feline dinner," as the manufacturer calls it, because of the enticing description of the contents in particular the words, "scrumptious, succulent chunks of real chicken in a gourmet sauce," caught my attention and made me long for Chef Antoine's specialty at my favourite French restaurant but the sticky, grey mess inside the tin was a bit of a letdown but, undeterred, I emptied the muck onto a plate and probed it with my fork, hoping for a glimpse of the "tender, savoury, prime cuts of real beef" or a whiff of the "aromatic, taste-tempting flavours of real liver," but the more closely I examined my cat's intended dinner, the more certain I became that the label's insistent repetition of the word "real" with respect to every ingredient was a deliberate attempt to delude the consumer and it certainly required a great deal more faith in the manufacturer's integrity than I could muster after a close visual and olfactory examination of the evidence.

Solving Modifier Problems

The thieves were caught before much of the loot could be disposed of *by the police.*

Stamping her feet and switching her tail to brush away flies, Josée led the mare out of the barn.

For sale: A complete set of first-year accounting texts *by a needy student in almost perfect condition.*

These sentences show what can happen to your writing if you aren't sure how to use modifiers. A **modifier** is a word or group of words that adds information about another word in a sentence. In the examples above, the italicized words are modifiers. Used correctly, modifiers describe or explain or limit another word, making its meaning more precise. Used carelessly, however, modifiers can cause confusion or, even worse, amusement. Few things are more embarrassing than being laughed at when you didn't mean to be funny.

You need to be able to recognize and solve two kinds of modifier problems: **misplaced modifiers** and **dangling modifiers.**

Misplaced Modifiers

Modifiers must be as close as possible to the words they apply to. Usually, a reader will assume that a modifier modifies whatever it's next to. It's important to remember this, because, as the following examples show, changing the position of a modifier can change the meaning of your sentence.

(Only) I love you. (No one else loves you.)

I (only) love you. (I don't have any other feelings for you.)

I love (only) you. (You are the only one I love.)

I love you (only.) (You are the only one I love.)

> To make sure a modifier is in the right place, ask yourself, "What does it apply to?" and put it beside that word.

When a modifier is not close enough to the word it refers to, it is said to be misplaced. A **misplaced modifier** can be *a single word in the wrong place:*

The supervisor told me they needed someone who could use a word processor (badly.)

Is some company really hiring people to do poor work? Or does the company urgently need someone familiar with word processing? The modifier *badly* belongs next to *needed:*

The supervisor told me they (badly) needed someone who could use a word processor.

> Be especially careful with these words: *almost, nearly, just, only, even, hardly, merely, scarcely.* Put them right before the words they modify.

Misplaced: I (almost) ate the whole pie.
Correctly placed: I ate (almost) the whole pie.

Misplaced: When he was a defenceman for the Boston Bruins, Bobby Orr (nearly) had knee surgery in the off-season every year he played.

Correctly placed: When he was a defenceman for the Boston Bruins, Bobby Orr had knee surgery in the off-season (nearly) every year he played.

A misplaced modifier can also be *a group of words in the wrong place:*

(Scratching each other playfully,) we watched the monkeys.

The modifier, *scratching each other playfully,* is too far away from the word it is supposed to modify, *monkeys.* In fact, it seems to modify *we,* making the sentence ridiculous. We need to rewrite the sentence:

We watched the monkeys (scratching each other playfully.)

Look at this one:

I worked for my aunt, who owns a variety store (during the summer.)

During the summer applies to *worked* and should be closer to it:

(During the summer,) I worked for my aunt, who owns a variety store.

Notice that a modifier need not always go right next to what it modifies; it should, however, be as close as possible to it.

Occasionally, as in the examples above, the modifier is obviously out of place. The writer's intention is clear, and the sentences are easy to correct. But sometimes modifiers are misplaced in such a way that the meaning is not clear, as in this example:

Mara said (on her way out) she would deliver the package to Julio.

Did Mara *say* it on her way out? Or is she going to *deliver the package* on her way out? To avoid confusion, we must move the modifier and, depending on which meaning we want, write:

(On her way out,) Mara said she would deliver the package to Julio.

or:

Mara said she would deliver the package to Julio (on her way out.)

In the following exercises, rewrite the sentences that contain misplaced modifiers, positioning the modifiers correctly. Check your answers to each set before going on. Answers begin on p. 350.

EXERCISE 8.1

1. Fernando has almost insulted everyone he's gone out with.

2. The boss told me on Friday I was being let go.

3. They nearly decided to pay me $350 a week.

4. I will ask you only one more time.

5. My sister only could pray to win the lottery.

6. I hate parties where the food is served to the guests who are all standing around on tiny paper plates.

7. Elmo bought a cigarette lighter for his girlfriend costing $29.95.

8. The angry hippo chased me toward the exit in a rage.

9. Unless they are poodles or terriers, most pet owners don't bother having their dogs professionally groomed.

10. I appreciate a car designed for the safety and comfort of the driver with an air bag and soft seat.

EXERCISE 8.2

1. People who shoplift frequently get caught.

2. Stan almost watched television all night.

3. Dolly tried to convince the members of her fan club to wear two or three sets of false eyelashes enthusiastically.

4. Melted in a saucepan, stir the sifted flour into the butter.

5. As someone who is concerned about fitness, you really should stop smoking.

6. No one is allowed to dump any pollutants except petrochemical company executives into the river.

7. He took a stand against a tree while waiting for the bear with an old black-powder rifle.

8. Rosa passed the security guard and two workmen walking to school.

9. I am pleased to meet with student representatives from all of our colleges here in Petawawa.

10. Perhaps you're on your own in Vancouver, with a sparkling city to explore and a couple of tickets to an event at the covered stadium in your pocket. (B.C. travel flyer)

Dangling Modifiers

A **dangling modifier** occurs when there is no appropriate word in the sentence for the modifier to apply to. That is, the sentence does not contain a *specific word* or *idea* to which the modifier can sensibly refer. With no appropriate word to refer to, the modifier seems to apply to whatever it's next to, often with ridiculous results:

> (After a good night's sleep,) my teachers were impressed by my alertness.
> (This sentence seems to say that the teachers had a good night's sleep.)
> (Cycling close to the curb,) a minivan swerved and nearly hit me.
> (The minivan was cycling close to the curb?)

Dangling modifiers are trickier to fix than misplaced ones; you can't simply move danglers to another spot in the sentence. There are two ways to correct them. One way requires that you remember this rule:

> When a modifier comes at the beginning of a sentence, it modifies the subject of the sentence.

This rule means that you can avoid dangling modifiers by choosing the subjects of your sentences carefully. All you have to do is make the subject an appropriate one for the modifier to apply to. Applying this rule, we can correct both examples simply by changing the sentences' subjects:

After a good night's sleep, I impressed my teachers with my alertness.

Cycling close to the curb, I was nearly hit by a swerving minivan.

Another way to correct a dangling modifier is to change it into a dependent clause:

> After I had had a good night's sleep, I impressed my teachers with my alertness.

> While I was cycling close to the curb, a minivan swerved and nearly hit me.

Sometimes a dangling modifier comes at the end of a sentence:

> A picnic would be a good idea, not having much money.

Can you correct this sentence? Try it; then look at the suggestions at the bottom of the page.[1]

Here is a summary of the steps to follow in solving modifier problems:

> 1. Ask "What does the modifier apply to?"
> 2. Be sure there is a word or word group *in the sentence* for the modifier to apply to.
> 3. Put the modifier as close as possible to the word or word group it applies to.

Most of the sentences in exercises 8.3 and 8.4 contain dangling modifiers. Correct them by changing the subject of each sentence to one the modifier can appropriately apply to. There is no one "right" way to correct each sentence; our answers are only suggestions.

EXERCISE 8.3

1. As a college English teacher, dangling modifiers are annoying.

2. When writing, a dictionary is your best friend.

---

[1] Here are two suggestions:
  1. Add a subject: Not having much money, *I* thought a picnic would be a good idea.
  2. Change the dangler to a dependent clause: *Since I didn't have much money,* I thought a picnic would be a good idea.

3. Driving recklessly, the police stopped Sula at a roadblock.

4. Because they don't shed their hair, our neighbours love their Cornish Rex cats.

5. The surface must be sanded smooth before applying the varnish.

6. Upon entering, the store was empty.

7. Attempting to hotwire a '95 Mercedes 318, the police were called and made an arrest.

8. Having rotted in storage, the farmers could not sell their grain for the profit they were counting on.

9. In very cold weather, the engine should be thoroughly warmed up before attempting to drive.

10. Driving through the desert, our mouths became drier and drier.

EXERCISE 8.4

1. After changing the tire, the jack should be released.

2. The next question is whether to order beer or wine, having decided on pizza.

3. After waiting for you for an hour, the evening was ruined.

4. Jogging through Stanley Park, a cluster of totem poles came into view.

5. Most of the spare keys, after spending nine dollars on them, have been lost.

6. Having set the microwave on automatic, the turkey was quickly cooked to perfection.

7. Having completed the beginning, the ending is the second most important part of the essay.

8. Convicted of aggravated assault, the judge sentenced her to two years in Kingston.

9. After scoring the goal in overtime, a huge victory parade wound through the city.

10. It was a great moment: after making the speech of a lifetime, the election put him in the leader's office.

EXERCISE 8.5
Correct the dangling modifiers in exercise 8.3 by changing them into dependent clauses.

EXERCISE 8.6
Correct the dangling modifiers in exercise 8.4 by changing them into dependent clauses.

Correct the misplaced and dangling modifiers in exercises 8.7 through 8.8 in any way you choose. Our answers are only suggestions.

EXERCISE 8.7

1. Although he lives more than 50 km away, he nearly manages to come to every class.

2. The sign said that students are only admitted to the pub.

3. The lion was recaptured before anyone was mauled or bitten by the trainer.

4. While asleep, the blankets were kicked off the bed.

5. I saw the Queen and her entourage arrive through a plate-glass window.

6. Having ruled out the other two Japanese imports, the Mazda is the one we chose.

7. Swimming isn't a good idea if polluted.

8. The man wore a hat on his head which was hideous.

9. I learned about Joan's having a baby in last week's letter.

10. The counsellor who admitted he was not familiar with the college's harassment policy recently has alienated the students.

EXERCISE 8.8

1. Gnawing on a bone, Joe found his dog.

2. He said on Tuesday we would have a test.

3. Left over from last week's party, our guests didn't find the food very appetizing.

4. Employees who are late frequently are dismissed without notice.

5. Having forgotten to pick me up twice this week, I'm quitting Jim's car pool.

6. Although badly bruised, Maria turned the avocados into great guacamole.

7. Before going to bed, the alarm should be set for 6:00 A.M.

8. Though drunk daily, many people don't trust Lake Ontario water.

9. It is traditional to pay one's respects to friends and relatives after they have died in a funeral parlour.

10. After completing the study of staffing requirements, an assistant to the personnel manager will be hired.

EXERCISE 8.9

To test your mastery of modifiers, try this final exercise, for which no answers are provided.

1. While still in kindergarten, my parents moved me to Red Deer.

2. After finishing high school, college seemed like a good idea.

3. Having been overfertilized, my sister thinks our cactus may not survive.

4. A person who blacks out while drinking nine times out of ten is an alcoholic.

5. Hiking out into the wilderness, the weather grew ominous.

6. Gino asked Maria to marry him during the evening.

7. If caged, you can bring your Great Dane on the flight.

8. Being overinflated, I think the balloon will burst.

9. Weighing at least 80 kg, even Bettina couldn't move the baggage.

10. There is a sign in the lobby of a Moscow hotel that reads, "You are welcome to visit the cemetery where famous Russian composers, artists, and writers are buried daily except Thursdays."

CHAPTER 9

The Parallelism Principle

When writing about items in a series, you must be sure all the items are **parallel;** that is, they must be written in the same grammatical form.

> I like camping, fishing, and to hike.

The items in this sentence are not parallel. Two end in *ing,* but the third *(to hike)* is the infinitive form of the verb. To correct the sentence, you must make all the items in the series take the same grammatical form—either

> I like to camp, to fish, and to hike.

or

> I like camping, fishing, and hiking.

> Correct faulty parallelism by giving all items in a series the same grammatical form.

One way to tell whether all the items in a series are parallel is to write the items in list form, one below the other. That way, you can make sure that all the elements are the same—that they are all words, or all phrases, or all clauses.

NOT PARALLEL	PARALLEL

Sula is pleasant,
    attractive and
  likes to help.

Sula is pleasant,
    attractive, and
  helpful.

I support myself by delivering pizza,
        poker,
          and
   shooting pool.

I support myself by delivering pizza,
       playing poker, and
      shooting pool.

Kheeran is neat,
   polite, and
  an obnoxious person.

Kheeran is neat,
   polite, and
  obnoxious.

Claude tries to do what is right,
     different things, and
   make a profit.

Claude tries to do what is right,
     what is different, and
   what is profitable.

With his sharp mind,
by having the boss as his uncle, and
   few enemies,
       he'll go far.

With his sharp mind,
   the boss as his uncle, and
   few enemies,
       he'll go far.

or

Having a sharp mind,
   the boss as his uncle, and
   few enemies,
       he'll go far.

As you can see, achieving parallelism is partly a matter of developing an ear for the sound of a correct list. Practice and the exercises in this chapter will help. Once you have mastered parallelism in your sentences, you will be ready to develop ideas in parallel sequence and thus to write clear, well-organized prose. Parallelism, far from being a "frill," is a fundamental characteristic of good writing.

In the following exercises, correct the sentences where necessary. As you work through these exercises, try to spot faulty parallelism and correct it from the sound of the sentences before you examine them closely for mistakes. Check your answers to each set of ten before going on. Answers begin on p. 353.

EXERCISE 9.1

1. The three main kinds of speech are demonstrative, informative, and

   the kind persuading someone of something.

2. The single mother faces many problems. Two of the most difficult are supporting her household and sole parent to her child.

3. She advised me to take two aspirins and that I call her in the morning.

4. Books provide us with information, education, and they're entertaining to read.

5. To make your court appearance as painless as possible, prepare your case thoroughly and maintaining a pleasant, positive attitude.

6. The apostrophe is used for two purposes: contraction, and it shows possession.

7. Swiftly and with skill the woman gutted and scaled the fish.

8. I am overworked and not paid enough.

9. You need to develop skill and strategy and be agile to be a good tennis player.

10. The two main responsibilities of a corrections officer are security and controlling the inmates.

EXERCISE 9.2

1. A part-time job can develop your decision-making skills, your sense of responsibility, and you feel more self-confident and independent.

2. The three keys to improving your marks are study, you must work hard, and bribing the teacher.

3. I couldn't decide whether I should become a chef or to study data processing.

4. The recent increase in teenage suicides can be attributed primarily to two causes: the widespread lack of strong religious beliefs and there are no strict moral codes either.

5. A course in logical reasoning will help us evaluate what we read and making sound decisions.

6. My supervisor told me that my performance was generally satisfactory but to improve my writing.

7. Ms. Hencz assigns two hours of homework every night, and we're expected to do an essay each week.

8. The two most important characteristics of a personal work space are how neat and well organized it looks and the privacy.

9. Playing with small construction toys is beneficial to young children because it develops their fine motor skills, encourages concentration and patience, and their creative imagination is stimulated.

10. When you're buying a new car, you should look at more than just the size, style, and how much it costs. The warranty, how much it costs to run, and trade-in value should also be taken into consideration.

EXERCISE 9.3

1. The role of the health instructor is to teach preventive medicine, care of the sick, and how to go about rehabilitating the injured.

2. The most common causes of snowmobile accidents are mechanical failure, the weather conditions might be poor, and the driver careless.

3. The portable classrooms are ill-equipped, poorly lighted, and there isn't any heat.

4. The advantages of a thesis statement are that it limits your topic, the contents of the paper are made very clear, and you show how your paper will be organized.

5. Unemployment deprives the individual of purchasing power, and the country's national output is reduced.

6. A good nurse is energetic, tolerant, sympathetic, and can be relied upon.

7. The money spent on space exploration should be used to provide aid to underdeveloped countries, and medical research could be funded.

8. The best house cats are quiet, clean, affectionate, and should be somewhere else.

9. Springtime brings out some interesting emotions along with the flowers and leaves: a new appreciation for the beauty of nature, and members of the opposite sex are newly admired.

10. You can conclude a paper with a summary of main points, by posing a question, or you could end with a quotation.

EXERCISE 9.4

1. Our winter has not been very pleasant: we've had vicious ice storms, followed by heavy snowfalls, followed by freezing rain that is dangerous.

2. Baseball is a game that requires a high level of skill with natural talent in large measure.

3. Many foreigners see conservatism, a pride in our country, and an interest in being orderly as characteristic of Canadians.

4. Patience and dexterity will make you a good person who plays the piano, or cutter of meat, or Lego builder.

5. Being a dutiful son, loyal husband, and treating his children with affection made Jason so stressed that he took up boxing as an outlet for his aggression.

6. There are some parents who think that rock music is dangerous and causes an addictive reaction.

7. Selena has three passions in her life: to dance with her boyfriend, listening to Charlie Major's music and fast cars.

8. After this year at school, I intend to go into nursing or I'll become a teacher.

9. After nine years of making up faulty sentences for students to fix, Brian can no longer write properly or correctly express himself.

10. Both those in management positions and workers must make compromises if this joint committee is to succeed.

EXERCISE 9.5

Correct the faulty parallelism in the following paragraph.

When they buy a car, most people consider a number of factors, such as safety, style, how fast they go, whether or not they are reliable, how much they cost. For some buyers, the most important consideration is the impression their new car will make on their relatives and people they like.

Unfortunately, these would-be buyers often make an unfavourable impression on their loans officer or the manager of their bank by choosing a vehicle that is beyond their means. Another kind of car buyer will settle for nothing less than the loudest, flashiest vehicle available with loads of power. As I plug along in my aged, rusted out, underpowered Ford, I console myself with the thought that people who drive flashy sports cars with too much power are trying to make up for other inadequacies.

EXERCISE 9.6

As a test of your ability to correct faulty parallelism, fix the errors in the sentences below. No answers are provided for this exercise.

1. My cat is noisy, smells, and suffers from arthritis, but the whole family loves her anyway.

2. Tonight's show has all the ingredients of a successful television series: lots of sex, greedy characters, and it's violent.

3. The computer is helping me write faster, I find it easier, and it is certainly more accurate.

4. Anna is trying to decide whether she wants to be an actress, to practise medicine, or playing golf professionally.

5. When I'm canoeing, I value the silence most, but catching fish and bird-watching, and taking pictures are important to me, too.

6. As I watched the Commonwealth Games, I found I could classify the athletes into three categories: the able-bodied, those who were physically challenged, and the chemically enhanced.

7. Jean is comfortable with her decision to be a wife, a mother, and pursue a career.

8. Rudolf's being selfish, unkind to others, and a cheapskate are the reasons why everyone dislikes him.

9. Travel teaches us to be tolerant of others, patient, how to be resourceful, and independence.

10. Forests are to British Columbia what grain is to the Prairies, their language is to the people of Quebec, and fish to Newfoundland—a battleground for competing economic interests and the interests of politicians.

EXERCISE 9.7

For each of the topics below, list five descriptive features in grammatically parallel form. Here is an example for the topic "insurance sales representative":

SINGLE WORD	PHRASE/CLAUSE
talkative	talks incessantly
aggressive	won't take "no" for an answer
knowledgeable	knows the insurance business
enthusiastic	is full of energy
inflexible	refuses to consider another opinion

1. pop music (or rap, or classical, or any other kind of music)

2. the English language

3. your hardest course

4. your favourite restaurant

5. a grandmother (*or* grandfather)

CHAPTER 10

Refining by Combining

To reinforce what you've learned about sentence structure, try your voice and your hand (preferably with a pencil in it) at sentence combining. You've rid your writing of fragments; you've cast out comma splices; you're riding herd on run-ons. But you may still find that your sentences, although technically correct, are choppy or repetitious. And you may be bored with conveying the same idea in the same old way. Sentence combining will not only confirm your mastery of sentence structure but also enable you to refine and polish your writing.

What is sentence combining? Sometimes called sentence generating or embedding, **sentence combining** is a technique that enables you to avoid a choppy, monotonous style while at the same time producing correct sentences.

Let's look at an example of two short, technically correct sentences that could be combined:

Our paper carrier collects on Fridays.

He delivers the *Winnipeg Free Press* on Saturdays.

There are several ways of combining these two statements into a single sentence.

---

1. You can connect them with an appropriate linking word, or phrase:
   - (comma +) coordinating conjunction (*and, but, or, for, now, so, yet*)
   - semicolon + conjunctive adverb + comma (see list on p.165)

Our paper carrier delivers the *Winnipeg Free Press* on Saturdays <u>and</u> collects on Fridays.

Our paper carrier delivers the *Winnipeg Free Press* on Saturdays<u>, but</u> he collects on Fridays.

Our paper carrier delivers the *Winnipeg Free Press* on Saturdays<u>; however</u>, he collects on Fridays.

---

2. You can change one of the sentences into a subordinate clause. (See list of dependent-clause cues on p.52)

Our paper carrier, <u>who delivers the *Winnipeg Free Press* on Saturdays,</u> collects on Fridays.

On Fridays, our paper carrier collects for the *Winnipeg Free Press,* <u>which he delivers on Saturdays.</u>

<u>Although he delivers the *Winnipeg Free Press* on Saturdays,</u> our paper carrier collects on Fridays.

---

3. You can change one of the sentences into a modifying phrase.

Having collected his money on Friday, our paper carrier delivers the *Winnipeg Free Press* on Saturday.

On Fridays, our paper carrier collects for the *Winnipeg Free Press,* a Saturday paper.

> 4. Sometimes it is possible to reduce one of your sentences to a single-word modifier.

On Fridays, our paper carrier collects for the (Saturday) *Winnipeg Free Press*.

In sentence combining, you are free to move parts of the sentence around, change words, add or delete words, or make whatever other changes you find necessary. Anything goes: just make sure you don't drastically alter the meaning of the base sentences. Keep in mind that your aim in combining sentences is to make effective sentences—not long ones. Clarity is essential and brevity has force. Here's another example for you to consider.

Correct but stilted sentences conveying an idea:

Malcolm X was an influence.
He influenced American culture.
His influence was strong in the 1960s.

Correct and smooth sentences conveying the same idea:

Malcolm X had a strong influence on American culture in the 1960s.
Malcolm X strongly influenced American culture in the 1960s.
In the 1960s, American culture was strongly influenced by Malcolm X.

The skills that you learn by combining sentences identify you as a perceptive and sensitive writer. They are useful not only in writing and speaking, but also in reading, listening, and problem solving.

Before you turn to the exercises at the end of this chapter, you may wish to review conjunctions and relative pronouns, both of which can cause problems for ESL students.

Using Conjunctions to Combine Clauses

Whether you are using coordinating or subordinating conjunctions, be sure to use only ONE conjunction to connect two clauses. The main clause needs no conjunction, but the dependent or coordinate clause does need a conjunction to link it to the main clause. For example, let's say you want to combine "I enjoy school" with "I also like my part-time job." Look at the following possibilities:

Correct:	*Although* I enjoy school, I also like my part-time job.
Also correct:	I enjoy school, *and* I also like my part-time job.
Incorrect:	*Although* I enjoy school, *and* I also like my part-time job.

Now test your understanding of this important point by doing the following exercise.

EXERCISE 10.1

Put a check mark (✔) before each sentence that is correct. Put an X before each sentence that contains too many conjunctions, and cross out the unnecessary conjunction(s). Be sure to check the capitalization and punctuation of your corrected sentences. Turn to p. 354 to check your answers.

1. _____Though it was a difficult decision, but we made it.

2. _____After the test was over, so we went to the cafeteria.

3. _____Since Maia works every night until 2:00, and she is tired.

4. _____When you first move into an apartment, you are usually required to pay a deposit.

5. _____Even though you have apologized, yet I am still angry with you.

6. _____If I win the lottery, the first thing I will buy is a Porsche.

7. _____Before I came to college, when I worked as a nanny.

8. _____Because I want to see the dean today, so I am prepared to wait all afternoon, if necessary.

9. _____Before we meet for lunch, perhaps you could buy a new cartridge for our printer.

10. _____Though my mother has told me many times before, and she will undoubtedly tell me again.

Using Relative Pronouns to Combine Clauses

You can combine two clauses by using a relative pronoun (*who, whom, whose, that, which*) to join them. The relative pronoun can function in several ways:

SEPARATE SENTENCES
The man is standing at the bus stop. He is my father.

COMBINED SENTENCE
The man who is standing at the bus stop is my father. (*Who* is the subject of the subordinate clause.)

I need a copy of *Frankenstein*. Ms. Lee assigned this novel last week.

I need a copy of *Frankenstein*, which Ms. Lee assigned last week. (*Which* is the direct object of the subordinate clause.)

Chandra is going to propose to Jenny. He loves her very much.

Chandra is going to propose to Jenny, whom he loves very much. (*Whom* is the direct object of the subordinate clause.)

The computer is the tool of the Information Age. We are all familiar with the computer.

The tool of the Information Age is the computer, with which we are all familiar. (*Which* is the object of the preposition *with*.)

Yesterday Gina met Raffi. Raffi's family lives in Beirut.

Yesterday Gina met Raffi, whose family lives in Beirut. (*Whose* functions as a possessive modifying *family*.)

A common error is to fail to delete the word the relative pronoun replaces. We do NOT write

> The man who is standing at the bus stop, he is my father. (*Who* replaces *he*.)
> I need a copy of *Frankenstein*, which novel Ms. Lee assigned last week. (*Which* replaces *novel*.)
> Chandra is going to propose to Jenny, whom he loves her very much. (*Whom* replaces *her*.)

EXERCISE 10.2

Combine the following sentences, using the relative pronoun given in parentheses to link the two clauses.

1. Matti has a friend. The friend's locker was broken into. (whose)
2. Anna is wearing a ring. Rudi gave her the ring. (that)
3. The clerk in the Registrar's office was most helpful. She provided me with a new timetable. (who)
4. Co-op programs are popular among students. The students are enrolled in college full time. (who)
5. Rene speaks often about his daughter. He is very proud of her. (whom)
6. I handed in the homework two weeks ago. The professor still hasn't returned it. (that)
7. Today our class attended a lecture on financial management. We knew nothing about financial management. (which)
8. The train station is in the centre of the city. It is easy to find. (which)
9. I enjoy talking with my classmates. I have learned a great deal about other countries from them. (whom)
10. Some children were eating a watermelon. They were having a seed-spitting contest. (who)

Turn back to p. 85 and review the four ways to combine clauses into sentences before you do the following exercises. Try out your answers aloud before you write them. (You may want to look over Chapters 17 and 18 before you tackle these exercises.)

EXERCISE 10.3

Combine the following sentences, using the cues in parentheses as your guide to linking the sentences. Answers begin on p. 355.

1. The picketers left the streets.
   The police arrived. (when)

2. The angry bystanders knocked down the assassin.
   The angry bystanders tore him limb from limb. (and)

3. Maria is forty-one years old.
   She looks about twenty. (but)

4. He always quits.
   You need him. (just when)

5. Newspapers distort facts.
   Politicians complain about this. (that)

6. Football is violent.
   North Americans love football. (even though)

7. Television manipulates feelings.
   Many people are not aware of this fact. (that)

8. Eazy-E was a gangsta rapper.
   He died in 1994.
   He died of AIDS. (who)

9. Vesna hates zucchini.
   She planted some anyway.
   She planted zucchini to please her husband. (although)

10. Scientists in the ancient world looked to the stars for guidance.
    Modern scientists may travel to the stars. (whereas)

EXERCISE 10.4

Using all four ways of combining clauses into sentences, combine the following statements into longer, more interesting units. (*Hint:* Read each set
of statements through to the end before you begin to combine them, and
try out several variations aloud or in your head before writing down your
preferred solution.) There are many ways to combine these statements in
effective sentences. Our answers (p. 355) are only suggestions.

1. The chocolate sauce was rich.
   It was dark.
   It covered my dessert.
   The chocolate sauce was like a thick blanket.

2. Matthew stumbled down the stairs.
    He was horrified by the sight.
    Sadik and two of his friends were wrestling in the living room.

3. I don't get there by noon.
    Come looking for me.
    I may be in trouble.

4. Key glanced at first base.
    He went into his windup.
    Then he threw a curve ball.
    Murray hit the ball over the right field wall.

5. The student begged for mercy.
    She threw herself at her instructor's feet.
    She had been caught plagiarizing.

6. The moon was full.
    We sat huddled in our sleeping bags.
    We sat for a long time.
    The sleeping bags were warm.
    We finally fell asleep.

7. The old train station was once the hub of the city.
    It is now the dilapidated refuge of rats.

8. The moose sensed danger.
    The moose lifted its head.
    It was ready to explode into action at the slightest sound.

9. Jamie was lonely.
    Jamie was miserable.
    Jamie stumbled into the classroom.
    Her school books were heavy in her hand.

10. Philosophy 101 is Monika's favourite course.
    Few students register for philosophy.
    Students think philosophy is a tough course.

EXERCISE 10.5

This set of exercises is more challenging. In some questions you may need to combine the given statements into two or more sentences. Again, be sure to read through all the statements in each question to identify related ideas before you begin revising. Turn to p. 356 to compare your sentences with our suggested revisions.

1. Each year more Canadians buy mutual funds.
   Mutual funds diversify investment.
   Mutual funds make purchasers feel secure.

2. The city of Toronto boasts about its CN Tower.
   It is 555 metres high.
   The CN Tower holds a record.
   It is the world's tallest freestanding structure.

3. It was 10:15.
   The concert was supposed to begin at 10:00.
   The band had not arrived.
   The audience was growing restless.
   The band's van was stuck in traffic.

4. The patient complained of pain.
   The patient thought she had broken her ankle.
   The intern examined her.
   The intern ordered X-rays.
   The intern was young.

5. A vegetarian diet is healthy.
   Peas contain protein.
   Beans contain protein.
   Lentils contain protein.

Iron is found in spinach.
People do not need to eat meat.

6. Fall is Canada's most beautiful season.
In fall, the leaves turn red.
The leaves turn yellow and orange.
The days are cold.
The days are sunny.
There are no mosquitoes or black flies.

7. The mail carrier walked up the path.
The dog began to bark.
The mail carrier walked up the path.
The mail carrier pushed the letters through the mail slot.
The dog grabbed the letters in his mouth.
The dog began shaking the letters.

8. Many people go to night school.
Some people go to learn a new skill.
Other people go to qualify for a promotion at work.
Some students go just to socialize with other students.

9. Cricket and baseball are very different.
Baseball is played with a round bat.
Cricket is played with a flat bat.
A baseball team has nine players.
A cricket team has eleven players.
Both are summer games.

10. Citizenship is an abstract term.
To most people, it means loyalty.
It also means obedience and conformity.
To a few people, it means thinking for themselves.
It means acting independently.
It means taking control of their own lives.

11. Nursing is a discipline.
    The discipline is concerned with promoting the well-being of the individual.
    A good nurse respects the dignity of each human being.
    She respects the autonomy of each person.
    She respects everyone's individuality.

12. Canada has some unusual place names.
    We find these names all across the country.
    Saskatchewan has a particularly large number of peculiar place names.
    One example is Cut Knife.
    Another example is Moose Jaw.
    Climax is perhaps the most famous example.

13. Newfoundland, too, has some strange-sounding names.
    These names all sound amusing to people who don't live there.
    Jerry's Nose is an example of a strange-sounding name.
    Bumble Bee Bight and Come-by-Chance are other examples.

14. The new Exclusiva is a luxury automobile.
    It is priced for the successful executive.
    It is the ultimate in luxury automobiles.
    It is engineered for safety.
    The new Exclusiva is built for comfort.
    It is powered by a state-of-the-art engine.
    The new Exclusiva looks sleek.
    It looks sophisticated.

15. Lawyers are professionals.
    Doctors are professionals.
    Businesspeople are professionals.
    These professionals make up less than 10 percent of the Canadian workforce.
    They occupy almost 75 percent of the seats in the House of Commons.

16. Blue-collar workers make up nearly 50 percent of Canada's population.
    They hold less than 10 percent of the seats in the House of Commons.
    Women are underrepresented in government.
    Native people and minorities are also underrepresented.
    This fact calls into question our nation's commitment to democracy.

17. Tiananmen Square is in Beijing.
    Beijing is in China.
    Three thousand students began a hunger strike in the square.
    They began their strike on May 13, 1989.

18. The students' demonstration lasted four weeks.
    The students erected a homemade replica of the Statue of Liberty.
    Their statue was 10m tall.
    They called it the Goddess of Democracy.

19. Thousands of armed troops descended on the square.
    The troops fired off tracer bullets and tear gas.
    The soldiers used loudspeakers to urge the students to leave the square.
    The soldiers opened fire directly on the crowds.
    The soldiers charged them with bayonets.

20. Hundreds of demonstrators were killed.
    Hundreds of demonstrators were wounded.
    It was Sunday morning, June 4, 1989.
    It was a massacre.

After you have combined a number of sentences, you can evaluate your work. Read your sentences aloud. How they *sound* is important. Test your work against these six characteristics of successful sentences:

1. MEANING   Have you said what you mean?
2. CLARITY   Is your sentence clear? Can it be understood on the first reading?

3. COHERENCE   Do the parts of your sentence fit together logically and smoothly?

4. EMPHASIS   Are the most important ideas either at the end or at the beginning of the sentence?

5. CONCISENESS   Is the sentence direct and to the point? Have you cut out all redundant or repetitious words?

6. RHYTHM   Does the sentence flow smoothly? Are there any interruptions in the development of the key idea(s)? Do any interruptions help to emphasize important points, or do they distract the reader?

If your sentences pass all six tests of successful sentence style, you may be confident that they are both technically correct and pleasing to the ear. No reader could ask for more.

_____ **UNIT THREE**

Grammar

CHAPTER 11

Choosing the Correct Verb Form

Errors in grammar are like flies in soup: most of the time, they don't affect meaning any more than flies affect flavour. But they are both distracting and irritating. You must eliminate grammar errors from your writing if you want your readers to pay attention to what you say rather than to how you say it.

Good writers pay particularly careful attention to verbs. A verb is to a sentence what an engine is to a car; it is the source of power and a frequent cause of trouble.[1]

In this chapter, we will look at three of the most common problems verbs present: identifying the principal parts of irregular verbs, using present and past participles as adjectives, and choosing between active and passive voice.

Every verb has four forms, called its **principal parts:**

1. The **base** form: used by itself or with do; *can, may, might, will, could, should, would, must; need to, have to, ought to, used to*
2. The **past tense** form: used by itself
3. The **present participle** (the **-ing**) form: used with *am, is, are; was, were; will be; have been,* etc. to form the progressive tenses
4. The **past participle** form: used with *have, has, had* to form the perfect tenses

---

[1] For a review of verb tenses, modals, and negative constructions, see Chapters 27 and 28.

Here are some examples:

BASE	PAST TENSE	PRESENT PARTICIPLE	PAST PARTICIPLE
dance	danced	dancing	danced
learn	learned	learning	learned
play	played	playing	played
seem	seemed	seeming	seemed

To use verbs correctly, you must be familiar with their principal parts. Knowing three facts will help you. First, you won't have trouble with the present participle, the *-ing* form. It is always made up of the base form of the verb + *ing*. Second, your dictionary will give you the principal parts of all **irregular** verbs. Look up the base form, and you'll find the past tense and the present and past participles given beside it, usually in parentheses. For example, if you look up "sing" in your dictionary, you will find *sang* (past tense), *sung* (past participle), and *singing*, (present participle) listed immediately after the verb itself. If the past tense and past participle are not given, the verb is **regular.** So, the third thing you need to know is how to form the past tense and the past participle of regular verbs: add *-ed* to the base form. The examples listed above—*dance, learn, play, seem*—are all regular verbs.

Unfortunately for native speakers and ESL speakers alike, many of the most common English verbs are **irregular.** Their past tenses and past participles are formed in unpredictable ways. The verbs in the list below are used so often that it is worth your time to memorize their principal parts. (We have not included the *-ing* form because, as we have noted above, it never causes any difficulty.)

The Principal Parts of Irregular Verbs

BASE (Use with *can, may, might, shall, will, could, would, should, must*, etc.)	PAST TENSE	PAST PARTICIPLE (Use with *have, has, had*)
awake	awoke/awaked	awaked/awoke
be (am, is)	was/were	been
bear	bore	borne
beat	beat	beaten
become	became	became
begin	began	begun
bid (offer to pay)	bid	bid
bid (say, command)	bid/bade	bid/bidden

BASE	PAST TENSE	PAST PARTICIPLE
(Use with *can, may, might, shall, will, could, would, should, must*)		(Use with *have, has, had*)
bite	bit	bitten
bleed	bled	bled
blow	blew	blown
break	broke	broken
bring	brought	brought
	(*not* brang)	(*not* brung)
broadcast	broadcast	broadcast
build	built	built
burst	burst	burst
buy	bought	bought
catch	caught	caught
choose	chose	chosen
come	came	come
cost	cost	cost
cut	cut	cut
deal	dealt	dealt
dig	dug	dug
dive	dived/dove	dived
do	did (*not* done)	done
draw	drew	drawn
dream	dreamed/dreamt	dreamed/dreamt
drink	drank	drunk
	(*not* drunk)	
eat	ate	eaten
fall	fell	fallen
feed	fed	fed
feel	felt	felt
fight	fought	fought
find	found	found
fling	flung	flung
fly	flew	flown
forget	forgot	forgotten/forgot
forgive	forgave	forgiven
freeze	froze	frozen
get	got	got/gotten
give	gave	given
go	went	gone (*not* went)
grow	grew	grown
hang (suspend)	hung	hung
hang (put to death)	hanged	hanged

BASE	PAST TENSE	PAST PARTICIPLE
(Use with *can, may, might, shall, will, could, would, should, must*)		(Use with *have, has, had*)
have	had	had
hear	heard	heard
hide	hid	hidden
hit	hit	hit
hold	held	held
hurt	hurt	hurt
keep	kept	kept
know	knew	known
lay (put or place)	laid	laid
lead	led	led
leave	left	left
lend	lent (*not* loaned)	lent (*not* loaned)
lie (recline)	lay	lain (*not* layed)
light	lit/lighted	lit/lighted
lose	lost	lost
mean	meant	meant
meet	met	met
pay	paid	paid
raise (to lift up, increase, bring up)	raised	raised
ride	rode	ridden
ring	rang	rung
rise	rose	risen
run	ran	run
say	said	said
see	saw (*not* seen)	seen
sell	sold	sold
set (put or place)	set	set
shake	shook	shaken (*not* shook)
shine	shone	shone
sing	sang	sung
sink	sank	sunk
sit	sat	sat
sleep	slept	slept
slide	slid	slid
speak	spoke	spoken
speed	sped	sped
steal	stole	stolen
stick	stuck	stuck
strike (hit)	struck	struck

BASE	PAST TENSE	PAST PARTICIPLE
(Use with *can, may, might, shall, will, could, would, should, must*)		(Use with *have, has, had*)
strike (affect)	struck	stricken
swear	swore	sworn
swim	swam	swum
swing	swung (*not* swang)	swung
take	took	taken
teach	taught	taught
tear	tore	torn
tell	told	told
think	thought	thought
throw	threw	thrown
wake	woke/waked	waked/woken
wear	wore	worn
weave	wove	woven
win	won	won
wind	wound	wound
wring	wrung	wrung
write	wrote	written

The sentences in the exercises below require both the past tense and the past participle of the verb shown at the left. Write the required form in each blank. Do not add or remove helping verbs. Be sure to check your answers after each set. Answers begin on p. 357.

EXERCISE 11.1

1. wear   We _____ the same thing we had _____

   to Wai and Anna's wedding.

2. build   The house was _____ in a matter of days by the

   same men who _____ my uncle's house.

3. lie   After reading for an hour, I _____ the book

   aside and _____ down for a nap.

4. blow   The wind _____ so hard that it tore the roof off

a shed that had been _____ down.

5. bear   Politely we _____ Tanya's complaining, until

we could not have _____ it another minute.

6. hit   After making four errors in left field, Mohamed came to

bat and _____ the ball harder than he'd ever

_____ it before.

7. ride   Having _____ a cow once, I wouldn't mind if I

never _____ one again.

8. spend   I _____ more on Panna's present than I have

_____ on my mother over the whole year.

9. win   When Omar _____ the contest, he was de-

lighted, for he had never _____ anything

before.

10. tell   Dina _____ her dog to lie down; she should

have _____ it to play dead.

EXERCISE 11.2

1. wind   Maria _____ the clock, not knowing that Janos

had _____ it the night before.

2. tear   Alberto _____ the sheet into strips; when the

sheet was all _____ , he tied the strips together

and escaped through the window.

3. lie   The cat _____ defiantly right where the dog

      had _____ all morning.

4. bite   Terence _____ his nails whenever he was ner-

      vous; as a result, his fingernails were _____ to the

      quick.

5. grow   The vine _____ until it had _____ over

      the window and onto the roof.

6. have   I _____ a funny feeling that I had been

      _____.

7. burst   The little boy _____ into tears when he saw

      that his balloon had _____.

8. run   With the neighbour's dog chasing me, I _____

      faster than I had ever _____ before.

9. make   The kite you _____ flies as well as mine, which

      was _____ in China.

10. bring   Visitors from Chile _____ us a copper tray,

      not knowing that we had _____ one back

      ourselves.

EXERCISE 11.3

1. bid   Lewis _____ $200 for the ceramic bear with a

      clock in its stomach; luckily, someone else had already

      _____ $225.

2. ring   The bell is supposed to be _____ every half hour,

             but the last time it _____ was nine o'clock.

3. see   I would not believe that you _____ a Sasquatch

             if I hadn't _____ it too.

4. break   The talks were _____ off yesterday, just after

             Canada _____ diplomatic ties with North Korea.

5. fight   At our last meeting, we _____ over the same

             issues that we have _____ over for years.

6. keep   The snow _____ falling, which meant that the

             children had to be _____ indoors.

7. put   Cesar _____ his paper in the pile in which the

             other students had _____ theirs.

8. write   I finally _____to my parents, who complained

             that I should have _____ weeks ago.

9. throw   Ahmed _____ the ball that Emilia had

             _____ over the fence.

10. take   Before anyone else could have _____ it, I

             _____ the last piece of cake.

EXERCISE 11.4

1. think   I _____ Jolanta would have _____ to

             ask you to dinner while your roommate was away.

2. begin   We had just _____ to unpack the lunch when

             the rain _____.

3. feel   When I had my tonsils out, I _____ worse than

I had ever _____ before.

4. buy   We _____ twenty lottery tickets, which was

more than we'd _____ the year before.

5. do   We ought not to have _____ it, but we

_____ it anyway.

6. give   For my birthday, Uncle Joseph _____ me the

tie I had _____ him for Christmas.

7. pay   We _____ what they asked for the car, but it

was more than I thought we should have _____ .

8. lend   I _____ her the money, even though I had

_____ her ten dollars a week earlier.

9. go   After everyone else had _____, I _____

home.

10. hurt   It _____ me to learn that you had been

_____ by my careless remark.

EXERCISE 11.5

Now try your hand at this mastery test. No answers have been given for
this exercise.

1. hang   The judge sentenced the prisoner to be _____

by the neck until dead, and they _____ him the

next morning.

2. choose   Despite the fact that we _____ carefully, I'm afraid

that we have _____ the wrong person for the job.

3. swear   Sula _____ she would never tell anyone, and I

               have _____ to pull her hair out if she does.

4. forgive   Boris _____ me, but I have not _____

               him yet.

5. fly   The plane we _____ in looked old enough to

               have been _____ by the Wright brothers.

6. freeze   I _____ the meat, as you asked me to, but I'm

               sure it's been _____ before.

7. shake   After Mei had _____ the money out of her hus-

               band's pants, she _____ them again to be sure

               she had got it all.

8. lay   Jaime _____ his passport on the official's desk

               where all the others had been _____ .

9. swim, dive   After not having _____ or _____

               for years, they _____ and _____ all

               afternoon in the Leungs' pool.

10. eat, drink   We _____ and _____ until we could

               have _____ and _____ no more.

Using Present and Past Participles Correctly

Are you *interested*?   Are you *amused*?
Are you *interesting*?   Are you *amusing*?

Choosing the correct participle form (-*ing* or -*ed*) is often a problem for ESL writers. The passage and statements that follow illustrate the difference between the two:

I hadn't been to the movies in weeks, so last night I treated myself to a recent film starring my favourite actor, Jim Carrey. Like most of his movies, this one was fast-paced, funny, and filled with extraordinary physical stunts. Unlike most of Carrey's movies, this film included a love story and ended happily. I loved it.

> The movie was *entertaining*.   I was *entertained* by the movie.
> The movie was not *boring*.   I was not *bored* by the movie.

To remember when to use the present participle and when to use the past as an adjective, memorize this rule.

> Someone or something is **-ed** if something or someone is **-ing**.

In other words, *-ing* causes *-ed*. The present participle is an **active** adjective: it indicates that the word modified causes a response. The past participle is a **passive** adjective: it indicates that the word modified has been affected by someone or something. For example, someone is *amused* because someone or something is *amusing*:

> Professor Bertrand was *amused* by Luc's question.
> Luc's question was *amusing*.

In the situation above, we don't say, "The movie was entertained; it was not bored," or "I was entertaining, not boring, by this movie." But, following the rule, we can say, "Jim Carrey was *entertaining*, and I was *amused*."

The list that follows contains some of the most often confused and misused pairs of participles.

PRESENT	PAST	PRESENT	PAST
amazing	amazed	frightening	frightened
amusing	amused	horrifying	horrified
annoying	annoyed	interesting	interested
astonishing	astonished	irritating	irritated
boring	bored	loving	loved
confusing	confused	overwhelming	overwhelmed
depressing	depressed	pleasing	pleased
disappointing	disappointed	satisfying	satisfied
disgusting	disgusted	shocking	shocked
disturbing	disturbed	surprising	surprised
embarrassing	embarrassed	terrifying	terrified
exciting	excited	tiring	tired
exhausting	exhausted	worrying	worried

EXERCISE 11.6

Choose the correct adjective in each of the following sentences.

1. Elvis Stojko is an (exciting, excited) skater to watch.
2. When Alex kissed Velma in front of her friends, she felt (embarrassing, embarrassed).
3. Being stuck in Friday afternoon traffic for an hour is an (exhausting, exhausted) experience.
4. Cao was (disappointing, disappointed) with the mark he received on the test.
5. Using an automated teller for the first time can be (confusing, confused).
6. I am (amazing, amazed) that I ever had problems with participles.
7. Saied follows the same routine every day; his life must be (boring, bored).
8. Since Saied follows the same routine every day, I don't understand why he isn't (boring, bored).
9. Are you (satisfying, satisfied) now that you have ruined my evening?
10. When the princess kissed the frog, he was (thrilling, thrilled), but she was (disgusting, disgusted).

EXERCISE 11.7

For each situation below, write two sentences using particples. Use the *-ing* form of the verb given in parentheses in one of your sentences and the *-ed* form in the other. Here's an example:

I spent nine hours working in the library on Saturday. (tire)

   a) Saturday was a *tiring* day.
   b) I was *tired* after spending nine hours in the library.

No answers are given for this exercise.

1. The winter has been long and cold this year. (depress)
2. Professor Jamalian gave us an extra week to do the assignment. (surprise)
3. When the car skidded off the road, Jean managed to stop safely. (terrify)
4. Every Tuesday, the cafeteria offers tuna casserole for lunch. (bore)
5. I have not studied enough for today's test. (worry)
6. Everyone passed the last grammar quiz. (satisfy)
7. We didn't finish watching the video. (bore)
8. I wish Sabira would stop tapping her fingernails on the table. (annoy)
9. Kanga discovered cockroaches in the kitchen and bathroom of his new apartment. (disgust)
10. Basketball has quickly become one of Canada's most popular sports. (amaze)

Choosing between Active and Passive Voice

Most verbs can be classified according to **voice**; they can be either **active** or **passive**. If you want your writing to be effective, you need to know the difference between them. Here is the rule to follow:

> Always use an active verb UNLESS you have a specific reason to choose the passive voice.

You probably use verbs in the passive voice more often than you think you do, and you probably do so unconsciously. To be a better writer, you need to understand the different effects active and passive verbs have on a reader and to use the passive voice only when it is appropriate to your message.

When the subject of a clause performs the action of the verb, the verb is in the active voice. When the subject is being acted upon, the verb is in the passive voice. Sentences in the active voice emphasize *the person* who performs the action. Sentences in the passive voice emphasize *the action* or *the result of the action*, rather than the person who performs it. Study the following examples to see the difference between the two.

ACTIVE VERB	PASSIVE VERB
This tiny machine <u>replaces</u> two workers.	Two workers <u>are replaced</u> by this tiny machine.
The doctor <u>will see</u> you now.	You <u>will be seen</u> by the doctor now.
My father <u>has told</u> me I should be a stand up comedian.	I <u>have been told</u> by my father that I should be a stand up comedian.
After Guy <u>had submitted</u> his essay, his teacher <u>lost</u> it.	After the essay <u>had been submitted</u> by Guy, it <u>was lost</u> by his teacher.

Notice that the sentences with passive verbs have two things in common. First, their verbs consist of some form of *be* + a past participle. Second, the sentences containing passive verbs are longer than those with active verbs.

Because they lead to wordy sentences, you should avoid using passive verbs unless you have a special reason for choosing them. There are three situations in which you should choose the passive voice.

1. The person or agent that performed the action is not known.

Our telephone <u>had been left</u> off the hook for two days.

Primate Road is the name that <u>has been given</u> to our street.

This keyboard <u>is</u> not ergonomically <u>designed</u>.

2. You want to place the emphasis on the person, place, or object that was affected by an action rather than on the subject performing the action.

The computer lab <u>was broken</u> into by a group of angry students.

This sentence focusses the reader's attention on the computer lab rather than on the students. If we reconstruct the sentence in the active voice, we produce a quite different effect:

A group of angry students <u>broke</u> into the computer lab.

3. You are writing a technical report, a scientific report, or a legal document. Passive verbs are the appropriate choice when the focus is on the facts, methods, or procedures involved in an experiment, situation, or event rather than on the person(s) who discovered or performed them. Passive verbs establish an impersonal tone that is appropriate to these kinds of writing. Contrast the emphasis and tone of these sentence pairs:

Passive: The heat <u>was increased</u> to 300° and <u>was maintained</u> at that temperature .

Active: My lab partner and I <u>increased</u> the heat to 300° and <u>maintained</u> it at that temperature.

Passive: Our annual report <u>was approved</u> by the board on February 15.

Active: The board <u>approved</u> our annual report on February 15.

In general, because active verbs are more concise and forceful than passive verbs, they add focus and strength to your writing. When you find a passive verb in your writing, think about *who* is doing *what* to *whom*. Ask yourself why the *who* is not the subject of your sentence. If there is a good reason, then use the passive voice. Otherwise, change the verb.

EXERCISE 11.8

Rewrite the sentences below, changing the verbs from passive to active. You may need to add a word or word group to identify the doer of the action expressed by the verb.

1. The two dollar coin is called a "toonie" by some Canadians.
2. The magnetic strip on my Visa card was destroyed by the scanner at the airport.
3. During the summer, their dog was taken for long walks on the beach by Lucienne and Marcel.
4. The legalization of all recreational drugs was recommended by a panel of conservative thinkers.
5. This beer was brewed by a Bavarian brewmaster living in Burnaby.
6. Several records were broken by the Vancouver Grizzlies during their first season.
7. Some of the most interesting talks at our college this term were given by returning graduates.
8. Our company's letterhead and business cards were designed by a graphics artist who is colour-blind.
9. The police were told by me that my car had been hit by a drunken pedestrian.
10. My wallet was stolen by that woman! She should be stopped!

EXERCISE 11.9

Rewrite the sentences below, changing their verbs from passive to active. Then compare your revision to the original and decide which is more effective.

1. Muhsin's car was driven by him over to Farida's place.
2. All obstacles in the way to my success have been overcome by my unique combination of brains, beauty, and talent.
3. The body had been dragged for approximately 2 k before being hidden in the underbrush.
4. In a photo finish, the race was won by an unknown horse with an unpronounceable name.
5. After a few minutes of panic, Tina's nosebleed was stopped by the bartender's applying an ice cube to her nose.
6. Sears 70% discount sale was taken advantage of by those of us who had waited until January to buy winter clothing.
7. The fact that I had done no homework since the beginning of the term was discovered by a substitute teacher.
8. With only three seconds left in the overtime period, the winning goal was scored by Felix.
9. After the court order had been filed by Aida, it was never seen again.
10. The telephone call was made by our translator, but we were not told what was agreed to.

EXERCISE 11.10

Rewrite the following paragraph, changing passive verbs to active where appropriate. No answer is given for this exercise.

(1) After graduation, Sati was hired by a large publishing company to sell humanities textbooks to college professors. (2) Her first call was made at a university with a huge arts faculty. (3) Her company's books were being used by many of the professors, so Sati was not too worried about having to sell aggressively. (4) The popular history text on her list, however, had not been adopted by all faculty in the history department, so that is where her visit was begun. (5) A list of all the faculty members in the department was provided to Sati by the secretary. (6) Her book was not being used by professors Maheu, Jaffer, and Vacant, so the search for their offices was begun. (7) According to the schedule posted on his door, a class was being taught by Professor Maheu for the next two hours. (8) Professor Jaffer was found by Sati to be receptive and pleasant, but the text was not appropriate for the courses being taught by her. (9) Last, Sati went to find Professor Vacant, and his office was finally located by her. (10) She knocked on the door and was told to come in. (11) When Professor Vacant was asked for by Sati, the woman at one of the desks in the office looked blank. (12) She said there was no person in the history department by that name. (13) The fact that Professor Vacant's name was on the list Sati had been given was politely pointed out by her. (14) The woman at the desk looked at the list and began to laugh. (15) Finally, the joke was understood by Sati. (16) There was no Professor Vacant; the history department had a vacant position.

CHAPTER 12

Mastering Subject–Verb Agreement

One of the most common grammatical errors is failure to make the subject and the verb in a sentence agree with each other. Here is the rule for subject–verb agreement:

> Singular subjects take singular verbs.
> Plural subjects take plural verbs.

Singular and Plural

Here's an example of the singular and plural forms of a regular verb in the present tense:

	SINGULAR	PLURAL
1st person	I work	we work
2nd person	you work	you work
3rd person	*she (he, it, one, the student) works	*they (the students) work

From this example, you can figure out what the word **person** means. We have asterisked the third person singular and plural forms of the verb because these are the only forms likely to cause you trouble. In the third person, the endings of verbs and their subjects do not match. Singular verbs end in "s" *(works)*, but singular subjects do not *(student)*. Plural subjects regularly end in "s" *(students)*, but plural verbs do not *(work)*. When you are using a regular verb in the third person, remember that *either* the subject *or* the verb ends in "s," but not both.

Singular words concern one person or thing.

> The <u>phone</u> <u>rings</u>. <u>Claude</u> <u>sleeps</u>.

Plural words (and multiple subjects) concern more than one person or thing:

> The <u>phones</u> <u>ring</u>. The <u>boys</u> <u>sleep</u>. <u>Claude and Saied</u> <u>snore</u>.

The rule governing subject–verb agreement will cause you no difficulty so long as you make sure that the word the verb agrees with is really the subject of the sentence. To see how problems can arise, look at this example:

> One of the boys write graffiti.

The writer of this sentence forgot that the subject of a sentence is never in a prepositional phrase. The verb needs to be changed to agree with the true subject, *One*:

> <u>One</u> of the boys <u>writes</u> graffiti.

If you're careful about identifying the subject of your sentence, you'll have no difficulty with subject–verb agreement.

EXERCISE 12.1

Rewrite each sentence below, switching the position of its two main elements. Answers begin on p. 358.

Example: <u>Doritos</u> <u>are</u> my favourite snack.
     My favourite <u>snack</u> <u>is</u> Doritos.

1. What Vinh spends most of his money on is clothes.
   Clothes
2. Hostess Twinkies are the only junk food Tim eats.
3. Brown rice and tofu are my least favourite meal.

4. What Canada needs now is strong leadership and more jobs.
5. The reason for Eugene's failure was too many absences from class.
6. Vince's favourite pastime is computer games, especially *Doom* and *Myst*.
7. Disputes over wages and benefits are often the cause of strikes.
8. What I find fascinating is the differences between the Chinese and the Canadian attitudes toward the elderly.
9. Something Tanh always enjoys is political discussions.
10. Garlic, a cross, and a stake through the heart are the only known protection against a vampire attack.

So far, so good. You can find the subject, even when it's hiding on the far side of the verb or buried under a load of prepositional phrases. You can match up singular subjects with singular verbs, and plural subjects with plural verbs. Now let's take a look at a few of the complications that make subject–verb agreement such a disagreeable problem.

Six Special Cases

Some subjects are tricky. They look singular but are actually plural, or they look plural when they're really singular. There are six kinds of these slippery subjects, all of them common, and all of them likely to trip up the unwary writer.

---

1. Multiple subjects joined by *or; either . . . or; neither . . . nor;* or *not . . . but.*

All the multiple subjects we've dealt with so far have been joined by *and* and have required plural verbs, so agreement hasn't been a problem. But watch out when the two or more elements of a compound subject are joined by *or; either . . . or; neither . . . nor;* or *not . . . but.* In these cases, the verb agrees in number with the nearest subject. That is, if the subject closest to the verb is singular, the verb will be singular; if the subject closest to the verb is plural, the verb must be plural, too.

Neither the <u>federal government</u> nor the <u>provinces</u> <u>accept</u> responsibility for the deficit.

Neither the <u>provinces</u> nor the <u>federal government</u> <u>accepts</u> responsibility for the deficit.

EXERCISE 12.2
Circle the correct verb.

1. Not the parents but the child (seems seem) to control the family.
2. Either "Mrs." or "Ms" (is are) fine with me.
3. Onions, sad movies, or happiness (is are) likely to make her cry.
4. Either your friend or you (is are) lying about the accident.
5. Not cheap liquor but friendly people (is are) what I miss most about the States.
6. The oil company informed me that neither they nor their representative (is are) responsible for the damage to my car.
7. Neither the practical training nor the courses I took (was were) able to prepare me for the job.
8. According to a recent survey, not sexual incompatibility but disagreements over children (cause causes) the most strain in a marriage.
9. Not high unemployment but high interest rates (remain remains) Canadians' first concern.
10. Neither the landlord nor the tenants (know knows) who is responsible for the break-in.

> 2. Subjects that look multiple but really aren't.

Don't be fooled by phrases beginning with such words as *with, like, as well as, together with, in addition to, including.* These phrases are NOT part of the subject of the sentence. Mentally cross them out; they do not affect the verb.

> My math professor, as well as my counsellor, has advised me to change my major.

Two people were involved in the advising; nevertheless, the subject (<u>professor</u>) is singular, and so the verb must be singular (<u>has advised</u>).

> All my courses, including English, are easier this term.

If you mentally cross out the phrase "including English," you can easily see that the verb (<u>are</u>) must be plural to agree with the plural subject (<u>courses</u>).

EXERCISE 12.3
Circle the correct verb.

1. Eddie Vedder, with Pearl Jam, (is are) beginning a North American tour soon.
2. Margaret Atwood, like many contemporary Canadian authors, (write writes) novels with political themes.
3. My accounting assignment, not to mention my psychology and English homework, (is are) enough to drive me to drink.

4. The whole computer package, including monitor, disk drive, printer, and software, (is are) too expensive for us.
5. In spite of the efforts of parents and educators, television, with its mix of adventure shows, comedies, and rock videos, (remain remains) the most popular pastime for young people.
6. My brother, as well as my parents, (want wants) me to move out.
7. The food he serves, along with the drinks he mixes, (is are) delicious.
8. This play, in addition to the ones she wrote in her youth, (is are) guaranteed to put you to sleep.
9. The waiter, along with two busboys and the wine steward, (expect expects) us to tip generously.
10. Full employment, like lower taxes, (has have) become an impossible dream.

---

3. Words ending in *-one, -thing,* or *-body.*

When used as subjects, the following words are always singular. They require the singular form of the verb:

anyone	anything	anybody
everyone	everything	everybody
no one	nothing	nobody
someone	something	somebody

The last part of the word is the tip-off here: every*one*, any*thing*, no*body*. If you focus on this last part, you'll remember to use a singular verb with these subjects. Usually, these words cause trouble only when modifiers crop up between them and their verbs. For example, you would never write "Everyone are here." The trouble starts when you sandwich a group of words in between the subject and the verb. You might, if you weren't on your toes, write this: "Everyone involved in implementing the company's new policies and procedures are here." The meaning is plural: several people are present. But the subject (every*one*) is singular, so the verb must be *is.*

EXERCISE 12.4
Circle the correct verb.

1. Everybody on the fourth and fifth floors (was were) questioned by the police inspector.
2. No one who had seen the murderer (was were) found.
3. Everyone, including the victim's husband, (believe believes) the butler did it.

4. Anyone with information leading to an arrest (is are) entitled to a reward.
5. So far, no one but Jessica Fletcher (seem seems) entitled to the money.
6. Everything she had discovered, including the clue of the blood-stained Adidas, (is are) to be revealed tonight.
7. Until then, absolutely nothing in the victim's rooms (is are) to be touched.
8. Nobody (dare dares) challenge Ms. Fletcher's explanation of the crime.
9. *Murder, She Wrote* (has have) for years been one of television's most popular mystery programs.
10. Its star, Angela Lansbury, after numerous facelifts, (look looks) younger with every passing year.

> 4. *Each (of), either (of), neither (of).*

Used as subjects, these take singular verbs. (Remember, the subject is never in a prepositional phrase.)[1]

> Either <u>was</u> suitable for the job.
> Each of the boys <u>dreams</u> of scoring the winning goal.
> Neither of the stores <u>is</u> open after six o'clock.

EXERCISE 12.5
Circle the correct verb.

1. Neither of the singers (work works) very hard.
2. Either (is are) likely to be fired.
3. Neither of the proposals (interest interests) me.
4. Each of the contestants (hope hopes) to be chosen.
5. Either of the available seats (is are) very close to the stage.
6. I am sorry to say that neither (is are) ready to be used.
7. Each of the instructors (was were) eccentric in both method and appearance.
8. We were astonished to learn that each of them (has have) won a full-tuition scholarship.
9. If either of the candidates (answer answers) my questions honestly, then that person will get my vote.

---

[1] Note that the object in these prepositional phrases is always plural. We do NOT write "One of the student was late for class," or "Each of the boy dreams of scoring the winning goal."

10. Each of the leads in the *Star Trek* series, William Shatner, Patrick Stewart, and Avery Brook, (has have) played Shakespeare and other classical roles in live theatre.

---

5. Collective nouns.

A collective noun is a word naming a group. Some examples are *band, gang, orchestra, company, class, committee, team, crowd, public, family, audience, group,* and *majority.* When you are referring to the group acting as a unit, use a singular verb. When you are referring to the members of the group acting individually, use a plural verb.

> The <u>team</u> <u>is</u> sure to win tomorrow's game. (Here *team* refers to the group acting as a whole.)
>
> The <u>team</u> <u>are</u> getting into their uniforms now. (The separate members of the team are acting individually.)

EXERCISE 12.6
Circle the correct verb.

1. The nuclear family (is are) the fundamental unit of society.
2. The electorate (seem seems) to be in an ugly, vengeful mood.
3. My department (pride prides) itself on a high degree of efficiency.
4. The budget committee (fight fights) among themselves continually.
5. (Has Have) the jury reached a verdict?
6. Having waited for almost an hour, the crowd (was were) growing restless.
7. Our office (give gives) a farewell party whenever anyone leaves.
8. The majority of immigrants (find finds) Canada a tolerant country.
9. The entire gang, without exception, (is are) getting together this weekend.
10. The audience (sit sits) impatiently, waiting for the concert to begin.

---

6. Units of money, time, mass, length, and distance.

These require singular verbs.

> <u>Six dollars</u> <u>is</u> too much to pay for a hamburger.
> <u>Two hours</u> <u>seems</u> like four in our sociology class.
> <u>Five kilometres</u> <u>is</u> too far to walk.
> <u>Eighty kilograms</u> <u>is</u> the weight of an average man.

EXERCISE 12.7

Circle the correct verb.

1. Three hours (seem seems) to pass very quickly when I'm at the movies.
2. Patients who suffer from anorexia nervosa find that even 40 kg (seem seems) like too much weight.
3. Ninety-nine cents (seem seems) a fair price.
4. Thirty dollars (is are) all I need for a ticket to Barenaked Ladies.
5. Forty years in the desert (is are) a long time to delay one's gratification.
6. Twenty centimetres of snow in six hours (was were) enough to paralyze the city.
7. Six dollars an hour for babysitting (is are) not bad.
8. Seven hours of classes (is are) too much for one day.
9. Thirty years of working at the same job from nine to five, five days a week, fifty weeks a year, (go goes) by very slowly.
10. When you are cooking your turkey, remember that twelve kilos (take takes) about seven hours in a 170° oven.

In exercises 12.8 and 12.9, correct the errors in subject–verb agreement. Check your answers to each exercise before going on.

EXERCISE 12.8

1. A group of unbiased students and faculty are trying to solve the problem.

2. Anybody who really want to succeed will do so.

3. Over the past ten years, the number of couples living together has increased greatly.

4. Every one of the contestant think winning a week in Lackawanna would be wonderful.

5. You'll find that not only ragweed but also cat hairs makes you sneeze.

6. If there is no bubbles, then you have patched your tire successfully.

7. Neither Amelash nor I is a very strong swimmer.

8. The lack of things to write about cause the headaches.

9. Michael Jackson, along with his handlers, pets, and bodyguards, have begun another world tour.

10. The amount of money generated by rock stars on concert tours are enormous.

EXERCISE 12.9

There's many good reasons for staying fit. The diminished strength, flexibility, and endurance that results from lack of exercise are very compelling factors, but everyone who joins the many health clubs in this city have individual reasons as well. The people I talked with says appearance or weight loss are their main motivation for working out. No one among the two hundred patrons of a local health club were there for the social life, according to my poll. Either weightlifting or daily aerobics was what they · wanted from their club, and the intensity of the workouts were clear evidence that they were serious. The manager of the club, along with all the members of the staff, were careful to point out that supervised exercise is essential for best results, but neither she nor her staff was in favour of fad diets or sweat programs.

EXERCISE 12.10

Complete the sentences using present-tense verbs. Then check the answer section to see whether your verbs should be singular or plural.

1. Neither my boss nor the receptionist

2. Everybody with two or more pets

3. Not the lead singer but the musicians

4. A flock of birds

5. Every one of his employees

6. Ten dollars

7. The whole family, including two aunts and six cousins,

8. The actors, as well as the director,

9. Either a Big Mac or a Whopper

10. No one among the hundreds present

EXERCISE 12.11

As a final check of your mastery of subject–verb agreement, correct the following sentences. No answers are provided for this exercise.

1. All of Ravi's courses, including drafting and architectural history, is easier for him this term.

2. Either the class or the instructor were mistaken about the due date for the project.

3. Although you are unsure of your position on the issue, everyone else in my classes want to ban Rush Limbaugh from the airwaves.

4. A losing coach, together with his hapless players, are often abused by the media.

5. Each of those outfits give Laszlo a seedy, disreputable look.

6. There is a buxom woman and two beefy gentlemen lurking in the parking lot waiting for you.

7. Did you know that a "pride" of lion are what a group of them are called?

8. Twenty dollars seem like a lot to pay for a portrait of Elvis on velvet.

9. Everyone who fear for the life of this planet are concerned about global warming and the depletion of the ozone layer.

10. Either Ngoc or Liang, together with the children, are going to the Galaxyland on Saturday.

CHAPTER 13

Keeping Your Tenses Consistent

Verbs are time markers. Changes in tense express changes in time: past, present, or future.

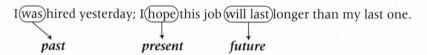

I was hired yesterday; I hope this job will last longer than my last one.

     past   *present*   *future*

Sometimes, as in the sentence above, it is necessary to use several different tenses in a single sentence to get the meaning across. But most of the time, whether you're writing a sentence or a paragraph, you use one tense throughout. Normally, you choose either the past or the present tense, depending on the nature of your topic. (Very few paragraphs are written completely in the future tense.) Here is the rule to follow:

> Don't change tense unless meaning requires it.

Readers like and expect consistency. If you begin a sentence with "I argued, protested, and even attempted an appeal to his masculine pride," the reader will tune in to the past-tense verbs and expect any other verbs in the sentence to be in the past tense too. So, if you finish the sentence with ". . . but he looks at me with those big blue eyes and gets me to pay for dinner," your readers will be jolted abruptly out of one time frame into another. This sort of jolting is uncomfortable, and readers don't like it.

Shifting tenses is like shifting gears: it should be done smoothly and when necessary—never abruptly, out of carelessness, or on a whim. Avoid causing verbal whiplash; keep your tenses consistent.

Problem: Meiling goes into the garage and tried to start the car.
Solution 1: Meiling went into the garage and tried to start the car.
Solution 2: Meiling goes into the garage and tries to start the car.

Problem: Rudolf delayed until the last possible minute, but then begins to write his paper. When he gets halfway through, he decided to change his topic.
Solution 1: Rudolf delayed as long as possible, but then began to write his paper. When he got halfway through, he decided to change his topic.
Solution 2: Rudolf delays as long as possible, but then begins to write his paper. When he gets halfway through, he decides to change his topic.

In the exercises for this section, most of the sentences contain unnecessary tense shifts. Use the first verb in each sentence as your time marker and change the tense(s) of the other verb(s) to agree with it. Answers begin on p. 360.

EXERCISE 13.1

1. Allan went home and tells Guljan what happened.

2. Kristi was so tired that, about ten minutes after class started, she goes right to sleep.

3. The umpire stands there, rubbing his eyes, unable to believe what he was seeing.

4. The goalie must not move from his stand until the penalty kicker makes contact with the ball.

5. When I answered the phone, there is yet another person on the line soliciting a contribution to some worthy cause.

6. First, gently fry the onion, garlic, and seasonings; then you will brown the meat.

7. Kyra watched TV all evening until she finally fell asleep at about midnight.

8. My deadline is next Thursday, by which time I had to have an outline and a rough draft ready for my prof's inspection.

9. I drank a half-litre of milk, then I eat two protein- and veggie-stuffed sandwiches, and I am ready for anything.

10. When Roch Voisine came on stage, the crowd goes crazy.

EXERCISE 13.2

1. First, backcomb your hair into spikes, then you'll coat your head with glue.

2. The guard walked over and punches me in the stomach.

3. The Peter Principle states that every employee will rise to his or her level of incompetence.

4. Amin and Mia go on their first date and it is a disaster; however, they decided to try again.

5. The couple living in the next apartment had a boa constrictor that keeps getting loose.

6. Even though I spoke to Rudolf just last week about being on time for class, this morning he wanders in twenty minutes late.

7. Prejudice is learned and will be hard to outgrow.

8. As usual, Professor Campbell began by asking a rhetorical question that he proceeds to answer without waiting for anyone in the class to attempt to respond.

9. Are you going to this week's game? It'll be sure to be the best one of the series.

10. Just as time runs out, Emir launched a shot at the basket from the centre line. It missed the rim by about two metres.

EXERCISE 13.3

Correct the faulty tense shifts in this paragraph. Use the italicized verb as your time marker.

As a boy, Ralph *had* a remarkable knack for making accurate predictions about the future. When he was 7, he announces to anyone who would listen that he would be a millionaire by the time he is old enough to vote. When he was 11, he predicts that he would star in a major motion picture by the time he reaches the legal driving age. At the age of 14, he prophesies that he would be elected mayor before his twenty-third birthday. Incredibly, his predictions come to pass, one after the other. At 16, he becomes the youngest person ever to play James Bond in a movie, and this role leads to other projects and a salary well into six figures. Good financial advice and careful investing make him a millionaire in two years. With all that money behind him, there will be no stopping Ralph's campaign to have become, at 22, the youngest mayor in Red Deer's history. However, his amazing early successes are not sustainable, and Ralph becomes a has-been by the time he turns 25.

EXERCISE 13.4

Test your mastery of tense consistency by correcting the following sentences. No answers are given for this exercise.

1. When the fax machine broke down, the whole office goes into a state of panic.

2. Lisa sat in front of the computer for two hours trying to detect the bug in her program, and when finally she sees it, she knew immediately how to correct it.

3. After school, Terry went straight to the fast-food restaurant where she is a cashier and gets into her uniform.

4. I was so sick that I go to bed and don't get up for three days.

5. The building manager agreed to rent us an apartment only after we offered her a substantial bribe.

6. We knew that Rudolf would fail math; he keeps skipping class.

7. It was not until the Constitution Act of 1982 that Canada becomes fully responsible for its own destiny.

8. Ron says there were none left, but I wanted to see for myself, so I drive to the store and find he was right.

9. The detective climbs the stairs as the music got louder and louder. Just when you can't stand it any more, the old woman leaped out at him and stabs him to death.

10. A new era was upon us. No more are we at the mercy of invisible bureaucrats and politicians. Now we are at the mercy of invisible experts and poll takers.

CHAPTER 14

Choosing the Correct Pronoun Form

After verbs, pronouns are the class of words most likely to cause problems for writers. In this chapter and the two following, we will look at the three aspects of pronoun usage that can trip you up if you're not careful: pronoun **form, agreement,** and **consistency.** We will also consider the special problems of usage that lead to sexist language.

English has eight different kinds of pronouns, but only three kinds are potentially troublesome for the writer:

> *personal pronouns: I, you, we, she, they,* etc.
> *relative pronouns: who, that, which,* etc.
> *indefinite pronouns: anyone, somebody, none, each,* etc.

Consider these examples of incorrect pronoun usage:

Her and me decided to rent a video.

Between you and I, I think Biff is cheating again.

How do you know which form of a pronoun to use? The answer depends on the pronoun's place and function in your sentence.

There are two forms of personal pronouns. One is used for subjects and one is used for objects. Pronoun errors occur when you confuse the two. In Chapter 5, you learned to identify the subject of a sentence. Keep that information in mind as you learn this basic rule:

> When the subject of a sentence is (or is referred to by) a pronoun, that pronoun must be in **subject form;** otherwise, use the **object form.**

SUBJECT PRONOUNS

Singular	*Plural*
I	we
you	you
he, she, it, one	they

<u>She</u> and <u>I</u> <u>decided</u> to rent a video. (The pronouns are the subject of the sentence.)

The lucky <u>winners</u> of the all-expenses-paid weekend in Pelvis, Saskatchewan, <u>are</u> *they.* (The pronoun refers to the subject of the sentence, "winners.")

The only <u>person</u> who handed in the assignment on time <u>was</u> *she.* (The pronoun refers to the subject of the sentence, "person.")

We serious <u>bikers</u> <u>prefer</u> Harleys to Hondas. (The pronoun refers to the subject of the sentence, "bikers.")

OBJECT PRONOUNS

Singular	*Plural*
me	us
you	you
him, her, it, one	them

Between you and *me,* <u>I</u> <u>think</u> Biff is cheating again. ("Me" is not the subject of the sentence; it is one of the objects of the preposition "between.")

<u>Karim</u> <u>asked</u> both *her* and *me* to the semiformal. ("Her" and "me" are not the subject of the verb "asked"; they are the direct object of "asked.")

The <u>police</u> <u>are</u> always suspicious of *us* bikers. ("Us" does not refer to the subject of the sentence, "police"; it refers to "bikers," the object of the preposition "of.")

Be especially careful with pronouns in multiple subjects or after prepositions. If you can remember these two rules, you'll be able to eliminate most potential errors in pronoun form:

---

1. A pronoun that is part of a multiple subject is *ALWAYS* in subject form.
2. A pronoun that follows a preposition is *ALWAYS* in object form.

Examples:

She and *I* <u>had</u> tickets to The Tragically Hip. (The pronouns are used as a multiple subject.)

We are counting on *you* and *him* to finish the project. (The pronouns follow the preposition "on.")

Here's a practically foolproof way for native English speakers to tell which pronoun form is needed. (ESL speakers, unfortunately, must rely on memorizing the rules.) When the sentence contains a pair of pronouns, mentally cross one out. Applying this technique to the first example above, you get "*She* had tickets" and "*I* had tickets," both of which sound right and are correct. In the second sentence, if you try the pronouns separately, you get "We are counting on *you*" and "We are counting on *him*." Again, you know by the sound that these are the correct forms. You would never say, "*Her* had tickets," or "*Me* had tickets," or "We are counting on *he*." If you deal with paired pronouns one at a time, you are unlikely to choose the wrong form.

EXERCISE 14.1

Choose the correct pronouns from the words given in parentheses.

1. Those videotapes belong to Patrick and (I me).
2. I can't believe that the committee would choose Bennie along with (we us).
3. Neither (they them) nor (us we) deserve to be treated like this.
4. Danny and (he him) think no one knows they smoke in the stairwell.
5. Just between you and (I me), the engagement between Yolande and (he him) is off.
6. If I have to choose between (he him) and you, I'm afraid it is (he him) who will be going to the lake with me.
7. As devoted television watchers, (us we) love it when (us we) and the program producers share similar tastes.

8. It would be preferable for (them they) to come here rather than for (us we) to go there.
9. I can't believe Chandra would break up with me after (her she) and (I me) got matching tattoos and navel rings.
10. It is likely that (us we) musicians would get more favourable reviews from the critics if we and (them they) met socially more often.

EXERCISE 14.2

Correct the errors in pronoun form in the following sentences.

1. Her and me have completely different tastes in music, though we agree on practically everything else.
2. There aren't many vegetarians besides Ettore and I who are so strict that they will not wear leather or wool.
3. It is not for you or I to decide whether they go to the game or stay home.
4. Iain and her are the best curlers on our team; if it weren't for they, we would be in last place.
5. Her and Marie took the magazines before either Tom or me had had a chance to read them.
6. Us and them were exhausted from studying all night, so we can't be blamed for the explosion.
7. Fate has put we two together and no matter what her or your father says, it is us who will live happily ever after at the end of the story.
8. Have you and him finally finished your project, or must us seniors do your work for you again?
9. It is up to you and he to piece together the clues and come up with the solution to the crime so that us innocent victims can be set free.
10. I don't need to see my doctor because I know that my chiropractor and her agree that I should not play in the championship game tonight, and they are both fans of we "Fighting Treefrogs."

Choosing the correct pronoun form is more than just a matter of not wanting to appear ignorant or careless. Sometimes, the form you use determines the meaning of your sentence. Consider these two sentences:

> Lin treats her dog better than *I*.
> Lin treats her dog better than *me*.

There's a world of difference between the meaning of the subject form: "Lin treats her dog better than *I* [do]" and the object form: "Lin treats her dog better than [she treats] *me*."

When using a pronoun after *than,* or *as well as,* or *as,* decide whether you mean to contrast the pronoun with the subject of the sentence. If you do, use the subject form of the pronoun. If not, use the object form.

Example:

Tammy would rather listen to Jim Witter than I. (*I* is contrasted with *Tammy.*)

Tammy would rather listen to Jim Witter than me. (*Me* is contrasted with *Jim Witter.*)

EXERCISE 14.3

Correct the following sentences where necessary.

1. Nobody hates English more than me.

2. She is more frightened of being alone than him.

3. Everyone wanted to go to the movies except Yvon and I.

4. More than me, Yuxiang uses the computer to draft and revise his papers.

5. Only a few Mexican food fanatics can eat jalapeno peppers as well as him.

6. At last I have met someone who enjoys barbecued eel as much as me!

7. After our instructor handed out the papers, Rudolf and me got into a fight.

8. Since he had copied his essay from me, he shouldn't have got a better grade than me.

9. Rudolf's thinking is that since he is better looking than me, he deserves the higher mark.

10. I have a real problem with a teacher who gives good marks to they who are blessed with a winning smile and great hair.

EXERCISE 14.4

Correct the pronouns where necessary in the following sentences. No answers have been given for this exercise.

1. No one feels worse about your loss than my family and me.

2. I decided not to apply for the position because both Pol and Stella wanted it more than me, and I didn't want to risk losing our friendship by being selected over they.

3. Quint likes our local talk-show host better than me and often calls in to her show. My roommate and me, on the other hand, have little interest in current affairs and just listen to music all day long.

4. My mother would rather cook for my brother than I because, unlike me, he never complains when dinner is burned or raw.

5. It is foolish to suppose that both the Flyers and us will finish out of the playoffs, so you will have to meet either they or us before you can claim the cup.

6. The responsibility for the shortfall in sales this month falls on marketing and we, even though I think it's clear they were more negligent than us.

7. I enjoy talking to Rogelio more than them, but if there's no one else around, I'll endure a conversation with they.

8. The major difference between Eugene and me is that he thinks he's perfect, while I am.

9. Us full-time computer programmers are curious to know why the person who was awarded the contract for designing the new software was her, a part-timer without qualifications.

10. To increase your chances of getting the raise you want, you should speak to your supervisor first, then she, but between you and I, it's a good idea to wait until she's had her morning coffee.

Mastering Pronoun– Antecedent Agreement

Now that you know how to choose the correct form of pronouns within a sentence, let's look at how to use pronouns consistently throughout a sentence and a paragraph.

Pronoun–Antecedent Agreement

The name of this pronoun problem may sound difficult, but the idea is very simple. Pronouns are words that substitute for or refer to the name of a person, place, or thing mentioned elsewhere in your sentence or your paragraph. The word(s) that a pronoun substitutes for or refers to is called the **antecedent.**

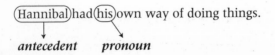

Hannibal had his own way of doing things.

antecedent   pronoun

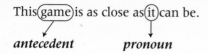

This game is as close as it can be.

antecedent   *pronoun*

Normally, as in these two examples, the antecedent comes before the pronoun that refers to it. The rule to remember is this:

> A pronoun must agree with its antecedent.

You probably follow this rule most of the time without even realizing that you know it. For example, you would never write

Hannibal had *its* own way of doing things.
or
This game is as close as *she* can be.

You know that these pronouns don't agree with their antecedents.

There are three kinds of pronoun–antecedent agreement, however, that you need to watch out for. They involve **relative pronouns**; **indefinite pronouns ending in** *-one, -body,* **or** *-thing*; and **vague references**.

1. Relative Pronouns

The first potential difficulty with pronoun–antecedent agreement is how to use the relative pronouns—*who, whom, which,* and *that*—correctly. Relative pronouns can be used only to refer to someone or something already specifically mentioned in the sentence. Here is the guideline to follow:

> *Who* and *whom, whoever* and *whomever* refer to people.
> *That* and *which* refer to everything else.

The player *who* was injured had to be taken to the hospital.

The students *who* were present supported the dean's proposal.

The moose *that* I met looked hostile.

Her report, *which* is due today, will address most of the concerns *that* the union has raised.

Whether you need *who* or *whom, whoever* or *whomever,* depends on the pronoun's place and function in your sentence. Apply the basic pronoun rule:

> If the pronoun is acting as, or refers to, the subject, use *who/whoever.* Otherwise, use *whom/whomever.*

It was he *who* filled out the form that won us the trip to Pelvis.
(The pronoun refers to the subject of the sentence, "he.")

The trip's promoters were willing to settle for *whomever* they could get.
(The pronoun does not refer to the subject, "promoters"; it is the object of the preposition "for.")

An even simpler solution to this problem is to rewrite the sentence so you don't need either *who* or *whom:*

He filled out the form that won us the trip to Pelvis.

The trip's promoters were willing to settle for anyone they could get.

That is required more often than *which.* You should use *which* only in a clause that is separated from the rest of the sentence by commas.

The moose *that* I met looked hostile.

The moose, *which* was standing right in front of my car, looked hostile.

EXERCISE 15.1

Correct the following sentences where necessary. Answers begin on p. 362.

1. Clive is the only one that wants his picture hung in the board room.

2. Everyone that went to the party had a good time, though a few had more punch than was good for them.

3. Is this the dog which bit the mail carrier that carries a squirt gun?

4. The path led me past the home of a hermit that lives all alone in the forest which surrounds our town.

5. A filmmaker that stays within budget on every production will always have work, no matter how mediocre his movies might be.

6. The open-office concept is one which makes sense to anyone that has worked in a stuffy little cubicle all day.

7. One advantage of the open office is that it lets you see who is working hard and who is taking it easy. It also allows you to spot people that you'd like to meet.

8. The four tests which we wrote today would have defeated anyone that wasn't prepared for them.

9. Sales clerks that want to make good commissions must have good people skills as well as knowledge of the products which they are selling.

10. The winning goal, that was made with only two seconds left in the game, was scored by a player that I used to know in high school.

2. Pronouns Ending in *-one, -body, -thing*

The second tricky aspect of pronoun–antecedent agreement involves these pronouns:

anyone	anybody	anything
everyone	everybody	everything
no one	nobody	nothing
someone	somebody	something
each (one)		

In Chapter 12, you learned that when these words are used as subjects, they are singular and require singular verbs. So it makes sense that the pronouns that stand for or refer to them must also be singular.

> Antecedents ending in *-one, -body,* and *-thing* are singular. They must be referred to by singular pronouns: *he, she, it; his, her, its.*

Each of the students must buy *his* or *her* own lab coat.

Every mother deserves a break from *her* children now and then.

Everybody is expected to do *his* share of the cleaning up.

No one could say that in *his* heart *he* believed she was guilty.

But take another look at the last two sentences. Until about twenty years ago, the pronouns *he, him, his* were used with singular antecedents and referred to both men and women. Today, however, many readers are sensitive to sex bias in writing and feel that it is not appropriate to use the masculine pronoun when referring to both sexes. As a writer, you should be aware of this sensitivity. If you want to appeal to the broadest possible audience, you should avoid what some readers may consider sexist language.

In speech, it has become acceptable to use plural pronouns with *-one, -body,* and *-thing* antecedents. Although these are grammatically singular and take singular verbs, they are often plural in meaning, and in conversation we find ourselves saying

Everybody is expected to do their share of the cleaning up.

No one could say that in their hearts they believed she was guilty.

This usage is acceptable only in speech; it is not acceptable in standard written English. Writers sometimes make errors in pronoun–antecedent agreement because they are trying to write without indicating whether the person referred to is male or female. "Everybody is expected to do *their* share" is incorrect, as we have seen; however, it does avoid making "everybody" male. The writer could replace the plural *their* with the singular and nonsexist *his or her*—"Everybody is expected to do *his or her* share"—but *his or her* sounds clumsy, especially if it is used frequently.

There are two better ways to solve the problem.

1. Revise the sentence to leave the pronoun out.

Everybody is expected to help clean up.

At heart, no one really believed she was guilty.

Such creative avoidance of sex-specific language or incorrect constructions can be an interesting intellectual challenge. The results sometimes sound a little artificial, however. The second solution is easier to accomplish.

2. Revise the sentence to make both the antecedent and the pronoun plural.

> You are all expected to do your share of the cleaning up.

> In our hearts, we did not believe she was guilty.

Here are a couple of examples for you to study:

> **Problem:**   Each of the students has been given his assignment.
> **Revision 1:**   Each of the students has been given an assignment.
> **Revision 2:**   All of the students have been given their assignments.

> **Problem:**   Everyone is looking forward to seeing his or her former classmates again.
> **Revision 1:**   Everyone is looking forward to seeing former classmates again.
> **Revision 2:**   All the graduates are looking forward to seeing their former classmates again.

Tip: If you compose on a word processor, it's easy to find this kind of pronoun-antecedent problem. Use the search function to locate every *they* and *their* in your writing, and check to be sure the antecedent is plural.

EXERCISE 15.2

Identify the most appropriate word(s) from the choices given in parentheses. Check your answers carefully before continuing.

1. Each of the women would prefer to answer the charges (herself, themselves.)
2. Would someone kindly lend (his, their, a) copy of the text to Jan?
3. Any one of us would be happy to take (his, her, his or her, their, the) time to help you.
4. I expect everyone to do (his, her, his or her, their) best in this course.
5. Everyone is expected to pay (his or her, their, a) portion of the expenses.
6. Everybody enjoys getting together with (his or her, their, the) family on Thanksgiving.
7. No one I know is willing to allow (his, her, his or her, their) name to appear on the ballot.
8. None of the pictures we took could be called great by (itself, themselves), but together they make an impressive collection.

9. So far, no one on the football team has been able to get (his, their) parents to donate (his or her, their) house for the party.
10. Any man (that, who) would buy an orange and purple tie should have (his, their) head examined.

EXERCISE 15.3
Correct the errors in the following sentences, being careful to avoid awkward repetition and sexist language.

1. Every child is a product of their environment as well as their heredity.

2. Anyone who would write a sentence like that last one should give up their computer.

3. The team agreed that everyone would have to show up for their practices.

4. Everybody must get in their places for the game to begin.

5. Anybody without a partner will have to try to find one approximately his height.

6. Golf is a game that is good for anyone who wants to enjoy outdoor exercise without getting their body sweaty or hurt.

7. We have asked every student with a complaint to see their instructor.

8. Do you know whether anyone in your neighbourhood wants their house painted or their grass cut this summer?

9. Few people I know enjoys himself on a squash court, but they like to play tennis whenever they can.

10. We're looking for someone whose intelligence and creativity are so outstanding that they can work unsupervised.

3. Vague Reference

Avoiding the third potential difficulty with pronoun–antecedent agreement requires common sense and an ability to put yourself in your reader's place. If you look at your writing from your reader's point of view, it is unlikely that you will break this rule:

A pronoun must *clearly* refer to the correct antecedent.

The mistake that occurs when you fail to follow this rule is called **vague reference.**

> Jules pointed to his brother and said that he had saved his life.

Who saved whom? Here's another:

> Sabina felt that Mary should have been more careful with her car when she lent it to her because she was a good friend of her husband.

Who owns the car? Who has the husband?

In sentences like these, you can only guess the meaning because you don't know who is being referred to by the pronouns. The antecedents are not clear. You can make such sentences less confusing either by using proper names (Jules, Sabina, Mary) more frequently or by changing the sentences around. These solutions aren't difficult; they just take a little time and some imagination. Try them on our examples.

Another type of vague reference occurs when there is no antecedent in the sentence for the pronoun to refer to.

> He loves watching off-road rallies and would love to do it himself one day. (Do what?)

> Snowboarding is her favourite winter sport, so it's odd that she doesn't own one. (One what?)

How would you revise these sentences?

Make sure that every pronoun has a clear antecedent, and that every pronoun agrees with its antecedent. Both must be singular or both must be plural. Once you have mastered this principle, you'll have no trouble with pronoun–antecedent agreement.

EXERCISE 15.4

Correct the following sentences where necessary. There are several ways to fix these sentences. In some cases, the antecedents are missing and you won't know what is being referred to. In other cases, the antecedents are so vague that the meaning of the sentence can be interpreted in more than one way.

1. Max is a good skater, which he practises daily.

2. He didn't hear her cry for help, which was due to his wearing earplugs.

3. That Miss Grundy would be Betty's teacher never occurred to her.

4. Every time David looked at the dog, he barked.

5. In a rage, Biff threw his ghetto blaster on the floor and cracked it.

6. Carla told her mother she was sure to get a job soon.

7. Whenever Rudolf and Biff met, he acted in a relaxed, friendly fashion so that no one would suspect he hated him.

8. Krystal told Sparkle she was losing her looks.

9. At our college, they introduced a "no smoking" policy three years ago.

10. I am writing this letter in response to your ad for a waiter and bartender, male or female. Being both, I wish to apply for the position.

EXERCISE 15.5

Correct the problems in the following paragraph, which contains all three kinds of pronoun–antecedent agreement errors. Part of the challenge in this exercise is to make the paragraph not only grammatically correct, but also free of sexist language.

Anyone that has competed in a triathlon (a three-part race consisting of swimming, cycling, and running) knows that proper training is an absolute necessity, not only to their success, but also to their survival. Swimming is one of the toughest contests, because it demands cardiovascular fitness as well as strength, and it makes demands on the whole body. While each of the three segments has their own challenges, the cycling part of the triathlon is the event which separates serious athletes from part-time fitness buffs. Here, he will find he can't summon enough energy after his swim to stay close to his opponent if he has trained harder than he. The serious athlete will begin to assert their dominance now, and by the end of the bike ride, anyone that has achieved a high level of physical efficiency through their training will still have a chance of a high placing. For the competitor in a triathlon, survival is often the primary goal. The body's reserves are called on, and only the dedicated, well-trained athlete will be able to do it. For most, reaching the finish line is a personal test, and the only competition is against one's previous finish times. The person that still has winning in mind after the swim, the cycle race, and the run has physical and mental reserves beyond the ordinary.

EXERCISE 15.6

Check your mastery of pronoun–antecedent agreement by correcting the errors in the following sentences. No answers have been provided for this exercise.

1. Each of the boys tried their best, so it was difficult for them to decide who should receive the "most enthusiastic player" award.

2. When it comes to snacking, Sharon can't resist those which are loaded with butter and sugar.

3. His scoring is the reason he was added to the team, but he hasn't got one in the last six games.

4. Anyone that wants to understand the Internet needs to have lots of time on their hands to spend exploring and experimenting.

5. The disagreement between Karin and Marie has finally gone too far; if she doesn't ask her to go, the rest of us will have to leave.

6. Attila is the one that asked all those at a party to divulge his or her most personal fantasies, and then wrote a movie script based on their stories.

7. "Is there *anyone* in the class that has finished their experiment yet?" Professor Bunsen asked testily.

8. We want to thank everyone that was so kind to us with their good wishes and generous wedding gifts, and also to inform them that, in spite of the recent divorce, we do sincerely appreciate their thoughtfulness.

9. Since I discovered the efficiency and fun of computing, all I dream about is getting one with a CD-ROM, a colour laser printer, and about three hundred games.

10. The lawyers directed the accountants to get their books in order so that, when the tax auditors checked their records, they could prove they had suffered substantial business losses during the past year.

CHAPTER 16

Maintaining Person Agreement

So far, we have focussed on using pronouns correctly and clearly within a sentence. Now let's turn to the problem of **person agreement,** which means using pronouns consistently in number and gender throughout a sentence or a paragraph. There are three categories of person that we use when we write or speak:

	SINGULAR	PLURAL
First person:	I; me	we; us
Second person:	you	you
Third person:	she, he, it, one; her, him; and all pronouns ending in *-one, -thing, -body*	they; them

Here is the rule for person agreement:

> Do not mix "persons" unless meaning requires it.

In other words, be consistent. If you begin a sentence using a second-person pronoun, you must use second person all the way through. Look at this sentence:

If *you* wish to succeed, *one* must work hard.

This is the most common error—mixing second-person *you* with third-person *one.*

Here's another example:

> *One* can live happily in Vancouver if *you* have a sturdy umbrella.

We can correct this error by using the second person throughout:

> *You* can live happily in Vancouver if *you* have a sturdy umbrella.

or by using the third person throughout:

> *One* can live happily in Vancouver if *one* has a sturdy umbrella.
> *or*
> *One* can live happily in Vancouver if *he or she* has a sturdy umbrella.

These last three sentences raise two points of style that you should consider.

1. Don't overuse *one.* Although all three revised sentences are correct, they affect the reader differently. The first sentence, in the second person, sounds the most informal and natural—like something you would say. It's a bit casual for general writing purposes. The second sentence, which uses *one* twice, sounds the most formal—even a little stilted. The third sentence falls between the other two in formality and is the one you'd be most likely to use in writing for school or business. It's grammatically correct and nonsexist, but it raises another potential problem.
2. Don't overuse *he or she.* If this construction occurs frequently, the reader cannot help shifting focus from what you're saying to how you're saying it. The best writing is transparent—that is, it doesn't call attention to itself. If your reader becomes distracted by your style, your meaning gets lost. Consider this sentence:

> A student can easily pass this course if he or she applies himself or herself to his or her studies.

Awkward, isn't it? Imagine being the unfortunate reader who has to struggle through a paragraph filled with this clumsy construction!

The solutions to this problem are the same as those for making pronouns ending in *-one, -body,* or *-thing* agree with their antecedents. You can either change the whole sentence to the plural:

> Students can easily pass this course if they apply themselves to their studies.

or you can rewrite the sentence without using the pronouns:

A student can easily pass this course by applying good study habits.

EXERCISE 16.1
Choose the correct word(s) from the parentheses for each of the following sentences. Answers begin on p. 364.

1. You mustn't annoy the instructor if (one wants, you want, he or she wants) to leave class on time.
2. Any woman will be irresistible if (you, one, she) uses our line of Beautifem products!
3. If you do the homework regularly and hand in all assignments on time, the chances are (one, you) will do well in the course.
4. You'd do better if (one, she, you) were to try harder.
5. When we came up for air, (one, we, you) couldn't see the boat!
6. If you want to avoid the winter flu, (one, you, they) should get a flu shot in the fall.
7. (One, You) mustn't push Biff too far, because he will either lose his temper or become hysterical, and that isn't what you want.
8. When we analyzed the situation, (one, they, we) realized that the problem would never have arisen if (one, they, we) had been more careful in (our, their) planning.
9. When you're bright and talented, (one doesn't, you don't, they don't) have to try very hard to impress (one's, your, their) elders, especially if (one is, you are, they are) also handsome.
10. You can't really enjoy a sport unless (one knows, you know) the basic rules. How can (one, you) understand the game unless (one knows, you know) what's going on?

Correct the following sentences where necessary. Check your answers to each set of ten before going on.

EXERCISE 16.2

1. A great worry is lifted from one's mind when you learn your application has been accepted.

2. If only one had read the instructions carefully, I wouldn't have messed up the answer on the test.

3. If any of you are planning to go to the class party, they can pick up their tickets now.

4. Men who don't think women are their equals may have to get used to living on your own.

5. It has taken most Canadians far too long to recognize the seriousness of our debt and deficit problems.

6. If one is convicted on that charge, a fine is the least of your worries.

7. After we had driven about 400 km, the lack of sleep made it hard to keep your eyes open.

8. If you can't cope with the pressure, one must expect to be replaced by someone who can.

9. The penalties for plagiarism are severe, but one doesn't usually think about penalties until after you are caught.

10. It's very difficult for a 14-year-old to control his or her temper when you feel frustrated or angry.

✳ EXERCISE 16.3

Rewrite the following paragraph in the third person singular.

Women who enjoy baseball may have difficulty explaining their passion to those who find the game boring. Each February, the serious fans begin to sharpen their watching and listening skills by tuning in to spring training games. If you have seen these fanatics watch a game, you will have noticed the alertness and intensity with which they follow the play. It is this single-minded dedication that the non-fans find themselves unable to comprehend. How can people be so interested in a game that they can watch for three hours or more, only to see so little take place? How can they get excited by a no-hitter, which, by definition, means that nothing has happened during the game? Baseball fans maintain that the game to which they are addicted offers many more pleasures than mere action. They cite fielding plays and the strategy of pitcher-versus-hitter matchups in defence of their game. To women who find such details meaningless, however, watching a baseball game is about as exciting as watching paint dry.

EXERCISE 16.4

The following paragraph contains a number of errors in person consistency. Rewrite the paragraph in the third person singular, making sure you maintain consistency in number, person, and gender. No answers are provided for this exercise.

(1) When a student arrives at college, it is often apparent to their teachers that they lack the study, writing, note-taking, and scheduling skills necessary for him to succeed at the post-secondary level. (2) Much of college work is independent, and you have to be able to function on one's own. (3) It is not unusual for students to be given an assignment at the beginning of term and be expected to hand it in weeks or even months later without your being reminded repeatedly of the deadline. (4) This requires the students to schedule his time effectively. (5) College study requires concentration and organization skills that students often have to develop for him or herself. (6) Having been given notes in handouts or on the board throughout high school, many students may find it difficult to take notes

in the lectures and seminars one encounters at college. (7) Students who are weak in any of these skills are at risk of failing your year. (8) Fortunately, at many colleges, help is available: you can sign up for a study skills or a mastery program, sometimes for course credit. (9) Part of success at college depends on one's level of preparation. (10) To acquire the knowledge and skills to do well academically, all of us first have to know how to budget our time, take notes, study, and write.

EXERCISE 16.5

Think of a significant experience you've had since coming to college. (If you don't like "significant," try embarrassing, funny, or frightening.) Write an account of this experience, telling your story in the third person: that is, instead of using *I*, use *he* or *she*. When you have finished your paper, reread it carefully. Check your sentence structure. Check your spelling. Check the agreement of your subjects and verbs, and of your pronouns and antecedents. And finally, check to be sure you have maintained consistency of verb tense and pronoun person in each paragraph of your paper.

UNIT FOUR

Punctuation

CHAPTER 17

The Comma

The comma is the most frequently used—and misused—punctuation mark in English. Leaving out a necessary comma can change the meaning of your sentence. Including unnecessary commas can distract the reader and interrupt the flow of meaning. Perhaps nothing is so sure a sign of a competent writer as the correct use of commas, so it is very important that you master them. This chapter presents four comma rules that will give you a good indication of when you should use a comma. If you apply these four rules faithfully, your reader will never be confused by missing or misplaced commas in your writing. And if, as occasionally happens, the sentence you are writing is not covered by one of our four rules, remember the first commandment of comma usage: when in doubt, leave it out.

Four Comma Rules

Here are the four essential rules that cover most instances in which you need to use a comma.

> 1. Use commas to separate items in a series of three or more.

The required subjects in this program are math, physics, and English.

Drive two blocks north of Main, turn left, go past two traffic signals, and turn right.

Tom went to the movies, Jan and Yasmin went to play pool, and I went to bed.

The comma before the *and* at the end of the list is optional; use it or leave it out, but be consistent.

EXERCISE 17.1

Insert commas where necessary in the following sentences, then check your answers on p. 365.

1. Does anyone remember John Paul George and Ringo?
2. Goldfish and gerbils make the best pets.
3. Krystal thinks she wants to get married, but she can't decide whether Dwight Rudolf or Eugene should be the lucky man.
4. Fans of rock folk and ska all enjoyed the Days of You concert.
5. MacDonald Laurier Borden and Pearson are four dissimilar men who have one thing in common.
6. Arnold is an all-round athlete; he enjoys skating skiing cycling tobogganing and showering.
7. Marieke has strong ambition a cool head good health and an inquiring mind; everyone hates her.
8. Careful investment of time and money can lead to a luxurious lifestyle international fame and early retirement.
9. Mowing the lawn shopping for groceries and doing my teenagers' homework are my least favourite activities.
10. Most of the world sees Canada as a land where French is spoken ice and snow are year-round hazards and violent hockey is the natives' favourite pastime.

> 2. Use comma(s) to separate from the rest of the sentence any word or expression that is not essential to the sentence's meaning *or* that means the same as something else in the sentence.

To find out whether a word, phrase, or clause is essential to the meaning of the sentence, try crossing it out. If the sentence remains complete and still makes sense, the crossed-out expression is *nonessential,* and should be set off by commas. Study the following four examples.

Writing a good letter of application isn't difficult, ~~if you're careful~~.

The phrase "if you're careful" is not essential to the meaning of the sentence, so it's separated from the rest of the sentence by a comma.

Writing a letter of application ~~that is clear and concise~~ is a challenge.

If you take out "that is clear and concise," the meaning of the sentence is completely changed. Not all letters of application are a challenge to write: only clear and concise ones. Writing vague and wordy letters is easy; anyone can do it. The words "that is clear and concise" are therefore essential to the meaning of the sentence, and so they are *not* set off by commas.

> ~~One of Canada's best-known novelists~~, Alice Munro spends the summer in Clinton, Ontario, and the winter in Comox, B.C.

The phrase "one of Canada's best-known novelists" means the same as "Alice Munro." The two expressions refer to the same person, so the first is set off by commas. When a nonessential word or phrase occurs in the middle of a sentence, rather than at the beginning or the end, be sure to put commas both before and after it.

> In *Selling Illusions*, ~~published in 1994~~, Neil Bissoondath explains why he thinks Canada's multiculturalism policy has done more harm than good.

Deleting "published in 1994" does not change the meaning of the sentence, so it is set off by commas.

EXERCISE 17.2

Insert commas where necessary in the following sentences. Check your answers before going on.

1. My mother's favourite singer is Gordon Lightfoot the former Elvis imitator from Orillia.
2. The winner of the 1994 Yorkton Film Festival Jury Award was Janis Lundman's documentary *Lawn and Order.*
3. The underlying message of the film is that whether you like it or not your lawn says a lot about who you are.
4. Listening to music is a perfect way to relax after a tough day at school.
5. Despite her reputation as an air head Leticia is we have discovered fairly bright.
6. To no one's surprise Professor Lam a popular mathematics instructor won the distinguished teacher award again this year.
7. No one who has seen Patrick Roy play can doubt that he is a superstar.
8. In a radical departure from tradition the bride wore a bright red gown and matching veil.
9. One of the wedding guests remarked rather cattily I thought that the bride looked like a Tomato Festival Queen.
10. Not surprisingly a recent study of driver stress shows that aggressive behaviour such as flashing high beams at other drivers increases during high-congestion traffic.

---

3. Put a comma between independent clauses when they are joined by these transition words:

and	nor	for
or	but	yet
so		

I like Céline Dion, but I prefer Sarah McLachlan.

We shape our tools, and our tools shape us. (Marshall McLuhan)

I knew I was going to be late, so I went back to sleep.

I hope I do well in the interview, for I really want this job.

Be sure that the sentence you are punctuating contains two independent clauses rather than one clause with a single subject and a multiple verb.

We <u>loved</u> the book but <u>hated</u> the movie. (<u>We</u> is the subject, and there are two verbs, <u>loved</u> and <u>hated</u>. Do not put a comma between two or more verbs that share a single subject.)

We both <u>loved</u> the book, but <u>Kim</u> <u>hated</u> the movie. (This sentence contains two independent clauses—<u>We</u> <u>loved</u> and <u>Kim</u> <u>hated</u>—joined by *but*. The comma is required here.)

EXERCISE 17.3

Insert commas where they are needed in the following sentences. Check your answers when you're done.

1. He and I are good friends yet we often disagree.
2. We have a choice: we could try bribery or we could resort to force.
3. We can't win this game nor can we afford to lose it.
4. The car swerved wildly and just missed the crossing guard.
5. Mona tried and tried to pass her driver's test and her persistence finally paid off.
6. My wife and I would like to buy a house but we don't have enough money for a down payment.
7. I'm bored and underpaid at work so I'm going back to school next fall.
8. Ravi and Denis are travelling to Whitehorse this summer and Sandy is going to St. John.
9. This is Bambi's last semester so she's concentrating on school for a change.
10. Please pay close attention for the instructions are a little complicated.

> 4. Put a comma after a word or group of words that comes before an independent clause.

Biff, you aren't paying attention.

No matter how hard I try, I will never be able to forget you.

Exhausted and cranky from staying up all night, I staggered into class.

If that's their idea of a large pizza, we'd better order two.

Until she got her promotion, she was quite friendly.

EXERCISE 17.4

Insert commas where they are needed in the following sentences. Check your answers when you have finished all ten.

1. In the end quality is what counts.
2. Second our department is required to cut costs by fifteen percent.
3. If there were any justice in this world I'd have been rewarded for my performance.
4. Moved beyond words the victorious candidate was able only to gesture his thanks to his supporters.
5. Carefully placing one foot in front of the other she managed to walk along the white line for several metres.
6. Where a huge hardwood forest had once stood only acres of tree stumps remained.
7. Finally it is clear that we must make our decision today.
8. While Rudolf may be short on brain he's long on brawn.
9. As her fortieth birthday approached Drusilla met the challenge by trading in her sedan for a sports car and her husband for a boyfriend ten years her junior.
10. When the first robin heralds the return of spring I begin to dream of lazy summer days lying beside the pool with a cool drink in my hand and a ball game on the radio.

The rest of the exercises in this chapter require you to apply all four comma rules. Before you begin, write out the four rules on a sheet of paper. Refer to them frequently as you punctuate the sentences that follow. After you've finished each exercise, check your answers and make sure you understand any mistakes you've made.

EXERCISE 17.5

1. Despite some excellent action sequences the movie was a failure because of the terrible script.
2. Your fall order which we received last week has been shipped.
3. These cold wet grey days are not good for the crops.
4. If starvation and lack of recognition made great artists Canada would be a land of Picassos.
5. What you hear what you read and what you experience all help to form your cultural background.
6. A few days after we sailed the boat sprang a leak.
7. Inside the band was playing at full blast.
8. The letter of application is one of the most important documents you will ever write yet you have spent only an hour composing it.
9. Despite some early problems Ottawa's National Gallery has become the home of one of the most interesting collections in North America.
10. Doing punctuation exercises is tedious work but is cleaner than tuning the car.

EXERCISE 17.6

1. There is something wrong with this proposal but I haven't yet figured out what it is.
2. Our hope of course is that the terrorists will be caught and punished.
3. George Washington the first president of the United States was an officer in the British army before he was engaged in the American Revolution.
4. Charlottetown Quebec and Kingston were the sites of the conferences that eventually led to Confederation in 1867.
5. If you can cope with overloaded logging trucks passing you at high speeds on narrow mountain roads you'll enjoy the spectacularly scenic drive from Hope to Princeton.
6. The Great Lakes form an inland passageway through which huge seagoing ships reach the heart of the North American continent.
7. A good dictionary consulted frequently is probably the most important resource for any student who wishes to develop a mature vocabulary.
8. While I respect your opinion and your right to express it that doesn't mean that I necessarily agree with you.
9. After our guests had gone home we discovered that they had drunk all the beer but had left most of the food so we'd be dining on leftovers for the next two weeks.
10. If there were any point in protesting the president's decision I would have complained long ago but I don't think anything will change her disastrous course of action.

EXERCISE 17.7

Insert commas where they are needed in the following sentences. No answers are provided for this exercise.

1. As long as you're prepared relaxed and confident you'll find that an employment interview is not necessarily a terrifying prospect.
2. Some people believe it or not actually enjoy interviews.
3. Others on the other hand are absolutely terrified at the prospect of confronting an interviewer or even worse a whole group of interviewers.
4. The first thing you should do to prepare yourself for an interview is to find out as much information as you can about the company.
5. Among the things you absolutely need to know are the title of the job you are applying for the name of the person or persons who will be conducting the interview the address of the company how long it will take you to get there and where the washrooms are.
6. Many employment consultants recommend that you visit the office of the firm to which you've applied to confirm how long it will take you to get there to check out the physical layout and to be sure you know where the interview room—and the washrooms—is located.
7. On your advance scouting trip you can also glean valuable information about the company's working conditions employee attitudes and even the dress code.
8. On the day of the interview be sure to show up ten or fifteen minutes in advance of your scheduled appointment.
9. When the interviewer greets you be sure to identify yourself and extend your hand. Your handshake should be brief and firm not limply passive or bone-crushingly aggressive.
10. And finally as one who has conducted hundreds of applicant interviews my advice to you is this: don't smoke even if you are invited to and say "No thank you" to an interviewer's offer of coffee or juice. There is nothing more embarrassing than dropping a lighted cigarette a hot cup of coffee or a bottle of grape juice into your lap during the course of an interview.

CHAPTER 18

The Semicolon

The colon and semicolon are often confused and used as if they were interchangeable. They serve very different functions, however, and their correct use can dramatically improve a reader's understanding of your writing. Here is one function of the semicolon:

> A semicolon can replace a period; in other words, it can appear between two independent clauses.

You should use the semicolon when the two clauses (sentences) you are joining are closely connected in meaning or when there is a cause-and-effect relationship between them.

> I'm too tired; I can't stay awake any longer.

> There's a good movie on tonight; it's a Canadian film called *Exotica.*

A period could have been used instead of the semicolon in either of these sentences, but the close connection between the clauses prompted the writer to use a semicolon.

Certain connecting or transition words are sometimes put between independent clauses to show a cause-effect relationship or the continuation of an idea. Words or phrases used in this way must be preceded by a semicolon and followed by a comma:

; also,	; furthermore,	; nevertheless,
; as a result,	; however,	; then,
; besides,	; in addition,	; therefore,
; consequently,	; in fact,	; thus,
; finally,	; instead,	
; for example,	; moreover,	

We had hiked for three hours; consequently, we were glad to rest.

There are only two of us; however, we're both pretty big.

The sun was very hot; therefore, we stopped for a drink and a swim.

In other words, ***a semicolon + a transition word/phrase + a comma*** = a link strong enough to come between two related independent clauses.

Note, however, that when the words and phrases listed in the box are used as *nonessential* expressions rather than as connecting words, they are separated from the rest of the sentence by commas (Comma Rule 2, p. 158).

However hard I try, I just can't seem to master particle physics.

Ten years from now, however, I'm sure I'll have no difficulty with the subject.

> To make a COMPLEX LIST easier to read and understand, put semicolons between the items instead of commas.

Here's an example:

We need to pack several things: matches to start a fire; an axe or hatchet to cut wood; cooking utensils and eating implements; and, of course, food.

In exercises 18.1 and 18.2, put a check mark (√) next to the sentences that are correctly punctuated. Consult the answers on p. 367 before continuing.

EXERCISE 18.1

1. ____ He sat down in a convenient bar; he was very thirsty.

2. ____ He sat down near a refreshing stream; for he was very tired.

3. ____ My cats get along fine with the dog; it's each other that they hate.

4. ____ It's a beautiful day; just right for a long walk.

5. ____ Six of the Indian nations joined together in a loose union, they were called Iroquois.

6. ____ The lawn, a little ragged, needs to be cut, the hedge, shrubs, and ivy need to be trimmed, the flowers need to be watered, and, most important, the gardener needs to be paid.

7. ____ I'd like to help, however, I'm supposed to rest all day.

8. ____ We reached Canoe Lake in time to meet the others; in fact, we arrived a little ahead of schedule.

9. ____ Halifax is my favourite city; someday I'm going to move there.

10. ____ Winter is something only Canadians really understand; it has shaped this country more than the railways, the politicians, and even the founding peoples.

EXERCISE 18.2

1. ____ It's far too expensive; besides, we really don't need one.

2. ____ There are only a few who could catch him; and I'm sure she isn't one of them.

3. ____ Coffee prices are ridiculous, yet I still must have my morning cup or three.

4. ____ Ninik wants to be an Olympic gymnast; consequently, she spends at least six hours a day in training.

5. ____ We'll have to go soon; for it's getting late.

6. ____ The weather is bad; I have a cold; the electricity is out; and, to top it all off, my in-laws are coming for dinner.

7. ____ If ever there were a time to act; it is now.

8. ____ Some people are skilled in many fields; Kumari, for example, is both a good plumber and a great cook.

9. ____ She disobeyed the rules; so, she will have to be punished.

10. ____ Krystal is always late, however, she's worth waiting for.

EXERCISE 18.3
Correct the faulty punctuation in exercise 18.1.

EXERCISE 18.4
Correct the faulty punctuation in exercise 18.2.

EXERCISE 18.5
Insert commas and semicolons where necessary in these sentences. Then check your answers carefully.

1. There seems to be no end to the work that must be done furthermore there isn't enough time in which to do it.
2. There must be a way or we're finished before we've even begun.
3. I can't afford a Porsche therefore I drive a Neon.
4. Jana is one of my favourite people she can always cheer me up.
5. There will be ample opportunity to finish your homework but right now I need your help.
6. The floor was knotty pine the furniture and walls were designed and finished to complement it.
7. Brock was killed early in the morning but the Americans were driven from Queenston Heights by nightfall.
8. Canada's history is not a very violent one however we've had several rebellions of note.
9. Jon has gone away to become a teacher Marta now has twin baby girls Kevin is unemployed Julie is a lawyer or stockbroker (I forget which) and Pavel is as usual drifting from job to job.
10. When the rain started they were trapped in the open nevertheless they stayed where they were until it let up and then made their way to the nearest shelter.

EXERCISE 18.6
Correct these sentences where necessary.

1. Please leave dinner in the oven for a little while I'll eat when I've finished this exercise.
2. Taking the corner at 90 kph, the police car swerved into the oncoming lane, fortunately no one was coming.
3. The chair called the meeting to order, however it quickly became apparent that none of us had done the background reading.

4. One of the products of the computer age is increased leisure, this, in turn, has led to increased opportunities for physical fitness.

5. A glance at the calendar will reveal that there are only 212 shopping days left until my birthday, that's just enough time for you to find the present I deserve.

6. Computers are marvellous tools they are fast efficient and accurate but they can't think. They remind me of a secretary I used to know, she's now my boss.

7. The Four Horsemen of the Apocalypse are; Conquest, Slaughter, Famine, and Death.

8. Some Biblical figures are familiar to people from many different cultures, for example the stories of Samson, and Delilah, and of David, and Goliath are widely known.

9. We're unhappy about our instructor's evaluation procedures, in fact we think they are irrational, arbitrary; and often unfair.

10. Every year at tax time, I am faced with the same problem: assembling my bills and receipts, figuring out my gas mileage, trying to recall which expenses were business-related and which were personal, finding my T4s T5s, and other T forms and organizing this mess so my accountant can attempt to keep me out of jail for another year.

EXERCISE 18.7

Correct these sentences as necessary. No answers are provided for this exercise.

1. I played squash, went jogging, and even tried weight-lifting this weekend, in addition I signed up for a six-month satisfaction-guaranteed fitness program.

2. I have mixed memories of my tour of Europe, for example, while I think fondly of gorgeous little towns like Gordes and Orvieto, I think less fondly of Venice, where I was robbed.

3. As I was buying a gelato at a little stand across from our hotel a man slipped his hand into my purse grabbed my passport and was promptly seized by two plainclothes detectives who had been keeping an eye on him.

4. I was required to fill out a complaint which took hours since it had to be translated from English to Italian and back to English, consequently the only view of Venice's famous canals that I got was from a police boat.

5. For my birthday last year, my husband gave me a dozen roses. This year he gave me a shovel, as a result I'm wondering if the romance has gone from our relationship.

6. For years, students complained that the English teachers couldn't calculate grades accurately, finally the Math Department offered to give

a seminar to introduce the English Department to the mysteries of addition and subtraction.

7. Louis Riel led a Métis rebellion in Manitoba in 1885 but he was defeated tried and executed the same year his death caused a deep rift between English and French Canada.

8. The Canadian political scene has become much less interesting since the departure of men like Pierre Trudeau and Brian Mulroney, whether you liked them or not, they both provoked a lot of public debate over political issues.

9. In preparation for the final exam, please bring your text and any notes you may have taken in class at least two pens a scientific calculator lots of scrap paper on which to work out the problems and a drafting set.

10. Reading spy novels is I admit a waste of time but it beats sitting in front of the tube being bombarded with ads for products I don't need, learning intimate even embarrassing details about the lives of people I don't know, will never meet, and would never want to know and being subjected to the so-called humour that is characteristic of the average American sitcom.

CHAPTER 19

The Colon

The **colon** functions as an introducer. When a statement is followed by a list or by one or more examples, the colon between the statement and what follows alerts the reader to what is coming.

> We have two choices: to go or to stay.

> Try to imagine yourself like me: young, gorgeous, brilliant, and rich.

> One person is responsible for your happiness in life: you.

The statement that precedes the colon must be a complete sentence (independent clause). Therefore, a colon can never come immediately after *is* or *are*. Here's an example of what *not* to write.

> Three things I am violently allergic to are: cats, ragweed, and country music.

This is incorrect because the statement before the colon is not a complete sentence.

The colon, then, follows a complete statement and introduces a list or example(s) that defines or amplifies something in the statement. The information after the colon often answers the question "what?" or "who?"

> I am violently allergic to three things: (what?) cats, ragweed, and country music.

> Business and industry face a new challenge: (what?) the global marketplace.

> The evil queen gazed into the mirror to admire the reflection of the fairest woman of them all: (who?) herself.

And finally, the colon is used after a complete sentence introducing a quotation.

> Stephen Leacock did not think very highly of his readers' tastes in literature: "There are only two subjects that appeal nowadays to the general public: murder and sex; and, for people of culture, sex-murder."

The uses of the colon can be summed up as follows:

> The colon follows an independent clause and introduces one of three things: examples, a list, or a quotation.

EXERCISE 19.1

Put a check mark (√) next to the sentences that are correctly punctuated, then turn to p. 368 to check your answers.

1. _____ Two of the most common causes of failure are laziness and lack of self-discipline.

2. _____ Only one thing was missing the boat.

3. _____ He tried three different tactics: phone calls, flowers, and flattery.

4. _____ On the list we must include: chips, mix, ice, and peanuts.

5. _____ The instructor's first words were not encouraging: "Half of you are going to fail, and the other half won't get jobs."

6. _____ Three qualities of a good quarterback are: leadership, intelligence, and physical strength.

7. _____ There are two things that every ambitious person strives for: money and power.

8. _____ The lake is: deep and cold.

9. _____ Dogs have many qualities that make them superior to cats; loyalty, intelligence, working ability, and friendliness.

10. _____ Let me give you an example, Louis Riel.

EXERCISE 19.2

Put a check mark (√) next to the sentences that are correctly punctuated.

1. ____ I'd like to help: but I can't.

2. ____ I'll take the following volunteers, Marie, Susan, Ngoc, and Lewis.

3. ____ We'll have to go back to get: tent poles, matches, and paddles.

4. ____ Two very good centres were Beliveau and Apps.

5. ____ The debate will be lively if they choose a certain topic: religion.

6. ____ No one wants to go with him, for two very good reasons money and time.

7. ____ He's involved in all types of athletics: skiing, hiking, hockey, and football, to name a few.

8. ____ My boss is so mean she must be: bitter or crazy.

9. ____ She won more medals at the Games than we expected: two golds and a bronze.

10. ____ They were unlucky twice: when they bought that car and when they sold it.

EXERCISE 19.3

Correct the incorrectly punctuated sentences in exercise 19.1.

EXERCISE 19.4

Correct the incorrectly punctuated sentences in exercise 19.2.

EXERCISE 19.5

As a test of your ability to use colons, correct the punctuation errors in the following sentences. No answers are given for this exercise.

1. There is only one thing worse than getting old; the alternative.
2. If I had unlimited amounts of money, the two things I would most like to do are: first, to sail around the world in a luxury yacht, and, second, to do it again.
3. According to my parents, I am: lazy, selfish, careless, and ignorant, but what do they know?

4. Since it's clear our essays will be late, we have three choices to beg for an extension, claim our computer malfunctioned, or forge a doctor's note.

5. One of the most memorable essays I've encountered in the past twenty years was a paper called: "How to Suck Seed in Starting You're Own Buisness."

6. After watching a program on genealogy, I began to trace my own family's history: however, I soon discovered that my family tree is a shrub best left unexamined.

7. Having listened faithfully to the CDs you recommended, I can now say without hesitation that: toxic thrash does nothing for me.

8. This course requires an enormous amount of work, but when we've finished, our rewards will be: a diploma, the chance of interesting employment, and a very valuable skill.

9. With astonishing speed, computers all over the globe are being linked into one network that will become the world's primary environment for: communication, research, commerce, and entertainment the Internet.

10. In 1995, fisheries minister Brian Tobin secured his place in Canadian history with an immortal comment; "We're down to one, lost, lonely, unloved, unattractive little turbot, clinging by its fingernails to the Grand Banks of Newfoundland."

CHAPTER 20

Quotation Marks

Quotation marks (" ") are used to set off direct speech or dialogue, short passages of quoted material, and some titles. They are a signal to the reader that the words in quotes are not your words, but someone else's. Quotation marks come in pairs; there must be a set to show where the dialogue, quotation, or title begins and a set to show where it ends. You must be absolutely sure that whatever you put between them is stated *exactly* as it is in the source you are using. The only other thing you need to know about quotation marks is how to punctuate what comes between them.

Dialogue

When you quote direct speech, include normal sentence punctuation. If the speaker's name or a comment about the speaker is included in your own sentence, set it off with commas. A comma or the end punctuation mark comes *inside* the final set of quotation marks.

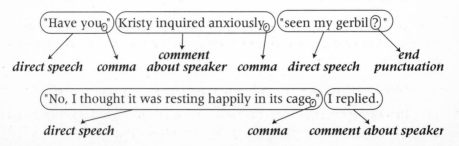

Be careful to put quotation marks only around direct speech (someone's exact words). Don't use quotation marks with indirect speech (a paraphrase of someone's words).

> Kristy inquired anxiously whether I had seen her gerbil. (These are not Kristy's exact words, nor is the sentence a question.)

A quotation *within* a quotation is punctuated by single quotation marks:

> "Diana," whined Charles, "I really do think it unkind of you to call poor Camilla 'The Rottweiler.'"

Quoted Material

When you quote a **short** passage (three lines of print or less), you can work it into your own sentence. Use a comma to introduce a quotation of one or more sentences, and include normal sentence punctuation within the quotation marks.

> According to Margaret Atwood, "If you like men, you can like Americans. Cautiously. Selectively. Beginning with the feet. One at a time."

> "As you grow old," wrote Richard Needham, "you lose your interest in sex, your friends drift away, your children ignore you. There are other advantages, of course, but these would seem to me the outstanding ones."

> "My idea of long-range planning is lunch," confesses Frank Ogden, Canada's foremost futurist.

If your own introductory words form a complete sentence, use a colon to introduce the quotation:

> Frank Ogden, Canada's foremost futurist, confesses that he has little respect for traditional business planning cycles: "My idea of long-range planning is lunch."

If the passage you are quoting is a couple of words, a phrase, or anything less than a complete sentence, do not use a comma or a colon to introduce it.

> Woody Allen's one regret in life is that he is "not someone else."

> Neil Bissoondath argues that racism is based on "willful ignorance and an acceptance of—and comfort with—stereotype."

All the lines of a *long* quoted passage (more than three lines of print) should be indented ten spaces from the left margin. Long quotations are not enclosed in quotation marks. The block indentation indicates to the reader that the words set off in this way are not yours, but some other writer's. (Turn to Chapter 25 to find examples of the treatment of long quotations.)

College writing normally requires that you indicate the source of any material you quote. The easiest way to do this is to give the author's surname, if it's not already included in your sentence, and the page reference in parentheses at the end of the quote.

For example,

> In the 18th century, a lifelong bachelor observed, "Marriage has many pains, but celibacy has no pleasures" (Johnson 214).

> According to Dr. Samuel Johnson, "Marriage has many pains, but celibacy has no pleasures" (214).

These source identifications are called parenthetical citations.

Some instructors prefer footnotes or endnotes to parenthetical citations. Find out what format your instructor requires and follow it. In any library or bookstore, you will find a variety of style guides and handbooks that explain different styles of documentation. Your instructor will be happy to recommend one.

Titles

Unless you are using a word processor that prints *italics*, titles of books or other entire works should be <u>underlined</u>. Titles of parts of those books or works should be put in quotation marks. Thus, titles of books, magazines, pamphlets, newspapers, plays, films, and albums should be italicized or underlined. Titles of single articles, essays, stories, poems, or songs should be placed in quotation marks.

Below you will find an example of a bibliography (a list of works consulted or cited in a research paper) showing how titles of different kinds of publications are punctuated.

essay in an anthology   Atwood, Margaret. "Canadians: What Do They Want?" <u>The Act of Writing</u>. Ed. Ronald Conrad. 3rd ed. Toronto: McGraw-Hill, 1993. 302–305.

speech reprinted in a book   Brown, Rosemary. "Overcoming Sexism and Racism—How?" <u>Racism in Canada</u>. Ed. Ormond McKague. Saskatoon: Fifth House, 1991. 163–177.

song lyric reprinted in an anthology	Cohen, Leonard. "Suzanne Takes You Down." <u>An Anthology of Canadian Literature in English</u>. Eds. Donna Bennett and Russell Brown. 2 vols. Toronto: Oxford, 1983. 2:350.
book review in a periodical	Conway, J. F. "The Good, The Bad, The Ugly." <u>The Literary Review of Canada</u> April 1995:17–19.
article in a newspaper	Delacourt, Susan. "Losing Interest." <u>The Globe and Mail</u> 1 April 1995: D1.
encyclopedia entry	"Flag Debate." <u>The Canadian Encyclopedia</u>. 2nd ed. Edmonton: Hurtig, 1988. 2:789.
novel	Findley, Timothy. <u>Headhunter</u>. Toronto: HarperCollins, 1993.
article in a magazine	McMurdy, Deirdre. "Drugstore Cowboy." <u>Maclean's</u> 2 Dec.1991: 74.
chapter in a book	Norton, Sarah, and Brian Green. "Cracking the Sentence Code." <u>The Bare Essentials, Form A</u>. 4th ed. Toronto: Harcourt, 1996. 43–66.

In the following exercises, place quotation marks where they are needed and insert any necessary punctuation before and after each quote. The answers for this chapter begin on p. 369.

EXERCISE 20.1

1. Three thousand is a bargain for that coat said Drusilla, eyeing the floor-length mink.
2. Simone inquired whether Canadian trains were always late.
3. Put that gun down, shouted the officer or I'll shoot!
4. The time has come the Walrus said, to talk of many things.
5. Canada's national anthem, O Canada, was written by Calixa Lavallée.
6. My father likes to remind me of John F. Kennedy's words Too often we enjoy the comfort of opinion without the discomfort of thought.
7. In his novel, Generation X, Douglas Coupland warns, Less is a possibility.
8. Two singles from Sheryl Crow's first album, Tuesday Night Music Club, became hits All I Wanna Do and Strong Enough.
9. The Guinness Book of Records claims that the world's most-married man is former Baptist minister Scotty Wolfe, who got married 27 times.

10. When asked how many children were born of these marriages, Mr. Wolfe replied I think I had 41.

EXERCISE 20.2

1. Roman said that he'd like to meet you.
2. After his best player suffered another injury, the coach pleaded with him Please, Marcel, wear a face mask!
3. Our professor asked who had announced that today's class was cancelled.
4. Brian inquired When are we going to eat?
5. When you cook dinner Val replied.
6. Marshall McLuhan's insight, The medium is the message appears in his most famous book, Understanding Media.
7. The headline in today's Winnipeg Free Press is Canada's dollar sinks to new low.
8. We've decided to rent a video this evening, but we can't decide between The Lion King and Priscilla, Queen of the Desert.
9. This is the second time you've been thrown out of class the dean told Biff. I'm inclined to suspend you for a week.
10. Say you love me he pleaded. OK, she replied, You love me.

EXERCISE 20.3

Now test your understanding of quotation marks and the punctuation that goes with them. There are no answers provided for this exercise.

1. In the movie Forrest Gump, Mrs. Gump has a few words of wisdom for her son Life is like a box of chocolates. You never know what you're going to get.
2. At a go-kart track near Courtenay, B. C., a large sign warns drivers No Wreckless Driving Allowed.
3. Now I understand, said Minnie, as she strapped on her safety helmet, why the track is next to the hospital.
4. Foster Hewitt's words have echoed down through the years as the ultimate expression of hockey achievement He shoots! He scores!
5. Krystal isn't a big winter sports fan, but she says that there is one activity she really enjoys: aprés-ski.
6. After his first date with Rudolf's sister, Gordon swore Never again!
7. Our production of King Lear will be set in contemporary London, and the references will be updated to the 1990s our director told us in the first production meeting.
8. Frank magazine, the viciously satiric publication from Ottawa, refers to our prime minister as Jean Crouton.

9. Movie critic Dennis Dermody's article Sit Down and Shut Up or Don't Sit by Me will be reprinted in his forthcoming collection of essays on contemporary films How to Cook and Eat Macauley Culkin.

10. In Pure Punnishment, her article on wordplay, Professor Banerjee recounts the following example of a pun. A husband forgot to buy his wife her favourite flowers, anemones, for her birthday, and the florist had only some ferns left. When the husband presented the ferns, his wife remarked With fronds like these, who needs anemones?

CHAPTER 21

Question Marks, Exclamation Marks, and Punctuation Review

The Question Mark

Everyone knows that a **question mark** follows an interrogative, or asking, sentence, but we all sometimes forget to include it. Let this chapter serve as a reminder not to forget!

> Put a question mark at the end of every interrogative sentence.

The question mark gives your readers an important clue to the meaning of your sentence. "There's more?" means something quite different from

"There's more!", and both are different from "There's more." When you speak, your tone of voice conveys the meaning you intend; when you write, your punctuation tells your reader what you mean.

The only time you don't end a question with a question mark is when the question is part of a statement.

QUESTION	STATEMENT
Are you going?	I asked whether you were going.
Do you know them?	I wonder if you know them.
Is there enough evidence to convict him?	The jury deliberated whether there was enough evidence to convict him.

Supply the correct end punctuation for these sentences, then check your answers on p. 370.

EXERCISE 21.1

1. What more could I possibly do to help
2. Val asked Biff whether he was absolutely positive he had paid the bill
3. Why is there always a cop around when I'm speeding but never when I need help
4. Have you checked the weather forecast to see when the weather is expected to clear
5. I will always wonder whether Rhonda handed in my essay
6. Is it true that voters will act rationally only when all other possibilities have been exhausted
7. Did the committee consider all the options carefully before making this decision
8. I don't understand why sociology is so important in a business program
9. Eugene is still asking the math teacher to raise his mark to at least a pass
10. The question isn't whether there is intelligent life on Mars, it's whether there's intelligent life on earth

EXERCISE 21.2

1. I'm not sure whether there is a game tonight or not
2. Is there life after long days of boring classes, followed by long nights of homework
3. If we can't complete the project on time, will we be penalized
4. Our question was what to do after the boss had burst into tears and gone home

5. What good will it do if I continue to be pleasant to people who take such delight in making me look foolish

6. How can anyone just stand by while some innocent person is being attacked

7. Whoever would have thought that the Canadian dollar would fall below the U.S. seventy-cents mark

8. I am surprised and hurt that you would question my motives in asking you for help with my studying

9. Please take a look at these tests and tell me whether you think these two students were cheating

10. Why can't the sports fans who yell so loudly at players' mistakes try to put themselves in the same position as those they criticize and be a little more forgiving

The Exclamation Mark

Consider the difference in tone between these two sentences:

> There's a man behind you.
> There's a man behind you!

In the first sentence, information is being supplied, perhaps about the line of people waiting their turn at a grocery-store checkout counter. The second sentence might be a shouted warning about a mugger.

> Use an **exclamation mark** as end punctuation in sentences requiring extreme emphasis or dramatic effect.

Note that the exclamation mark will have "punch" or dramatic effect only if you use it sparingly. If you use an exclamation mark after *every other* sentence, how will your readers know when you really mean to indicate excitement? Overuse of exclamation marks is a technique used in comic books. The writers of comics use an exclamation mark after practically every sentence to try to heighten the impact of their characters' words. Instead, they rob their exclamation marks of all meaning.

Practically any sentence could have an exclamation mark after it, but remember that the punctuation changes the meaning of the sentence. Read the following sentences with and without an exclamation mark, and picture the situation that would call for each reading.

They've moved	Don't touch that button
The carriage was empty	Listen to that noise

EXERCISE 21.3

Supply appropriate end punctuation in these sentences.

1. Take that, you monster
2. Ready, aim, fire
3. I can't believe it   We've got the winning number
4. That's the last straw   I quit
5. There's a fly in my soup
6. Run   It's right behind you
7. "Slide " The whole team was screaming in unison
8. I can't believe it   The thing actually flies
9. Turn the heat up   I'm freezing
10. The girls descended on the mall waving their plastic and crying, "Charge "

EXERCISE 21.4

Correct the end punctuation in the following sentences.

1. The question was whether we would spend the night in Abbotsford or push on to Vancouver?
2. Just think!! We have two glorious weeks free of English class!!!
3. Bruce thought he looked absolutely irresistible (?) in his new leather pants
4. If you think you're confused, just imagine how I must feel?
5. If I ever hear him tell that joke again, I swear I'll hit him.
6. Katy asked Ramon if he'd like to stay over?
7. My Ph.D. didn't impress my co-workers at the doughnut shop.
8. Today we read a poem by Irving Layton, who was born in Rumania, I think?
9. After seeing your test results, I wonder if you even bought the text, let alone read it?
10. Congratulations. You've just mastered end punctuation marks.

EXERCISE 21.5

Supply appropriate end punctuation for the sentences in the following paragraph. No answers are given for this exercise.

I wonder why it is that I cannot dance   My girlfriend would go out dancing every night of the week if she didn't have morning classes   And can she ever dance   When she is really into the music, I've seen her receive applause from an entire club as she leaves the dance floor   They applaud me, too, but it's because they're glad to see me sit down   Why is it that every part of my body moves to a different rhythm   When my hips find the beat, my feet are a half-beat behind, and my shoulders move around on their own as if I had some horrible nervous disorder   If I kept it up for very long,

I suspect my body would tear itself apart Is it because I'm tall, and nerve impulses have to travel a long way to get from one part of my frame to an-other I've been told that, when dancing, I look like a stork with an un-controllable itch in a vital part of its anatomy Talk about embarrassing "What can I do " I ask myself Should I subject myself to weeks of torture and take dancing lessons when I suspect they wouldn't help in the least Is there no medical cure for my condition I must have been born without a rhythm gene I wonder if it's too late to get a transplant

Punctuation Review

The following exercises will test your mastery of all punctuation studied in Unit 4. Go through them carefully and check your answers to each set before going on to the next. If you make a mistake, go back to the chapter dealing with that piece of punctuation and review the explanations and examples.

EXERCISE 21.6

1. Enjoy the view we called out as they left for the mountaintop, we had wisely decided to wait for them in a meadow halfway up.
2. To be a millionaire by the time you are thirty, you will have to: take large risks, be lucky, and have creative ideas.
3. High school was indeed the best time of my life because I met the friends there that I would continue to see for many years and I learned the principles that were to guide me through later more difficult years.
4. The question of whether evolution is a fact or a myth doesn't worry most of the people in my class, they're more concerned about whether there's a dance on Friday night.
5. Why won't he listen Marsha whispered tearfully.
6. With the crowd chanting Out Out the referee had a hard time justify-ing his decision; a ten-minute misconduct.
7. Typing as though his life depended on the completion of the assign-ment, Ted managed to get through the first chapter before supper, this left him with Chapter Two The Next Day to complete before bedtime.
8. The rain looked as though it would never let up so Gary and the two girls packed up to go home their vacation plans ruined.
9. Don't go, Angela fell to her knees and begged her friend to stay. Why must you leave now she asked just when we're about to succeed.
10. You'll find he has just one fault my friend, he snores.

EXERCISE 21.7

   All too often it seems that the Canadian national pastime is complaining about the weather! Our summers are criticized because they're too hot while our springs are too wet our autumns too cool and our winters too long. If the climate is so bad here why does anyone live north of the U.S. border. Perhaps the problem is not that Canadians don't like living in Canada but that they love to complain.

   Two of the most popular sports teams in Canada were at one time those with the worst records; the Argonauts and the Maple Leafs. Could this popularity be due to the ample opportunity and scope they gave to their fans for complaint. Not only do we bemoan the record of such teams when they lose but when they win we dwell with glee on the possibilities of disaster for next year.

   The same syndrome can be seen in our attitude toward Canadian heroes, it has often been said that we are a nation without heroes but I suspect that we have plenty of candidates: it's just that we enjoy complaining so much we try to find fault wherever we can and prefer to focus on clay feet rather than great works. One cannot help but wonder how Canadians fare in heaven where everything is perfect. I suspect they must be desperately unhappy?

EXERCISE 21.8

This is the last test of your punctuation skills. Correct any punctuation errors and supply any missing punctuation in the following sentences. No answers are provided for this exercise.

1. The early bird gets the worm as the old saying goes and I have always used this proverb as encouragement to get up as late as I can often holding out until after 11 A.M.
2. That my friend is the way of the world birth life death.
3. A warm bath and a cold drink are second to only one thing in my opinion, barbecued steak well done and covered in mushrooms onions steak sauce and garlic.
4. It was Charlotte Whitton former mayor of Ottawa who first said To succeed a woman must be twice as good as a man, fortunately that isn't difficult.
5. The Telefest Award ceremony is held each year to honour excellence in student productions of television film and radio, last year the winner in the best long drama category was a film called: The Absolution.
6. Running Marcel said is bad for the knees weight-lifting puts strain on the back. I'd rather die in my bed with all my parts working than wear out my body bit by bit wouldn't you.

7. It's time to pack up the homework shut down the computer make some popcorn pull up the old easy chair and park myself in front of the TV set, the world series is on.

8. The professor cleared his throat to get the class's attention then told them "to read the chapter entitled The Principle of Space Flight in their textbook The Wonders of the Twentieth Century."

9. When I told him on first meeting him that he sure was tall he replied You certainly have a firm grasp of the obvious. But in spite of that bad beginning we gradually became friends!

10. This Wednesday I have English French and math but I'll gladly skip them if you'll take me to see Night of the Ghouls and Plan Nine from Outer Space two films by the famously bad moviemaker Ed Wood that are playing at our local theatre.

EXERCISE 21.9

Write a paper of approximately two pages explaining how to do or make something or how to get somewhere. When you've finished, review your paper carefully, checking spelling, sentence structure, and grammar. Pay particular attention to punctuation. Be sure you have put a question mark at the end of every interrogative sentence and used exclamation marks only when necessary, for emphasis. Here are some topics you might explore:

1. how to make one of your favourite dishes
2. how to choose a good professor (*or* spiritual adviser, vacation spot, place to live, etc.)
3. how to play a particular sport or game
4. how to survive winter (*or* unemployment, a family reunion, etc.
5. how to educate parents (*or* a lover, a teacher, a younger brother or sister, etc.
6. how to win (*or* lose) an argument
7. how to prepare for a job interview (*or* a parental interrogation, an interview with the dean, etc.)
8. how to cure a cold (*or* the blues, insomnia, an addiction, etc.)
9. how to choose a spouse (*or* a college, career, apartment, roommate, etc.)
10. how to raise a family while going to school

Organizing Your Writing

CHAPTER 22

Finding Something to Write About

Everybody knows that content is important in writing. Not so many writers seem to know that form is just as important. In fact, you can't really separate the two: *what you say is how you say it*. Writing a paper (or an essay, or a report, or a letter, or anything else) is like doing a chemistry experiment: you need the right amount of the right ingredients, put together in the right proportions and in the right order. There are five steps to follow:

1. Choose a satisfactory subject
2. Select the main points of your subject
3. Write a thesis statement *or*
   Write an outline
4. Write the paragraphs
5. Revise the paper

If you follow these steps faithfully, in order, we guarantee that you will write clear, organized papers.

Note that when you get to step 3, you have a choice. You can choose to organize your paper by means of a thesis statement or by means of an outline. The thesis-statement approach works well for short papers—those no longer than about 500 words. An outline is necessary for longer papers and is often useful for organizing shorter papers. Ideally, you should learn to use both methods of organizing your writing; in fact, your teacher may require that you do so.

Steps 1, 2, and 3 make up the planning stage of the writing process. Be warned: done properly, these three steps will take you at least as long as steps 4 and 5, which involve the actual writing. The longer you spend on the preliminary steps, the less time your writing will take, and the better your paper will be.

Step 1: Choose a Satisfactory Subject

Unless you are assigned a specific subject by a teacher or supervisor, choosing your subject can be the most difficult part of writing a paper. Apply the following guidelines carefully, because no amount of instruction can help you write a good paper on something you don't know anything about or on something that is inappropriate for your audience or purpose. Your subject should satisfy the **4-S test:**

> A satisfactory subject is SIGNIFICANT, SINGLE, SPECIFIC, and SUPPORTABLE.

1. Your subject should be **significant.** Write about something that your reader needs to know or might want to know. Consider your audience and choose a subject that will be significant to that audience. This doesn't mean that you can't ever be humorous, but, unless you're another Stephen Leacock, an essay on "How I Deposit Money in My Bank" will probably be of little significance to your reader. The subject you choose must be worthy of the time and attention you expect your reader to give to your paper.

2. Your subject should be **single.** Don't try to do too much in your paper. A thorough discussion of one topic is much more satisfying to read than a skimpy, superficial treatment of several topics. A subject like "The Problems of League Expansion in Hockey and Other Sports" includes too much to deal with satisfactorily in one paper. Limit yourself to a single topic, such as "The Problems of League Expansion in the NHL."

3. Your subject should be **specific.** This requirement is closely tied to the "single" requirement. Given a choice between a broad, general topic and a narrow, specific one, you should choose the latter. In a short paper, you can't hope to say anything new or significant about a very large topic: "Employment Opportunities in Canada," for example. But you could write an interesting, detailed discussion on a more specific topic, such as

"Employment Opportunities in Nova Scotia's Hospitality Industry." You can narrow a broad subject by applying one or more **limiting factors** to it. Try thinking of your subject in terms of a specific *kind*, or *time*, or *place*, or *number*, or *person* associated with it. To come up with the hospitality topic, for example, we limited the subject of employment opportunities in Canada in terms of both place and kind.

4. Your subject must be **supportable.** You must know something about the subject (preferably, more than your reader does), or you must be able to find out about it. Your discussion of your subject will be clear and convincing only if you can include examples, facts, quotations, descriptions, anecdotes, and other details. Supporting evidence can be taken from your own experience or from the experience of other people. In other words, your topic may require you to do some research.

EXERCISE 22.1

Test the following subjects against the guidelines we've given. Can you tell what's wrong with them? Check your answers on p. 372.

1. Employment equity
2. The theory of evolution
3. The five senses
4. Caring for your cuticles
5. Career possibilities in accounting and management
6. Television is both good and bad
7. Child care 50 years from now
8. My cat Fluffy
9. Democracy is good
10. The dangers of skin diving and sky diving

EXERCISE 22.2

Consider the following subjects in terms of the 4-S guidelines. Some are possibilities for satisfactory papers. Others are hopeless. Make good subjects out of all of them by revising to make them significant, single, specific, and supportable.

1. Air is necessary to life
2. Some people are intelligent
3. The censorship of books and movies
4. The economy in other countries
5. Famous Canadian women
6. How to use a pencil sharpener
7. Predicting the future
8. Today's teenagers have a hard time
9. Taking out the garbage
10. The disabled

EXERCISE 22.3

List five subjects that you might choose to write about. Be sure each subject is *significant, single, specific,* and *supportable.*

Step 2: Selecting the Main Points of Your Subject

Now that you have an appropriate subject for your paper, give some thought to the approach you're going to take to develop it. There are many possible ways of thinking and writing about a subject. In a short paper, you can deal effectively with only a few aspects of your topic. How do you decide which aspects of your subject to discuss, what **main points** to make and explain? One way is to make a list of everything you can think of that you might want to say about the subject. Some preliminary research may help, too. You may discover some points about the subject that you hadn't thought of.

Another way—especially useful if you find you're stuck for ideas—is to ask yourself questions about your subject. Run your subject through this list of questions and see which one "fits" it best. (The symbol S stands for your subject.)

---

1. How is S made or done? (What are the main steps to follow in accomplishing S?)
2. How does S work?
3. What are the main parts or components of S?
4. What are the main functions of S?
5. What are the important features or characteristics of S?
6. What are the main kinds or types of S?
7. What are some significant examples of S?
8. What are the causes of S?
9. What are the effects or consequences of S?
10. What are the main similarities and/or differences between S and _____ ?
11. What are the main advantages (or disadvantages) of S?
12. What are the reasons for (or against) S?

These questions suggest some of the various ways of looking at or thinking about a subject. Most subjects will yield answers to more than one of these questions. Focus on the question that produces the answers that are closest to what you want to say about your subject. The answers to that question are the main points you will discuss in your paper.

Here's how the procedure works. Assume you've been forced to accept as your subject "Writing Good Business Letters." Don't despair. Run down the list of questions until you find the one you can answer best. The process might go something like this:

1. *How is a business letter written?*

   No answer comes to mind. Scratch that question.

2. *How does a business letter work?*

   Silly question; it doesn't make sense.

3. *What are the main parts of a business letter?*

   Well, there are the inside address, the body, the salutation, and the complimentary close, but you don't know enough about these to write anything intelligent or original on them.

4. *What are the main functions of the business letter?*

   You can think of three: to request information, to place an order, and to complain about some product or service. This has possibilities, but you're not wildly enthusiastic about these aspects of your subject, so you go on.

5. *What are the important characteristics of a good business letter?*

   At last! Here's one you can answer satisfactorily. You know that a business letter should be clear, brief and to the point, and courteous. Assuming that you know or can find out some pertinent and interesting information about these characteristics, you're all set. *Clarity, conciseness,* and *courtesy* are the points you will discuss in your paper. (Before you go any further, though, it's a good idea to apply the remaining questions in the box to your subject, just to be sure there isn't another question that yields answers you like even better.)

Selecting the main points to write about isn't a difficult process, but it is time-consuming. Don't rush. Take the necessary time. This is a crucial stage in the writing process.

Here are a few sample subjects, together with some main points that were discovered by applying the list of questions in the box on p. 192. Study the chart below until you're sure you understand how to find suitable main points for any subject.

SUBJECT	SELECTED QUESTION	MAIN POINTS
A good teacher	5. What are the important characteristics of a good teacher?	• knowledge • ability to communicate this knowledge • respect for students

SUBJECT	SELECTED QUESTION	MAIN POINTS
Running for fitness	12. What are the reasons for people's interest in running?	• improvement of one's physical condition • improvement of one's mental condition • low-cost approach to fitness
Common-law relationships	11. What are the main disadvantages of common-law relationships?	• possible lack of commitment between partners • possible legal problems, should separation occur • possible lack of security for children born into such an arrangement
Mental retardation	8. What are the causes of mental retardation?	• genetic defects • brain damage • early environmental deprivation
A successful party	1. How do you hold a successful party?	• by inviting the right mix of people • by planning the entertainment carefully • by preparing the food ahead of time • by providing a relaxed, friendly atmosphere
The accounting profession	6. What are the main kinds of accountants?	• Chartered Accountant • Registered Industrial Accountant • Certified General Accountant

As a general rule, you should try to identify between *two* and *five* main ideas for your subject. If you have only one main idea, you have a subject suitable for a paragraph, not an essay. If you have more than five, you have too much material for a short paper. Select the most important aspects of the subject, or take another look at it to see how you can focus it more specifically.

EXERCISE 22.4

In this exercise, select a question from the box on p. 192 and generate good main points for each subject.

SUBJECT	SELECTED QUESTION	MAIN POINTS
1. My preparation for college		•
		•
		•
		•
2. My part-time/ full-time job		•
		•
		•
		•
3. My family's immigration to Canada		•
		•
		•
		•
4. Leaving home		•
		•
		•
		•
5. Pop music		•
		•
		•
		•

EXERCISE 22.5

For each of the five subjects you chose in exercise 22.3, list two to five main points. If suitable main points do not immediately come to mind, apply to your subject the twelve questions in the box on p. 192, one at a time, until you find the one that fits best. The answers to that question are your main points.

Testing Your Main Points

Now take a close look at the main points you've chosen in exercise 22.5. It may be necessary to revise some of them before going any further. Are some points really too minor to bother with? Do any of the points overlap in meaning? Are there any points that are not directly related to the subject?

Main points must be SIGNIFICANT, DISTINCT, and RELEVANT.

To be completely satisfactory, the main points you have chosen to write about must all be **significant:** worth writing a paragraph or more on. You shouldn't have any trivial ideas mixed in with the important ones.

Second, each of the main points you've chosen must be **distinct.** That is, it must be different from all the others. There must be no overlap in meaning. Check to be sure you haven't given two different labels to what is really only one aspect of the subject.

And finally, each main point must be **relevant**; it must be clearly **related** to the subject. It must be an aspect of the subject you are writing about, not some other subject. For example, if you're writing about the advantages of a subject, cross out any disadvantages that may have appeared on your list.

EXERCISE 22.6

Here is a list of subjects, each of which is followed by some possible main points. Circle the unsatisfactory point(s) in each group.

1. Reasons for teenage drug abuse
   - peer pressure
   - school pressure
   - alcohol
   - boredom

2. How homemade bread is made
   - prepare dough
   - large bakeries
   - kneading dough
   - saving money
   - bake loaves

3. The advantages of being physically fit
   - improved muscle tone
   - improved appearance
   - improved stamina
   - improved looks
   - improved social life

4. Characteristics of sharks
   - tiny brains
   - white shark
   - tough and durable beasts
   - several sets of needle-sharp teeth
   - hammerhead shark
   - not all are dangerous to humans

5. The functions of a travel counsellor
   - plan a client's itinerary
   - book the required arrangements
   - make travel plans
   - get a passport
   - ensure the client is satisfied

6. Popular fad diets
   - the Scarsdale diet
   - the Pritikin diet
   - may be dangerous
   - the Powter regime
   - weight is often gained back

7. The main kinds of daytime television
   - talk shows
   - quiz shows
   - soap operas
   - largely female audience
   - game shows

8. Effects of the postwar baby boom
   - growth of postsecondary institutions in 60s and 70s
   - surge in birth of children from 1947–1965
   - changing social norms due to size of boomer population
   - shortage of jobs for entry-level workers
   - lack of opportunities for career advancement in the 80s and 90s

EXERCISE 22.7

Circle the unsatisfactory point(s) in each group.

1. Why government lotteries
    are harmful

    - they encourage compulsive
      gambling
    - they are fun to play
    - Lottario, Lotto 6/49
    - they bilk money from people
      who have little
    - they foster a "something-for-
      nothing" attitude

2. Some differences between
    high school and college

    - practical training
    - college students must assume
      more responsibility for their
      learning
    - college students are treated like
      adults
    - college students cannot smoke
      in the building

3. Some benefits of biofeedback

    - the medical process by which
      a person learns to control
      autonomic body processes
    - may relieve asthma and ulcers
    - autonomic responses are
      involuntary, self-regulating
      processes
    - may control blood pressure
    - may relieve migraines and
      anxiety

4. The main points of comparison
    between football and rugby

    - both games are team ball games
    - football requires helmets
    - both games are rough
    - both games are played on a
      large field
    - football is more of a spectator
      sport than rugby

5. Ways to treat the hyperactive
    child

    - drug therapy
    - intensely active
    - psychiatric counselling
    - cannot concentrate for long
    - change in family routines
    - change in diet

6. How to find a job
- watch employment ads carefully
- prepare a first-class résumé
- send résumés and covering letters to possible employers
- finding a job may take a while
- prepare for interviews
- buy a suit

7. Different kinds of family structure
- nuclear family
- in-laws
- single-parent family
- communal family
- family breakdown
- polygamous family

8. Reasons for legalizing prostitution
- to save taxpayers money
- to control spread of sexually transmitted diseases
- to eliminate juvenile prostitution
- to ensure regular health check-ups for prostitutes
- to decriminalize prostitution

EXERCISE 22.8

Study the main points you chose in exercise 22.5 (p. 196). Cross out any that are not *significant*, *distinct*, or *relevant* to the subject. If necessary, add new main points so that you end up with at least three main points for each subject.

Organizing Your Main Points

Now that you've decided on three or four main points to discuss, you need to decide in what order you wish to present them in your paper. Choose the order that is most appropriate for your particular subject.

> There are four basic ways to arrange main points in an essay: CHRONOLOGICAL, CLIMACTIC, LOGICALLY LINKED, and RANDOM order.

1. **Chronological order** means in order of time sequence, from first to last. Here's an example:

SUBJECT	MAIN POINTS
The process of a relationship	• attraction
	• meeting
	• discovery
	• intimacy
	• disillusionment

2. **Climactic order** means saving your strongest or most important point for last. Generally, you would present your strongest point last, your second-strongest point first, and the others in between, like this:

SUBJECT	MAIN POINTS
Disadvantages of cigarette smoking	• danger to those around you
	• disapproval of others
	• expense
	• danger to yourself

3. **Logically linked order** means that the main points are connected in such a way that one point must be explained before the next can be understood. Consider this example:

SUBJECT	MAIN POINTS
Main causes of juvenile delinquency	• lack of opportunity for work
	• lack of recreational facilities
	• boredom

The logical link here is this: because of unemployment, recreational facilities are needed, and because of both unemployment and inadequate recreational facilities, boredom becomes a problem. The first two points must be explained before the reader can fully understand the third.

4. **Random order** means the points can be explained in any order. A random arrangement of points is possible only if the main points are *equally significant* and *not chronologically or causally linked*, as in this example:

SUBJECT	MAIN POINTS
Reasons for the waste disposal crisis	• disposal sites are hard to find
	• costs are high
	• new technologies are not yet fully developed

EXERCISE 22.9

Below we have identified eight subjects, together with several main points that could be used to develop them. For each subject, number the points so that they are arranged in the order suggested.

SUBJECT	ORDER	MAIN POINTS
1. How to start a gas lawnmower	chronological	____ make sure there is enough gas in tank ____ turn switch to start ____ put lawnmower on flat ground ____ when running, adjust to proper speed ____ pull cord ____ mow!
2. Differences between spoken and written language	climactic	____ speech is transitory; writing is permanent ____ speech is direct and personal; writing isn't ____ speech can't be revised; writing can
3. How to write a research paper	chronological	____ read and take notes on selected research sources ____ draft the paper ____ compile a working bibliography of research sources ____ define the subject ____ type and proofread paper ____ prepare footnotes, if needed, and bibliography ____ revise the paper
4. How colleges benefit society	logical	____ they provide the individual with a higher level of general education ____ society benefits from increased productivity and commitment of an educated populace ____ they provide the individual with job skills

SUBJECT	ORDER	MAIN POINTS
5. Some causes of World War II	chronological	____ World Depression in early 1930s ____ Hitler's rise to power in 1933 ____ heavy reparations demanded of Germany at end of World War I ____ German aggression in Europe
6. Effects of malnutrition	logical	____ malnutrition affects the productivity and prosperity of nations as a whole ____ malnutrition impedes the mental and physical development of children ____ undernourished children become sickly adults unable to participate fully in their society
7. Why pornography should be banned	chronological	____ it degrades the people involved in making it ____ it brutalizes society as a whole ____ it desensitizes the people who view it
8. Why pornography should not be banned	climactic	____ organized crime benefits from illegal distribution ____ censorship violates individual civil rights ____ banning pornography would lead to censorship of legitimate art and literature

EXERCISE 22.10

Using your list of subjects and main points from exercise 22.8, arrange the main points for each subject in the most appropriate order. (*Note:* Keep your answer sheet. You will need it in some of the exercises that follow.)

In this chapter, you've learned how to choose a satisfactory subject and how to select and arrange the main points of that subject—the first two steps in the five-step process we outlined at the beginning of the chapter. Now it's time to decide whether you'll develop your paper by the thesis-statement method or by the outline method. We think the former generally works best for short papers and the latter for long papers, but this distinction isn't hard and fast. Your wisest choice is to learn both ways to structure a paper. You will often get the best results if you use them together.

CHAPTER 23

Writing the Thesis Statement

In Chapter 22, you chose a topic and selected some aspects of it to discuss. Now you're ready for the third step in developing a paper. If you're writing a short paper, we recommend that you use the method presented in this chapter. If you're writing a longer paper or if your teacher prefers the outline method, you may prefer to turn now to Chapter 24, "Writing the Outline."

Step 3: Write a Thesis Statement

The key to a clearly organized paper is a **thesis statement**—a statement near the beginning of your paper that announces its subject and scope. The thesis statement is a tremendous help both to you and to your readers. It plans your paper for you, and it tells your readers exactly what they are going to read about. In fiction, letting readers know in advance what they are going to find would never do. But for practical, everyday kinds of writing, advance notice works very well. Term papers, technical reports, research papers, office memoranda, and business letters are no place for suspense or surprises. In these kinds of writing, you're more likely to get and keep your readers' attention if you indicate the subject and scope of your paper at the outset. The thesis statement acts like a table of contents, giving a clear indication of what follows. It's a kind of map of the territory covered in your paper: it keeps your reader (and you) on the right track.

> A thesis statement is a sentence that clearly and concisely indicates the **subject** of your paper, the **main points** you will discuss, and the **order** in which you will discuss them.

To write a thesis statement, you join your subject to your main points, which you have already arranged in order. To join the two parts of a thesis statement, you use a **link**. Your link can be a word or a phrase such as *are, include, consist of, because, since,* or it can be a colon.[1] Here is the simple formula for constructing a thesis statement:

S	consists of	1, 2, 3 . . . n.
subject	*link*	*main points*

Here's an example:

Three characteristics of a good business letter are conciseness, clarity, and courtesy.

subject	*link*	*main points*

EXERCISE 23.1

In each of the following thesis statements, underline the subject with a wavy line, circle the link and underline the main points with a straight line. Answers begin on p. 374.

1. There are three kinds of students whom teachers find difficult to teach: whiners, snoozers, and disrupters.

2. The most prolific producers of unnecessary jargon are politicians, sports writers, advertising-copy writers, and educators.

---

[1] Remember that a colon can be used only after an independent clause. See Chapter 19 if you need a review.

3. Dining in the cafeteria should be avoided if possible, for the food is high in cost, low in nutrition, and unappetizing in taste.

4. Because they lack basic skills, study skills, or motivation, some students run the risk of failure in college.

5. Pay television has faced challenges in Canada because of the relatively small market, the high monthly cost, and the stiff network competition.

6. Political violence has become ingrained in the social fabric of many Latin American countries including Nicaragua, El Salvador, Colombia, and Brazil.

7. The Canadian national character was shaped by early conflicts such as the battle for Quebec, the rebellion of 1837, and the Riel rebellion.

8. Canada is little more than an American satellite, for the United States influences our foreign policy, dominates our culture, and controls our economy.

9. The major improvements Western medical technology has made in impoverished parts of the world consist of widespread immunization, the availability of antibiotics, and improved sanitation.

10. Two cheers for democracy: one because it admits variety and two because it permits criticism. (E.M. Forster)

When you combine your subject with your main points to form a thesis statement, there is an important rule to remember:

> The main points should be **grammatically parallel**.

This rule means that if main point 1 is a word, then main points 2 and 3 and so on must be words, too. If main point 1 is a phrase, then the rest must be phrases. If your first main point is a dependent clause, then the rest must be dependent clauses. Study the model thesis statements you analyzed in exercise 23.1. In every example, the main points are in grammatically parallel form. For each of those thesis statements, decide whether words, phrases, or dependent clauses were used. If you feel your understanding of parallelism is a bit wobbly, review Chapter 9 before doing the following exercises.

EXERCISE 23.2

This exercise will test your grasp of the parallelism principle. In each question below, one main point is not parallel to the others. Circle the faulty main point and rewrite it to make it grammatically parallel.

1. I
   a. came
   b. saw
   c. conquered
   d. pack up and head for Rome

2. I am looking for a husband who is
   a. strength
   b. intelligent
   c. good-looking
   d. well-heeled

3. Her wicked stepsisters were
   a. ill-tempered
   b. ungrateful
   c. ugliness
   d. self-centered

4. Greg completed the requirements
   a. skilfully
   b. with intelligence
   c. correctly
   d. quickly

5. We enjoy travelling
   a. by car
   b. sailing
   c. by air
   d. by train

6. A politician should be
   a. well-liked by constituents
   b. respected by colleagues
   c. esteemed by the party
   d. even the media trust him

7. We have all been
   a. watching our diet
   b. learning to exercise
   c. not to watch so much television
   d. thinking of fitness

8. Excessive use of marijuana can
   a. make you eat more
   b. diminish ambition
   c. induce lethargy
   d. cause psychological dependence

9. Her family has a
   a. mansion in Westmount
   b. cottage in the Muskokas
   c. ski chalet in the Laurentians
   d. yacht that always seems to be in drydock

10. To lower the crime rate, we must ensure
    a. that citizens are involved in their communities
    b. that jobs and adequate housing are available
    c. enough fair-minded police visible
    d. that courts work justly and speedily

EXERCISE 23.3

Put a check mark (√) before the sentences that are grammatically parallel.
Check your answers when you have completed the exercise.

1. _____ His basement apartment was small, damp, cold, and lots of dirt.

2. _____ To be a good marriage counsellor, a person must have insight, pa-

   tient, compassion, and experience.

3. _____ Told to include "Activities and Interests" on his résumé, Elmo de-

   scribed his as chomping potato chips, guzzling beer, and watching

   TV.

4. ____ Too much coffee can give you nervous days, sleepless nights, and your heart may palpitate.

5. ____ We require our employees to be honest, reliable, disciplined, and they have to know something.

6. ____ Roderick is interested in the occult, so he spends his time reading about witches, warlocks, and wizards.

7. ____ We knew we would be suffering from a severe case of jet lag when we got back, so we took a cab home, unpacked our bags, and went right to sleep.

8. ____ Inflation is down, interest rates are up, and many people still don't have jobs.

9. ____ Hobbies are important because they provide recreation, stimulation, and relaxation.

10. ____ Writing acceptable college-level prose involves applying the principles of organization, sentence structure, spelling, and you have to punctuate, too.

EXERCISE 23.4
Now correct the faulty parallelism in the sentences in Exercise 23.3.

EXERCISE 23.5
Correct the faulty parallelism in the following sentences.

1. Do you know the difference among polygamy, bigamy, and marrying only one person at a time?

2. Ahmad has given up not only on the Liberals but also on the Conservatives and the Reform Party.

3. Rudolf decided he'd rather be a plumber than to teach school.

4. A good coach must train and discipline the team, and he must provide motivation.

5. Two features of the semester system are flexibility and it's economical.

6. Going to college is good for broadening one's social life as well as to learn career skills.

7. Compared to those of ten years ago, today's cars are smaller, more efficient, and they cost more.

8. We find it's more interesting to explore the tide pools at the seashore than lying in the sun all day.

9. Children who grow up in the city have a different outlook on life than the country.

10. Do Canadians really care if the United States dominates our economy, political life, and our culture?

EXERCISE 23.6

Correct the faulty parallelism in the following sentences.

1. The four kinds of prose writing are narration, description, exposition, and persuasive.

2. College fraternities and sororities have become less popular in the past twenty years because of expense, they are time-consuming, and they discriminate against some students.

3. Medical scientists are studying the link between weather and such diseases as colds, arthritic ailments, and cancer.

4. If I could have three wishes, I would wish to be gorgeous, absolutely brilliant, and the possessor of fabulous riches.

5. Roots products have won international favour because of their reasonable cost, the designs are fashionable without being faddish, and the quality is unfailingly high.

6. Intramural sports offer three important things to college students: a way to get involved in the school, an opportunity to meet friends, and they can stay fit.

7. Freud's psychoanalytic theories, developed in the early years of this century, not only have affected the course of psychology but also have had profound implications for education, artistic, and literary.

8. Many English words have similar meanings, but they come from very different root languages: for example, *spectre* comes from the Latin *spectrum* (appearance); *phantom* comes from the Greek *phantasm* (image); and *ghost,* Anglo-Saxon *gast*—spirit.

9. Geologists are exploring several phenomena that may lead to an early-warning system for earthquakes: the variation of electrical resistance of rocks under pressure, releasing gas trapped in the crystal lattice of a rock, and the appearance of eerie lights, or luminous flares, in the sky before a quake.

10. It was the best of times; it was the worst of times; it was the age of wis-

dom; it was the age of foolishness; it was the epoch of belief; it was the

age of incredulity; it was the season of Light; it was the season of Dark-

ness; it was the spring of hope; and there was a lot of despair that win-

ter, too. (With apologies to Charles Dickens, *A Tale of Two Cities*)

EXERCISE 23.7

This exercise is designed for those who wish to reinforce their understanding of thesis statement construction before proceeding. Turn back to Exercise 23.2. In that exercise, you made all the points grammatically parallel.
Now it's time to turn each subject with its list of points into a thesis statement. Before you write each sentence, arrange the main points listed below
the subject into an appropriate order: chronological, climactic, logical, or
random.

Answers to this exercise may vary. Just be sure you have a good rationale
for choosing the order you use in each case. When you've finished the exercise, turn to p. 376, where you will find suggested answers for some of the
items.

EXERCISE 23.8

Find the subjects and main points you produced for exercise 22.10 in Chapter 22. Combine each subject with its main points to make a thesis statement. Be sure the main points are expressed in parallel form.

We said at the beginning of this chapter that the thesis statement plans
your whole paper for you. Before we turn to the actual writing of the
paper, it will be useful for you to have a general idea of what the finished
product will look like. In a short paper, each main point can be explained
in a single paragraph. The main points of your subject become the **topics**
of the paragraphs, as is shown below in the model format for a paper that
has three main points.

Notice the proportions of the paragraphs in the model format. Since the
main points are approximately equal in significance, the paragraphs of the
body of the paper are approximately equal in length. (If your last main
point is more important than the other points, however, the paragraph that
explains it may be longer than the other paragraphs.)

Notice, too, that the beginning and ending paragraphs are much shorter
than the ones that explain the main points. Your introduction should not
ramble on, and your conclusion should not trail off. Get to your main
points as quickly as you can, and end with a bang, not a whimper.

Title

Paragraph 1: contains your introduction and thesis statement

<u>S consists of 1, 2, and 3.</u>

Paragraph 2: explains your first main point

<u>Topic sentence introducing main point 1.</u>

Paragraph 3: explains your second main point

<u>Topic sentence introducing main point 2.</u>

Paragraph 4: explains your third main point

<u>Topic sentence introducing main point 3.</u>

Paragraph 5: conclusion

EXERCISE 23.9

A good paper that follows the model format exactly is Brian Green's "Writing a Good Business Letter," which appears in Appendix A. Read it and underline the thesis statement and topic sentences. Then turn to Chapter 25.

CHAPTER 24

Writing the Outline

For longer compositions, business and technical reports, research papers, and the like, an outline is often necessary. A good outline maps out your paper from beginning to end. It shows you—before you begin to write—what you have to say about each of your main points. Outlining spares you the agony of discovering too late that you have too much information about one point and little or nothing to say about another.

Step 3: Write an Outline

Once you've chosen a satisfactory subject and main points to discuss, the next step is to expand what you have into an organized plan for your finished paper. To do this, you may need to do some further thinking or reading, to gather additional information and supporting facts. (For ideas about what kinds of information you might use, see "Developing Your Paragraphs," in Chapter 25.) After you've assembled all the information you think you'll need, prepare the outline.

First, write down your main points in the order you've decided is best for your presentation. Leave lots of space under each main point. Using Roman numerals (I, II, III, and so on), number your main points. Now, under each main point, indent and list the examples, facts, ideas, or other supporting information you're going to use to explain it. Again, leave lots of space. Check to be sure these items are arranged in an order that will be clear to your reader.[1] Label your supporting points, *A, B, C,* and so on.

If any of these supporting points need to be explained or developed, indent again and list the second level of supporting points, numbering them, *1, 2, 3,* and so on. Third-level supporting details, if there are any, are indented under the points to which they relate and are labelled, *a, b, c.* Add the introduction and conclusion, and you're done. Your outline might look something like this:

Introduction

    Attention-getter

    Thesis statement/statement of subject

  I. First main point

    A. item that develops first main point

    B. item that develops first main point

        1. supporting material that develops item B

        2. supporting material that develops item B

  II. Second main point

    A. item that develops second main point

    B. item that develops second main point

    C. item that develops second main point

 III. Third main point

    A. item that develops third main point

        1. supporting material that develops item A

            a. detail

            b. detail

        2. supporting material that develops item A

    B. item that develops third main point

Conclusion

    Summary

    Memorable statement

You'll probably find that before you can assign a number or a letter to a piece of information, you need to think carefully about where the item belongs in your paper. Questions about how to arrange your information under each main point and how much time to spend on a particular point should be cleared up at the outline stage. If, for example, you find you have

---

[1] The four kinds of order explained in Chapter 22 apply to the arrangement of ideas within a paragraph as well as to the arrangement of main points in a paper.

nine subheadings under main point I and only one under main point II, you need to do some rethinking to balance your paper. Main points should be supported by approximately equal amounts of information.

Preparing a satisfactory outline takes time. Be prepared to spend time adding, deleting, and rearranging your ideas and supporting details until you're completely satisfied with both the arrangement and the proportion of your outline. If you have access to a computer that has a word processing program with an outline feature, be sure to experiment with it. These programs can be very helpful to an inexperienced writer faced with a writing assignment and little knowledge of how to organize it.

EXERCISE 24.1

Below are the main points from a paper that explains, tongue-in-cheek, how to fail. Following the main points are eight statements that might be used to support and develop them. Read through the list and complete the outline by arranging the supporting details logically below the appropriate points. Discard any items that are not relevant to the main points. Turn to p. 377 to check your outline against ours.

I. Antagonize your teacher

-
-
-

II. Disdain your studies

-
-
-

III. Cheat on your work

-
-
-

- don't buy the text for the course
- aim an occasional snort or snicker in the teacher's direction
- copy research assignments out of an appropriate library book
- wear your Walkman to class and turn up the volume whenever the teacher speaks
- sit at the back during exams and try to read your classmate's paper
- never take notes in class
- stop going to class
- tattoo your answers on your forearms

With your outline in hand, all you have to do to draft your paper is to make the main points into paragraph divisions, assemble the supporting points into sentences, and add an introduction and conclusion. Chapter 25 explains how.

To show you the relationship between an outline and the final product, we've recreated the outline that was used to write "Writing a Good Business Letter" (reprinted in Appendix A):

Introduction
    Attention-getter: A good business letter is one that gets results.
    Thesis statement: A business letter should be concise, clear, and courteous.

  I. Concise
    A. The point should be made quickly
        1. assume your reader is busy
        2. assume your reader is not interested in trivia or personal messages
    B. Revision is necessary
        1. use precise language
        2. short letters have more impact than long letters
    C. There is still room for style and humour
 II. Clear
    A. Organization is important
        1. know what you want to say
        2. construct the paragraphs to guide the reader through to the conclusion
    B. Acceptable letter format should be used
    C. Rereading will aid clarity
        1. take the point of view of your reader
        2. ensure accuracy of facts, figures, explanations
III. Courteous
    A. Tone is important
        1. sarcasm and insults don't work
        2. be polite
    B. Writing and typing must be done with care
        1. correct grammar and spelling are part of courtesy
        2. mistakes will make the reader think less of you
Conclusion
    Summary: The business letter can pay big dividends on the time you invest in giving it a concise message, a clear structure, and a courteous tone.

Once you've mapped out your plan in an outline, the task of writing the essay is much easier. You can see where you're going and how to get there. Remember, the more time you spend on planning, the less time you will spend on writing—and the better your paper will be.

EXERCISE 24.2

Read "Writing a Good Business Letter" in Appendix A. Find the paragraphs that correspond to the various headings and subheadings in the outline (above). Label the paragraphs to show where they fit into the outline: I, A, B, 1, 2, and so on.

EXERCISE 24.3

Read Nell Waldman's "Flunking with Style" in Appendix A and write an outline for it. When you've finished, turn to p. 377 to compare your outline with ours.

EXERCISE 24.4

Turn to the subjects and main points you developed for exercise 22.10 in Chapter 22 and create an outline for a paper on one of those subjects.

CHAPTER 25

Writing the Paragraphs

You are now at step 4 in the writing process. Armed with either your thesis statement or your outline, you are ready to turn your main points into paragraphs. Does that sound like a magician's trick? It isn't. The "sleight-of-pen" involved requires only that you know what a paragraph looks like and how to put one together.

A paragraph looks like this:

Three or more sentences that specifically support or explain the topic go in here.

⎧
⎪
⎨
⎪
⎩

A sentence that introduces the **topic** (or main idea) of the paragraph goes here. _____ _____ _____ _____ _____ _____ _____

A sentence that concludes your explanation of the topic goes here.

Sometimes a main point can be explained satisfactorily in a single paragraph. If the main point is complicated and requires lots of support, several paragraphs are needed. Nevertheless, whether it is explaining a main point of a paper or an item supporting a main point, every paragraph contains two things: a topic sentence (usually the first sentence in the paragraph) and several sentences that develop the topic.

Beginning with a sentence that clearly states your main idea is a good way to start a paragraph. The sentences that follow support or expand on the topic. The key to making the paragraph *unified* (an important quality of English paragraphs) is to make sure that each of your supporting sentences relates directly to the main idea introduced in the topic sentence.

EXERCISE 25.1

Turn to Appendix A and read Bertrand Russell's "What I Have Lived For." Study the second, third, and fourth paragraphs and find in each the three basic components of a paragraph: the topic sentence, the supporting sentences, and the conclusion. Compare your answer with ours on p. 378.

Developing Your Paragraphs

How do you put a paragraph together? First, write your **topic sentence,** telling your reader what topic (main point or idea) you're going to discuss in the paragraph. Next, develop your topic. An adequately developed paragraph gives enough supporting information to make the topic completely clear to the reader. An average paragraph runs between 75 and 200 words (except for introductions and conclusions, which are shorter), so you can see you will need lots of supporting information for each point.

Unless you are writing from a very detailed outline and have all the supporting material you need listed in front of you, you need to do some more thinking at this point. Put yourself in your reader's place. What does your reader need to know in order to understand your point clearly? If you ask yourself the six questions listed below, you'll be able to decide what **kinds of development** to use to support a particular topic sentence. The kind of development you use is up to you. Decide on the basis of your topic and what the reader needs to know about it.

1. Is a **definition** necessary?

If you're using a term that may be unfamiliar to your reader, you should define it. Use your own words in the definition. Your reader needs to know what *you* mean by the term—and, besides, quoting from the dictionary is a very boring way to develop a paragraph. Below, Randy Walser defines "cyberspace":

> Cyberspace is a medium that gives people the feeling they have been transported, bodily, from the ordinary physical world to worlds purely of imagination. Although artists can use any medium to evoke imaginary worlds, cyberspace carries the worlds themselves. It has a lot in common with film and stage,

but is unique in the amount of power it yields to its audience. Film yields little power, as it provides no way for its audience to alter film images. Stage grants more power than film, as stage actors can "play off" audience reactions, but still the course of the action is basically determined by a playwright's script. Cyberspace grants ultimate power, as it enables its audience not merely to observe a reality, but to enter it and experience it as if it were real. No one can know what will happen from one moment to the next in a cyberspace, not even the spacemaker. Every moment gives every participant an opportunity to create the next event. Whereas film is used to show a reality to an audience, cyberspace is used to give a virtual body and a role to everyone in the audience. Print and radio tell; stage and film show; cyberspace embodies.

(from Howard Rheingold, *Virtual Reality.* New York: Simon and Schuster, 1991. 26.)

You should include a definition, too, if you're using a familiar term in a specific or unusual way. In the following paragraph, Andrew Nikiforuk defines how he interprets the familiar phrase, "back to the basics":

Let me reiterate what "back to the basics" means. It means teaching subjects that matter—such as English, math, history, geography, and science—because they contain the codes for power in a technological society as well as the only tools for criticizing and analyzing it. It means giving teachers more control over how their classrooms are organized and taught as well as making them more accountable for the results. It means skills in the context of disciplines (that's critical thinking) with the honest realization that not all students will become critical thinkers. It means fair tests and even standardized tests, because product matters in this culture. And finally, it means using the varied cultural backgrounds of students to explore common ground and Canadian realities.

(Andrew Nikiforuk, *School's Out: The Catastrophe in Public Education and What We Can Do About It.* Toronto: MacFarland, 1993.)

EXERCISE 25.2

Write a paragraph in which you define one of the following terms:

respect	friendship	happiness
community	stress	a good teacher
racism	a good job	wisdom

2. Would **examples** help clarify the point?

Listing a number of examples is probably the most common method of developing a topic. Readers become confused, even suspicious, when they read unsupported generalizations or statements of opinion. One of the most effective ways of communicating your idea is by providing clear, relevant examples. In the following paragraph, excerpted from a reading in Appendix A, Sun-Kyung Yi uses examples to explain why her job with a Korean company proved to be a "painful and frustrating experience."

> When the president of the company boasted that he "operated little Korea," he meant it literally. A Canadianized Korean was not tolerated. I looked like a Korean, therefore I had to talk, act, and think like one, too. Being accepted meant a total surrender to ancient codes of behaviour rooted in Confucian thought, while leaving the "Canadian" part of me out in the parking lot with my '86 Buick. In the first few days at work, I was bombarded with inquiries about my marital status. When I told them I was single, they spent the following days trying to match me up with available bachelors in the company and the community. I was expected to accept my inferior position as a woman and had to behave accordingly. It was not a place to practice my feminist views, or be an individual without being condemned. Little Korea is a place for men (who filled all the senior positions) and women don't dare to speak up or disagree with their male counterparts. The president (all employees bow to him and call him Mr. President) asked me to act more like a lady and smile. I was openly scorned by a senior employee because I spoke more fluent English than Korean. The cook in the kitchen shook her head in disbelief upon discovering that my cooking skills were limited to boiling a package of instant noodles. "You want a good husband, learn to cook," she advised me.

Sometimes, one example developed in detail is enough to allow the reader to understand what you mean. In the following paragraph, from "Surviving Your Daughter's Adolescence" (in Appendix A), Janet Read supports her topic "don't argue," with a familiar example: teaching an adolescent to drive.

> Finally we come to the hardest rule for a parent to follow: don't, under any circumstances, argue. Females between the ages of thirteen and eighteen are world-class debaters. They can argue black is white, rain is snow, or bitter is sweet. The most hazardous time is the period when your baby of a few short years ago is learning to drive. She will become, after only two driving lessons, an authority on rules of the road. We have all coped with

back-seat drivers, but nothing will have prepared you for this experience. The teenager feels a learner's permit is a licence to tell her parents how to drive. There are a few useful phrases you can employ to reduce the risk of argument: "Yes, dear." "Is that right?" "How astute of you to notice that!" These simple phrases can forestall an argument that would entertain your entire neighbourhood.

EXERCISE 25.3

Write a six- to ten-sentence paragraph based on the topic sentence below, using examples to develop it.

College is more than just a place to get an education.

3. Is a **series of steps** or **stages** involved?

Sometimes the most effective way to develop the main idea of your paragraph is by explaining how to do it—that is, by relating the process or series of steps involved. Make sure you break the process down into its component parts and explain the steps logically and precisely. Below, Brian Green explains the process of writing a good business letter:

> The business letter must be clear. You should have a firm idea of what you want to say, and you should let the reader know it. Use the structure of the letter—the paragraphs, topic sentences, and transitions—to guide the reader point by point from your introduction, through your reasoning, to your conclusion. Paragraph often, to break up the page and to provide visual cues to the organization of your letter. Use an accepted business-letter format. There are several, and they can be found in any book of business English. Reread what you have written from the point of view of someone who is seeing it for the first time, and revise to be sure that all necessary information is provided (including reference numbers, dates, and other identification) and that all explanations are clear. A clear message, clearly delivered, is the essence of business communication.

EXERCISE 25.4

Write a six- to ten-sentence paragraph developed as a series of steps telling your reader how to make or do something.

4. Would **specific details** be useful?

Providing your reader with concrete, specific, descriptive details can be a very effective way of developing your main point. In some paragraphs, numerical facts or statistics can be used to support your point effectively—just be sure your facts are correct and your statistics up-to-date! In the following paragraph, underline the specific details that help make Denise Chong's description of her grandfather an effective one:

> One Chinese man waiting for the passenger ship to dock at the pier at the foot of Granville Street stood out from the crowd by virtue of his nearly six-foot frame. He had a body that was all limbs, long even in his fingers, which gave his every gesture an elongated emphasis. A fedora graced his head, and he was attired in a custom-tailored three-piece gray suit. His shoes and wire-rimmed glasses were polished and his black hair meticulously combed to expose a high forehead, a physical trait the Chinese consider a sign of intelligence. He owned two suits—one gray, the other brown—and two fedoras. Believing one's appearance mirrored one's inner mind, his appearance today was, as always, immaculate. His manner, like his dress, was sober and serious. At thirty-seven, he was a year younger than the city of Vancouver.

> _____

> (from Denise Chong, *The Concubine's Children: Portrait of a Family Divided*. 1994. 11.)

Now consider the following paragraph, excerpted from a reading in Appendix A, in which Nell Waldman appeals to the reader's sense of hearing as well as sight to develop her point:

> [A]ntagonizing your teachers isn't difficult if you keep in mind what it is that teachers like: intelligent, interested, even enthusiastic faces in front row centre. Show that you're bored before the class begins by slouching in a desk at the back of the room. Wear your Walkman, and don't forget to turn up the volume when the teacher starts to talk. Carry on running conversations with your seatmates. Aim an occasional snort or snicker in the teacher's direction when she's putting a complex point on the board. Above all, never volunteer an answer and respond sullenly with an "I dunno" if the teacher has the nerve to ask you a question. Before long, you'll have that teacher bouncing chalk stubs off your head. Once you've earned the loathing of your instructors, you'll be well on your way to a truly memorable failure.

EXERCISE 25.5

Write a six- to ten-sentence paragraph describing one of the following topics. Try to include details that involve several of the physical senses: sight, hearing, touch, smell, and taste. Be sure to begin with a clearly identifiable topic sentence.

a fast-food restaurant
a place that makes you feel uncomfortable
your favourite space
a younger brother or sister
the most unusual-looking person you know
a favourite article of clothing or jewellery

5. Would a **comparison** or **contrast** help clarify your point?

A **comparison** points out similarities between objects, people, or ideas; it shows how two different things are alike. A **contrast** points out dissimilarities between things; it shows how two objects, people, or ideas are different. A **comparison and contrast** identifies both similarities and differences. In the paragraph below, Sun-Kyung Yi contrasts the two sides of her "split personality."

> When I was younger, toying with the idea of entertaining two separate identities was a real treat, like a secret game for which no one knew the rules but me. I was known as Angela to the outside world, and as Sun-Kyung at home. I ate bologna sandwiches in the school lunch room and rice and kimchee for dinner. I chatted about teen idols and giggled with my girlfriends during my classes, and ambitiously practiced piano and studied in the evenings, planning to become a doctor when I grew up. I waved hellos and goodbyes to my teachers, but bowed to my parents' friends visiting our home. I could also look straight in the eyes of my teachers and friends and talk frankly with them instead of staring at my feet with my mouth shut when Koreans talked to me. Going outside the home meant I was able to relax from the constraints of my cultural conditioning, until I walked back in the door and had to return to being an obedient and submissive daughter.

In the following paragraph, Don Gayton begins to develop his subject, how plants grow, by comparing the structure of a leaf to that of a factory:

> At a certain microscopic scale, a leaf begins to lose its biological elegance and starts looking more like a clanking, humming factory. The factory image, in fact, is not far off the mark: a grass leaf is essentially a four-story, double-sided solar-driven manufacturing plant, suspended in space. The roof of this factory is made from thick, transparent cuticle cells. Just below the roof,

on the fourth floor, is a palisade layer, where photosynthesis takes place. The third floor is the spongy mesophyll layer . . . where transpiration occurs. The second and first floors form the underside of the leaf, and they are a rough mirror image of the third and fourth. The stomata on the upper and lower roof vent gases and vapors to and from the mesophyll layer to the outside. Xylem and phloem liquid supply lines come in through the utility space between the second and third floors.

(Don Gayton, *The Wheatgrass Mechanism: Science and Imagination in the Western Canadian Landscape.* Saskatoon: Fifth House Publishers, 1990. 89.)

EXERCISE 25.6

Write a six- to ten-sentence paragraph comparing or contrasting two performers (or instructors or employers). Begin your paragraph with a topic sentence.

6. Would a **quotation** or **paraphrase** be appropriate?

Occasionally, you will find that someone else—an expert in a particular field, a well-known author, or a respected public figure—has said what you want to say better than you could ever hope to say it. In these cases, quotations—as long as they are kept short and not used too frequently—are useful in developing your topic. Notice how Martin Luther King uses a famous quotation to sum up the point of this paragraph.

As long as there is poverty in the world I can never be rich, even if I have a billion dollars. As long as diseases are rampant and millions of people in this world cannot expect to live more than twenty-eight or thirty years, I can never be totally healthy even if I just got a good check-up at Mayo Clinic. I can never be what I ought to be until you are what you ought to be. This is the way our world is made. No individual or nation can stand out boasting of being independent. We are interdependent. So John Donne placed it in graphic terms when he affirmed, "No man is an island entire of itself. Every man is a piece of the continent, a part of the main." Then he goes on to say, "Any man's death diminishes me because I am involved in mankind, and therefore never send to know for whom the bell tolls; it tolls for thee."

(from Martin Luther King, Jr., *The Measure of a Man.* Philadelphia: Christian Education Press, 1959.)

A paraphrase is a summary—in your own words—of someone else's idea. Don't forget to indicate whose idea you are paraphrasing, the way the author of "The Myth of Canadian Diversity" (in Appendix A) does in the following paragraph.

> . . . [O]ur much-discussed ethnic differences are overstated. Although Canada is an immigrant nation and Canadians spring from a variety of backgrounds, a recent study from the C.D. Howe Institute says that the idea of a "Canadian mosaic"—as distinct from the American "melting pot"—is a fallacy. In *The Illusion of Difference*, University of Toronto sociologists Jeffrey Reitz and Raymond Breton show that immigrants to Canada assimilate as quickly into the mainstream society as immigrants to the United States do. In fact, Canadians are less likely than Americans to favour holding on to cultural differences based on ethnic background. If you don't believe Mr. Reitz and Mr. Breton, visit any big-city high school, where the speech and behaviour of immigrant students just a few years in Canada is indistinguishable from that of any fifth-generation classmate.

College writing normally requires that you indicate the source of any material you quote. The easiest way to do this is to give the author's surname and the page reference in parentheses at the end of your quotation—for example: (King 287). At the end of your paper, include a Works Cited page, which is a list, in alphabetical order by authors' surnames, of all the books, articles, and other publications from which you have quoted in your paper. See p. 176 for examples of the format to use. Follow the instructions given in whatever style guide your instructor recommends, or consult Joseph Gibaldi and Walter S. Achtert, *MLA Handbook for Writers of Research Papers*, 4th ed. (New York: Modern Language Association, 1995).

In writing the paragraphs of your essay, remember that you will often need to use more than one method of development to explain your points. The six methods outlined above can be used in any combination you choose.

EXERCISE 25.7

Identify the kinds of development used in the following paragraphs (more than one kind may be present in each) in the readings in Appendix A. Then turn to p. 378 to check your answers.

1. "Writing a Good Business Letter," paragraph 1

2. "Surviving Your Daughter's Adolescence," paragraph 2

3. "Flunking with Style," paragraph 3

4. "Flunking with Style," paragraph 4

5. "What I Have Lived For," paragraph 2

6. "What I Have Lived For," paragraph 3

7. "The Myth of Canadian Diversity," paragraph 1

8. "The Myth of Canadian Diversity," paragraph 2

9. "An Immigrant's Split Personality," paragraph 4

10. "An Immigrant's Split Personality," paragraph 10

EXERCISE 25.8

Choose one of the following topic sentences or make up one of your own. Write a paragraph of about 100 words, using at least two different methods of paragraph development.

1. Some rock stars lead bizarre personal lives.

2. You are what you wear.

3. I will never forget the moment I ceased being a child.

4. If I had it to do over again, I would _____ .

5. Communicating clearly isn't easy.

Writing Introductions and Conclusions

Two paragraphs in your paper are not developed in the way we've just outlined: the introduction and the conclusion. All too often, these paragraphs are dull or clumsy and detract from a paper's effectiveness. But they needn't. Here's how to write good ones.

The introduction is worth special attention because that's where your reader either sits up and takes notice of your paper or sighs and pitches it into the wastebasket. Occasionally, for a very short paper, you can begin simply with your thesis statement or statement of subject. More usually, though, an **attention-getter** comes before the thesis statement. An attention-getter is a sentence or two designed to get the reader interested in what you have to say.

There are several kinds of attention-getter to choose from:

1. An interesting incident or anecdote related to your subject
2. A statement of opinion you intend to challenge (see "Flunking with Style," paragraph 1)
3. A definition (see "Writing a Good Business Letter," paragraph 1)
4. A quotation or paraphrase
5. A little-known or striking fact (see "An Immigrant's Split Personality," paragraph 1)

Add your thesis statement to the attention-getter and your introduction is complete.

The closing paragraph, too, usually has two parts: a **summary** of the main points of your paper (phrased differently, please—not a word-for-word repetition of your thesis statement or your topic sentences) and a **memorable statement.** Your memorable statement may take several forms:

1. Show the value or significance of your subject (see "Surviving Your Daughter's Adolescence," paragraph 5)
2. Refer back to the content of your opening paragraph (see "Writing a Good Business Letter," paragraph 5; also "What I Have Lived For," paragraph 5)
3. A relevant or thought-provoking quotation, statement, or question (see "The Myth of Canadian Diversity," paragraph 8)
4. A suggestion for change (see "An Immigrant's Split Personality," paragraph 10)
5. A challenge to the reader to get involved (see "Flunking with Style," paragraph 5)

EXERCISE 25.9

Using as many of the different kinds as you can, write an attention-getter and a memorable statement for each of the following topics.

1. I love (*or* hate) baseball (*or* hockey, football, or any other sport).

2. The media pay too much attention to the baby boomers and too little to the rest of us.

3. Movies today are better (*or* worse) than ever before.

4. Honesty is (*or* is not) always the best policy.

5. Cigarette smoking should (*or* should not) be prohibited in the workplace.

6. College students should (*or* should not) be paid to go to school.

7. Surfing the Internet is (*or* is not) great entertainment.

8. Teenagers are (*or* are not) too young to rear children effectively.

9. College professors should (*or* should not) be required to take courses in teaching methodology.

10. It's not easy being a man (*or* a woman).

Keeping Your Reader with You

As you write your paragraphs, keep in mind that you want to make it as easy as possible for your reader to follow you through your paper. Clear **transitions** and an appropriate **tone** can make the difference between a paper that confuses or annoys readers and one that enlightens and pleases them.

Transitions

Transitions are those words or phrases that show the relationship between one point and the next, causing a paragraph or a paper to read smoothly.

Like turn signals on a car, they tell the person following you where you're going. Here are some common transitions you can use to keep your reader on track.

---

1. ***To show a time relation:*** first, second, third, next, before, during, after, now, then, finally, last
2. ***To add an idea or example:*** in addition, also, another, furthermore, similarly, for example, for instance
3. ***To show contrast:*** although, but, however, instead, nevertheless, on the other hand, in contrast, on the contrary
4. ***To show a cause–effect relation:*** as a result, consequently, because, since, therefore, thus

---

Here is a paragraph that has adequate development but no transitions:

> There are several good reasons why you should not smoke. Smoking is harmful to your lungs and heart. It is annoying and dangerous to those around you who do not smoke. Smoking is an unattractive and dirty habit. It is difficult to quit. Most worthwhile things in life are hard to achieve.

Not very easy to read, is it? Readers are jerked abruptly from point to point until, battered and bruised, they reach the end. This kind of writing is unfair to readers. It makes them do too much of the work. The ideas may all be there, but the readers have to figure out for themselves how they fit together. After a couple of paragraphs like this one, even a patient reader can become annoyed.

Now read the same paragraph with the transitions added:

> There are several good reasons why you should not smoke. *Among them, three stand out as the most persuasive. First,* smoking is harmful to your lungs and heart. *Second,* it is *both* annoying and dangerous to those around you who do not smoke. *In addition to these compelling facts,* smoking is an unattractive and dirty habit. *Furthermore, once you begin,* it is difficult to quit; *but then,* most worthwhile things in life are hard to achieve.

In the revised paragraph, readers are gently guided from one point to the next. By the time they reach the conclusion, they know not only what ideas the writer had in mind, but also how they fit together. Transitions make the reader's job easier and more rewarding.

Tone

One final point. As you write the paragraphs of your paper, try to be conscious of your **tone.** Tone is simply good manners on paper. The words you use, the examples, quotations, and other supporting materials you choose to help explain your main points—all these contribute to your tone. When you are trying to explain something to someone, particularly if it's something you feel strongly about, you may be tempted to be highly emotional in your discussion. If you allow yourself to get emotional, chances are you won't be convincing. What will be communicated is the strength of your feelings, not the depth of your understanding or the validity of your opinion. To be clear and credible, you need to restrain your enthusiasm or anger and present your points in a calm, reasonable way.

We have two suggestions to help you find and maintain the right tone. First, never insult your reader, even unintentionally. Avoid phrases such as "any idiot can see," "no sane person could believe," and "it is obvious that. . . ." What is obvious to you isn't necessarily obvious to someone who has a limited understanding of your subject or who disagrees with your opinion. Don't talk down to your readers, as though they were children or hopelessly ignorant. Don't use sarcasm. Second, avoid profanity.

And don't apologize for your interpretation of your subject. Have confidence in yourself. You've thought long and hard about your subject, you've found good supporting material to help explain it, and you believe in its significance. Present your subject in a positive manner. If you hang back, using phrases such as "I may be wrong, but . . ." or "I tend to feel that . . . ," your reader won't be inclined to give your points the consideration they deserve. Keep your reader in mind as you write, and your writing will be both clear and convincing.

EXERCISE 25.10

Rewrite the following paragraph, adding transitions where necessary and correcting any lapses in tone. Compare your revision to ours on p. 378.

I'm new to college life. I hardly know anything about it. Don't consider me an expert. There are three ways to achieve academic success. I want to do well. A person doesn't have to go to class, which is nice. Going to class helps you learn more. Teachers don't bug you to do the work. It's easy to miss assignments or notes if they don't. The workload gets heavy all of a sudden in midterm. It sure is tough to keep up. I may be wrong but it seems to me that the keys to academic success are self-discipline and responsi-

bility for one's studies as a college student.

EXERCISE 25.11
Write a response to the prescription for academic success outlined in exercise 25.10 above. Remember to keep your tone consistent, and don't forget transitions.

EXERCISE 25.12
Do either A or B:

    A. Using one of the thesis statements you prepared in Chapter 23, exercise 23.8, write a paper of approximately 400 words.

    B. Using the outline you prepared in Chapter 24, exercise 24.4, write a paper of approximately 600 words.

CHAPTER 26

Revising Your Paper

No one can write in a single draft an essay that is perfectly organized and developed, let alone one that is free of errors in sentence structure, grammar, spelling, and punctuation. The purpose of the first draft is to get down on paper something you can work with until you're satisfied it will meet your reader's needs and expectations. Planning and drafting should take up about half the time you devote to writing a paper. The rest should be devoted to revision.

Revision is the process of refining your writing until it says what you want it to say in a way that enables your readers to understand your message and to receive it favourably. These two goals, clear understanding and favourable reception, constitute good communication. You can accomplish these goals only if you keep your readers in mind as you revise. Because it reflects the contents of the writer's mind, a first draft often seems all right to the writer. But in order to transfer an idea as clearly as possible from the mind of the writer to the mind of the reader, revision is necessary. The idea needs to be honed and refined until it is as clear to your reader as it is to you. By revising from your reader's point of view, you can avoid misunderstandings before they happen.

What Is Revision?

Revision means "re-seeing." It does *not* mean recopying. The aim of revision is to improve your writing's organization, accuracy, and style. Revising is a three-stage process. Each step requires that you read through your entire essay, painful though this may be. The goal of your first reading is to ensure that your reader's information needs are met. In your second reading, you focus on structure. Your third reading concentrates on correctness. Here are the steps to follow in revising a paper:

> 1. Improve the whole paper by revising its content and organization.
> 2. Refine paragraph and sentence structure, and correct any errors in grammar.
> 3. Edit and proofread to catch errors in word choice, spelling, and punctuation.

Inexperienced writers often skip the first two stages and concentrate on the third, thinking they will save time. This is a mistake. In fact, they waste time—both theirs and their readers'—because the result is writing that doesn't communicate clearly and won't make a positive impression.

The best way to begin revising is to do nothing to the early version of your paper for several days. Let as much time as possible pass between completing your first draft and rereading it. Ten minutes, or even half a day, is not enough. The danger in rereading too soon is that you're likely to "read" what you *think* you've written—what exists only in your head, not on the paper. But if, like many writers, you haven't allowed enough time for this cooling-off period, don't despair. There are two other things you can do to help you get some distance from your draft. If your first draft is handwritten, type it out. Reading your essay in a different form helps you "re-see" its content. Alternatively, read your paper aloud and try to hear it from the point of view of your reader. Listen to how your explanation unfolds, and mark every place you find something unclear, irrelevant, inadequately developed, or out of order.

Step One: Revising Content and Organization

As you read your paper aloud, keep in mind the three possible kinds of changes you can make at this stage:

1. You can **rearrange** information. This is the kind of revision that is most often needed, but least often done. Consider the order in which you've arranged your paragraphs. From your reader's point of view, is this the most effective order in which to present your ideas? If you are not already using a word processing program, now is the time to

begin. With a good word processor, moving blocks of text around is as easy as dealing a deck of cards.

2. You can **add** information. Adding new main ideas or more development is often necessary to make your message interesting and convincing as well as clear. It's a good idea to ask a friend to read your draft and identify what needs to be expanded or clarified. (Be sure to return the favour. You can learn a great deal by critiquing other people's writing.)

3. You can **delete** information. Now is the time to cut out anything that is repetitious, insignificant, or irrelevant to your subject and reader.

Use the checklist that follows to guide you as you review your paper's form and content.

Content and Organization Checklist

ACCURACY

Is everything you have said accurate?

- Is your information consistent with your own experience and observations, or with what you have discovered through research?
- Are all your facts and evidence up-to-date?

COMPLETENESS

Have you included enough main ideas and development to explain your subject and convince your reader? Remember that "enough" means from the reader's point of view, not the writer's.

SUBJECT

Is your subject

- significant? Does it avoid the trivial or the obvious?
- single? Does it avoid double or combined subjects?
- specific? Is it focussed and precise?
- supportable? Have you provided enough evidence to make your meaning clear?

MAIN POINTS

Are your main points

- significant? Have you deleted any unimportant ones?
- distinct? Are they all different from one another, or is there an overlap in content?
- relevant? Do all points relate directly to your subject?
- arranged in the most appropriate order? Again, "appropriate" means from the reader's perspective. Choose chronological, climactic, logical, or random order, depending on which is most likely to help the reader make sense of your information.

INTRODUCTION

Does your introduction

- catch the reader's attention and make him or her want to read on?
- contain a clearly identifiable thesis statement?
- identify the main points that your paper will explain?

CONCLUSION

Does your conclusion

- contain a summary or reinforcement of your main points, rephrased to avoid word-for-word repetition?
- contain a statement that effectively clinches your argument and leaves the reader with something to think about?

TONE

Is your tone consistent, reasonable, courteous, and confident through-out your essay?

When you have carefully considered these questions, it's time to move on to the second stage of the revision process.

Step Two: Revising Paragraphs and Sentences

Here, too, you should allow time—at least a couple of days—between your first revision and your second. Enough time must elapse to allow you to approach your paper as if you were seeing it for the first time. Once again, read your draft aloud, and use this list of questions to help you improve it.

Paragraph and Sentence Checklist

PARAGRAPHS

Does each paragraph

- begin with a clear, identifiable topic sentence?
- develop one—and only one—main idea?
- present one or more kinds of development appropriate to the main idea?
- contain clear and effective transitions to signal the relationship between sentences? Between paragraphs?

SENTENCES

Sentence Structure

- Is each sentence clear and complete?
  1. Are there any fragments or run-ons?
  2. Are there any misplaced or dangling modifiers?
  3. Are all lists (whether words, phrases, or clauses) expressed in parallel form?
- Are your sentences varied in length? Could some be combined to improve the clarity and impact of your message?

Grammar

- Have you used verbs correctly?
  1. Are all verbs in the correct form? the correct tense?
  2. Do all verbs agree with their subjects?
  3. Are all verbs in the correct tense?
  4. Are there any confusing shifts in verb tense within a paragraph?
- Have you used pronouns correctly?
  1. Are all pronouns in the correct form?
  2. Do all pronouns agree with their antecedents in person, number, and gender?
  3. Have any vague pronoun references been eliminated?

When you're sure you've answered these questions satisfactorily, turn to the third and last stage of the revision process.

Step Three: Editing and Proofreading

By now you're probably so tired of refining your paper that you may be tempted to skip **editing**—correcting errors in word choice, spelling, and punctuation—and **proofreading**—correcting errors in typing or writing that appear in the final draft. But these final tasks are essential if you want your paper to make a positive impression.

Misspellings, faulty punctuation, and messiness don't always create misunderstandings, but they do cause the reader to form a lower opinion of you and your work. Careful editing and proofreading are necessary if you want your writing to be favourably received.

Most word-processing programs now include both a grammar checker and a spelling checker, and it is worthwhile running your writing through these programs at the editing stage. The newer programs have some useful features. For example, they will question—but not correct—your use of apostrophes; they will sometimes catch errors in subject–verb agreement that you may have missed; and they will catch obvious misspellings and typos. But don't make the mistake of assuming the program will do all your editing for you. Many errors slip past a computer's checker; only you (or a knowledgeable and patient friend) can find and correct them.

If spelling is a particular problem for you, it is a good idea to read your paper, word by word, from the end to the beginning. Reading backward forces you to look at each word by itself and helps you spot those that look suspicious. Whenever you're in doubt about the spelling of a word, look it up! If you find this task too tedious to bear, ask a good speller to read over your paper for you and identify any errors.

Here are the questions to ask yourself when you are editing.

Editing Checklist

WORDS

Usage

Have you used words accurately?
- Have you used plurals where necessary?
- Have you included the correct forms of articles where they are needed?
- Have you checked all prepositions used in verb phrases?
- Have you used idioms appropriately?

Spelling

Are all words spelled correctly?
- Have you double-checked any irregular plurals?
- Have you double-checked any sound-alikes or look-alikes?
- Have you used capital letters where they are needed?
- Have you used apostrophes correctly for possessives and omitted them from plurals?

PUNCTUATION

Within Sentences
- Have you eliminated any unnecessary commas and included commas where needed? (Refer to the four comma rules as you consider this question.)
- Have you used colons and semicolons where appropriate?
- Are any quotations appropriately marked?

Beginnings and Endings
- Does each sentence begin with a capital letter?
- Do all questions—and only questions—end with a question mark?
- Are all quotation marks correctly placed?

Tips for Effective Proofreading

By the time you have finished editing, you will have gone over your paper so many times you may have practically memorized it. When you are very familiar with a piece of writing, it's hard to spot the small mistakes that may have crept in as you produced your final copy. Here are some tips to help you find those tiny, elusive errors:

1. Read through your essay line by line, using a ruler to guide you.
2. If you've been keeping a list of your most frequent errors in this course, do a scan of your essay looking specifically for the mistakes you know you are most likely to make.
3. Using the Quick Revision Guide on the inside front cover of this book, make a final check of all aspects of your paper.

Your "last" draft may need further revision after your proofreading review. If so, take the time to rewrite the paper so that the version you hand in is clean and easy to read. If a word processor is available to you, use it. Computers make editing and proofreading almost painless, since errors are so easy to correct.

At long last, you're ready to submit your paper. If you've followed the three steps to revision conscientiously, you can hand it in with confidence that it says what you want it to say, both about your subject and about you. One last word of advice:

> DON'T FORGET TO KEEP A COPY FOR YOUR FILES!

EXERCISE 26.1

Revise the following paragraph by applying the questions on the three checklists given in this chapter. Then compare your version with ours, on p. 379.

I came to Canada four years ago. There are many differences between Canada and my former country to adapt. The most difficult are social customs. Canadians take casual friendships for granted. Also even sexual relationships! This seem strange to me. The custom of dating is not known in my culture. And of course my parents are not approving. The relationship between parents and children is very different. In my former home, this relationship is formal. The way Canadians criticize their country and its leaders still surprises me. This would be considered unacceptable in most nonwestern countries. Possibly even criminal. These are hard to adjust to now. In a few years they will probably be familiar for me, like hamburgers and french fries do already.

EXERCISE 26.2

Using the Quick Revision Guide on the inside front cover, revise the paper you wrote for exercise 25.12 in Chapter 25.

UNIT SIX

Mastering Your New Language

Introduction

As a college student, you are preparing for the career of your choice. By now, at this level of study, your command of spoken English is good. You participate in conversations with English-speaking friends, and you are advanced enough to receive instruction in English.

But fluency in spoken English is not enough if you want to succeed in college and on the job. While it takes only two or three years for many ESL learners to become fluent in conversation, it takes most learners five to seven years to learn to read and write on a level equivalent to that of native English speakers. The language skills you need, of course, depend on the kind of career you want. The level of English required of managerial and technical personnel is very different from that required of unskilled workers. And, as we all know, unskilled jobs are fast disappearing. Now is the time for you to learn how to adapt your *spoken* English to *written* English.

There is a big difference between oral and written English. The spoken language takes many forms. The English used in Britain is different from that used in the United States; people in the Ottawa valley speak differently from those in Saskatchewan, or Trinidad, or New Delhi. These different forms of spoken language are called dialects, and they vary from country to country, even from place to place within a country.

Unlike speech, written language does not change much from region to region. There is a form of English that is recognized and accepted around the world called standard written English (SWE). The ability to use SWE well helps you in three ways. First, it improves your power to express your ideas clearly. Second, it helps you win the respect of your readers. And third, it increases the number of people with whom you can communicate. That's why employers hire and promote people who can use SWE effectively.

In Unit 6, you will find explanations of and exercises on the most common problems ESL students experience when they are learning to master standard written English. One of the most important keys to good writing is a strong vocabulary. If you compare an English-language dictionary to any other language dictionary, you'll see from the difference in thickness that English contains more words. The enormous size of the English vocabulary is a result of the fact that English has adopted many thousands of words from languages around the world.

Building your vocabulary is not a problem, however, because you are presented with opportunities to learn new words every day. In addition to watching TV or listening to the radio, you should read as much as you can—not just your textbooks, but also newspapers, magazines and books. When you come across a new word, look it up to see what it means and how it is pronounced. Note its spelling, and then use it in your own speech and writing. There is an old saying that you don't "own" a word (that is, it does not become part of your active vocabulary) until you have used it correctly three times. If your first language is Latin-based— French, Spanish, Italian, or Rumanian, for example—look for familiar root words that can help you guess and remember the meaning of unfamiliar words. For example, can you figure out what *pedestrian, bi-polar, extemporaneous*, and *manipulate* mean?

Every ESL student should own a good, comprehensive dictionary. Ideally, you should have two: a Canadian reference (we recommend the *Gage Canadian Dictionary* (Gage, 1996)), and an international reference (we recommend the *Cobuild English Dictionary* (HarperCollins 1995)). We find the *Cobuild* especially useful for ESL students because it defines words and phrases in full sentences and also highlights the 16,000 words that form the core of the English language. These words make up 95 per cent of all spoken and written English, so you need to pay special attention to them.

Both the *Gage* and the *Cobuild* label words that are restricted in some way: they may be regional, or archaic, or slang, or have offensive or sexual meanings in some contexts. You need a good dictionary not only to help expand and refine your vocabulary, but also to save you from making potentially embarrassing mistakes!

CHAPTER 27

Choosing the Correct Tense

The predicate (a verb or verb phrase) lies at the heart of every English sentence. It expresses an action or a state of being:

> My uncle *sells* cars.
> This weather *is* awful.

A sentence with no verb has no meaning. In English, the **tense** of a verb signals the time of an action: present, past, or future. To write well, you need a thorough understanding of the tense system.

Some languages, like Spanish, have a tense system even more complex than that of English. Others, like most Oriental languages, do not use verbs to indicate when an action takes place. If your native language does not use different verb forms to indicate time, you will not only have to memorize the various English tenses, but also learn to think in a different way about your message and how to communicate it. If you were to write "She come home tomorrow," or "The baby is sick last week," your message will probably be understood, but your audience will know that your command of English is weak. "She *will come* home tomorrow" and "The baby *was sick* last week," on the other hand, correctly place the events in time (future and past). The verbs themselves indicate time: "She will come" is unmistakably a future action, and "The baby was sick" is clearly an event that occurred in the past. The modifiers "tomorrow" and "last week" serve to locate the events more precisely in time than the verbs can do alone.

To see at a glance how the English tense system expresses past, present, and future time, study the Time Line on the inside back cover of this book. The little vertical arrow (↑) indicates the present moment, "now." A black dot (●) represents *a completed action or state of being*, both of which are expressed by the **simple forms** of a verb. A circle (○) indicates an event that occurred (or will occur) sometime after the action represented by the black dot took place. A wavy line (∿∿) represents *a continuing action or condition*, both of which are expressed by the **progressive forms** of a verb. A dotted line (----) indicates that the action or condition may continue into the future.

Now that you have an overview of the six basic tenses and the timing they represent, let's look more closely at each one. We will deal first with tenses that are used to talk about events that are taking place now (the present), then those used to express events that have already taken place (the past), and conclude with the various tenses used to indicate events that have not yet taken place (the future).

I. Tenses that Express Present Time

English expresses the idea of something occurring *now*, in the present, in two ways:

TENSE	EXAMPLE
Simple present	Jean *sings* in the shower. (Jean regularly sings while he is showering.)
Present progressive	Jean *is singing* in the shower. (Jean is singing at this moment.)

A. Simple Present

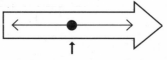

The simple present is used to indicate a regular or habitual activity, a fact, or a circumstance that does not change. For example:

Yves *drives* me to school. (Yves regularly drives me.)

Water *boils* at 100° C. (fact)

Charlottetown *is* the capital of Prince Edward Island. (fact)

Quebec *takes* pride in its status as a Founding Nation. (circumstance that does not change)

B. Present Progressive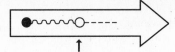

Progressive tenses are used to emphasize the *duration* of an activity or condition rather than the act or condition itself. The present progressive[1] (*(be)* + *present participle*) signifies an activity that is happening in the present moment, or one that is in progress or ongoing. The action or condition is temporary; it began before the present moment and will probably end sometime in the near future. Consider these examples:

I *am boiling* some water to make tea. (activity in progress)

Angelo *is visiting* Charlottetown. (right now)

A committee *is studying* the status of French in Montreal. (ongoing activity)

Usually, I *walk* (habitual activity) to school, but because it *is raining* (right now), today I *am taking* (activity in progress) the bus. The bus *is* expensive (fact), which is why I *prefer* to walk (circumstance that does not change).

In the exercises that follow, fill in each blank with the appropriate tense—simple present or present progressive—of the verb given in parentheses. Then turn to p. 379 to check your answers.

EXERCISE 27.1

1. It (snow) _____ again today. In my country, it often

   (rain) _____ , but it never (snow) _____.

2. Marc usually (work) _____ as a lifeguard, but this

   summer he (work) _____ in his family's restaurant.

3. Ravi (want) _____ to fix his car, but he (need)

   _____ someone to help him.

4. A ticket home (cost) _____ so much that I (doubt)

   _____ I can afford the trip.

---

[1] In some contexts, the present tenses are used to express future time. See p. 264.

5. We still (believe) _____ we have a good team, and

   now we (try) _____ to develop a winning strategy.

6. My mother usually (telephone) _____ me every day at

   6 o'clock, but it is now 6:30, and I (still wait) _____

   for her call. I wonder what she (do) _____.

7. The baby (cry) _____ again. He always (cry)

   _____ when his mother (leave) _____

   for work, but he (stop) _____ when his grand-

   father (pick) _____ him up.

8. Danuta (look) _____ out of the window and watching

   the snow fall, so she (not listen) _____ to Professor

   Dasgupta, who (explain) _____ our research assignment.

9. I (try) _____ to decide how to vote in the coming

   election. My family always (vote) _____ for the Lib-

   erals, but I (think) _____ that it is time for a change.

10. Jamala (study) _____ in the library most evenings.

    Tonight she (have) _____ difficulty concentrating be-

    cause the student who (sit) _____ at the information

    desk (talk) _____ loudly on the phone.

Some English verbs are not normally used in the progressive. These verbs express *states of being, cognition* (knowing), *emotions, possession,* and *perception* (information gained through our five senses).

STATE OF BEING	COGNITION	EMOTION	POSSESSION	PERCEPTION
be	think	love	have	see
seem	believe	like/dislike	own	hear
exist	know	hate	belong	taste
need	understand	appreciate		smell
cost	prefer	want		feel
owe				
weigh				

Incorrect: I am believing you when you say you are loving me.

Correct: I believe you when you say you love me.

Note that some of these verbs can be used to describe actions as well as states. When this is the case, the progressive form is appropriate. Consider these sentences:

STATE	ACTION
The curry *smells* delicious.	The chef *is tasting* the curry.
Solaya *weighs* 65k.	Solaya *is weighing* herself to see how much weight she has lost.
Tom *has* a motorcycle.	Tom *is having* trouble with statistics.

Can you fix the errors in the sentences below? Try it, then check your answer at the bottom of this page.[2]

I am hearing that you are owning a laptop. I am needing to borrow one for today's class. I am knowing you are hating to lend your things, but I am promising to return it by 4:00.

II. Tenses that Express Past Time

A. *Simple Past*

The simple past is used to indicate a completed action or state, one that began and ended in the past:

I *worked* as a computer technician last summer.

Most of my customers *knew* very little about their computers.

---

[2] I *hear* that you *own* a laptop. I *need* to borrow one for today's class. I *know* you *hate* to lend your things, but I *promise* to return it by 4:00.

B. Past Progressive

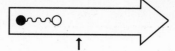

The past progressive tense (*was/were + present participle*) is used to indicate an action that took place or a condition that existed over a period of time in the past:

> I *was stocking* the shelves with the new shipment of software.

> The children *were misbehaving.*

It is also used to indicate an action that was taking place when another action occurred:

> The students *were talking* when the professor entered the room.

In this example, both actions, *were talking* and *entered,* occurred in the past, and at more or less the same time. But the idea conveyed by the past progressive tense is that the students' talking took place over a period of time, while the simple past tense indicates that the professor entered the room at one moment in the past.

EXERCISE 27.2

Fill in each blank with the appropriate tense—simple past or past progressive—of the verb given in parentheses.

1. Three of us (smoke) _____ in the upstairs washroom

   when the president (walk) _____ in.

2. The cat (hide) _____ behind the fish tank when I (see)

   _____ his tail twitch and (catch) _____ him.

3. While their sister (prepare) _____ their lunch, the

   children (rush) _____ into the house and (turn)

   on the television.

4. When *Burnt by the Sun,* a wonderful Russian film, (play) _____

   _____ in our local theatre, I (see) _____ it

   four times. Then I (try) _____ to find a copy on video.

5. Vinh (try) _____ to park his new van in the narrow

    driveway when he (hit) _____ the neighbour's hedge.

    The branches (make) _____deep scratches all along

    the side of the van.

6. For a moment, Vinh (think) _____ of complaining to

    his neighbour, but then he (realize) _____ that the

    accident (be) _____ his own fault.

7. Julio (tell) _____ his friends about his new job when

    one of the group (ask) _____ him how he (hear)

    _____ about the position.

8. When I finally (find) _____ my passport, I (understand)

    _____ why my search (take) _____

    so long. It (be) _____ in my sock drawer.

9. Wai-Lan (walk) _____ home when the rain

    (begin) _____. In an effort to stay dry, she (wait)

    _____ under a tree until finally a taxi (drive)

    _____ by and rescued her.

10. I (study) _____ at the local library when I (discover)

    _____ that the travel section (be) _____

    right behind my desk. I (try) _____ to continue

    studying, but the travel books (tempt)_____ me so

    much that I finally (put) _____ my homework aside

    and (read) _____ a book about the Queen Charlotte

    Islands.

C. Present Perfect and Present Perfect Progressive

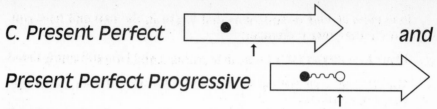

The **present perfect** (*have/has + past participle*) is used to express an action or state that occurred at some unspecified point in the past, or one that occurred repeatedly in the past. That is, it happened some time before "now," but the exact time or the duration of the activity is not given. If the specific time is identified, or if the activity occurred only once, the simple past tense is used. To see the difference in meaning of these two tenses, study the following paired sentences.

a) Josef *has found* a new job. (When Josef found the job is not mentioned, so the present perfect is required.)

Josef *found* a new job last month. (When he found the job is given, so the simple past is required.)

b) Natalie *has* already *seen* that movie. (When she saw it is unknown.)

Natalie *saw* that movie yesterday. (The time is specified.)

c) Canadian peacekeeping forces *have carried* out many missions around the world. (They have performed this duty repeatedly in the past.)

Canadian peacekeeping forces *carried* out a mission in Bosnia. (The activity occurred only once.)

There is one exception to this general rule. When you use a phrase beginning with *for* or *since* to express an activity that began in the past and continued into the present, the verb must be in the present perfect (or the present perfect progressive) tense. For example:

Mari *has been* in Canada <u>for</u> four years.

She *has gone* to school <u>since</u> she arrived.

Note that *for* and *since* mean different things. *For* is used to identify a period of time, while *since* is used to identify the time when the action or condition began: e.g., Surinder *has lived* in Montreal <u>for several years</u>, but his wife *has lived* here only <u>since January</u>.

The **present perfect progressive** tense (*have/has + been + -ing* form of the verb) is used in three ways.

1. To express actions or situations that began in the past and have continued up to the present moment:

> I *have been sitting* in this room all morning. (And I am still sitting here.)
>
> The class *has been working* on progressive tenses. (And the class is still working on them.)[3]

2. To stress the duration of an activity or event:

> I *have been waiting* for you for more than half an hour.
>
> For years now, Danuta *has been longing* to visit Rome.

Time phrases such as *for, since, all day, all morning,* etc. are often used with the present progressive tense to emphasize the period of time over which the activity took place.

3. To describe a regular activity that started in the recent past and continues in the present:

> Alain *has been working* hard.
>
> I'*ve been driving* to school.

These statements imply that the *working* and the *driving* began only recently.

Now practise using the past, present perfect, and present perfect progressive tenses by completing the following exercises.

EXERCISE 27.3

Fill in the blanks with the appropriate form of the verbs given in parentheses.

1. This morning my father (make) _____ me go to the

    barber who (cut) _____ his hair for the past twenty

    years.

---

[3] If you replace the present perfect progressive with the present perfect, the meaning changes slightly:

> I *have sat* in this room. (The action was completed some time in the past; I am no longer sitting here.)
> The class *has worked* on progressive tenses. (The class is no longer working on them.)

2. While I (wait) _____ for my turn, I (notice)

   _____ that I (be) _____ the only

   person in the shop under fifty.

3. We (plan) _____ to renovate our house for a long

   time now, but we (decide) _____ on a contractor only

   last week.

4. The telephone (ring) _____ at least twenty times

   while you were out.

5. Although Ali (live) _____ in Toronto since he was ten,

   he (never, visit) _____ the CN Tower.

6. My mother (manage) _____ her own business for

   three years now and (make) _____ a profit for the

   last two.

7. Hockey (always be) _____ Canadians' favourite sport;

   we (play) _____the game for more than 150 years.

8. To my surprise, sociology (turn) _____ out to be a lot

   of work. Our professor (give) _____ us four tests al-

   ready, and it's only the middle of the term.

9. Since 1977, when the government (introduce) _____

   Bill 101, the use of French in Montreal (increase) _____.

10. The use of French in Montreal (increase) _____ over

    the past twenty years, but the percentage of people who use French in

    the workplace (change) _____ very little.

EXERCISE 27.4

Fill in each blank with the most appropriate tense of the verb. To complete this exercise, you will need to use all four past tenses we have covered so far: simple past, past progressive, present perfect, and present perfect progressive. In some cases, more than one answer is possible. When you have completed the exercise, compare your answers with our suggestions on p. 380.

1. We (close) _____ the office early today because we

   (work) _____ overtime yesterday.

2. Ky and Shona (meet) _____ last September and (go)

   _____ out together since that time.

3. Gunter (watch) _____ *Star Trek* since he (be) _____

   in grade school. Now that the series has been cancelled, he feels as

   though he (lose) _____ his best friends.

4. For weeks now, I (wait) _____ for my transcript

   to come in the mail. I wonder if the Registrar's Office (go)

   _____ on strike.

5. Maria (plan) _____ to visit Newfoundland for a long

   time. Her sister (live) _____ there for a year, and, ever

   since she came home, she (tell) _____ Maria that the

   Rock is well worth the trip.

D. Past Perfect and Past Perfect Progressive

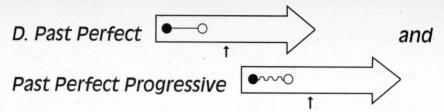

English makes a distinction between two actions or events that happened in the past when one event clearly preceded the other. The **past perfect** and **past perfect progressive** are used to indicate the event that occurred *first*. The simple past is used to describe the one that occurred *second*.

The past perfect (*has/had + past participle*) usually refers to a more distant time in the past than the present perfect represents. It is required in two circumstances:

1. Use the past perfect to describe an event that occurred before another event was completed.

> I *had ordered* a Caesar salad, but the waiter brought me fettuccine.
>   1   2

> Val got home to find that his dog *had chewed* up two cushions and
>   2   1
> his jacket.

2. Use the past perfect to describe an activity or state that was completed before a specified time in the past. The phrase *by the time* is often used to introduce the second of the two events.

> The class *had left* <u>by the time</u> the professor got there.
>   1   2

The **past perfect progressive** (*has/had been + past participle*) is used in the same situations as the past perfect, only it describes a completed action or condition that continued over a period of time in the past. Like all progressive tenses, it indicates *duration*. Look at these examples:

> Tom *had been waiting* for two hours when Rosemary finally returned his call.

> We were exhausted because our neighbour's dog *had been barking* and *howling* all night.

EXERCISE 27.5

Fill in each blank with the most appropriate tense—past, past perfect, or past perfect progressive—of the verb given in parentheses. (In some sentences, more than one answer is possible.) Then compare your answers with ours.

1. By the time I (realize) _____ I needed an elective to

   graduate, I (already drop) _____ the course.

2. Aunt Mina (promise) _____ to leave her fortune to

   Julio, but unfortunately she (die) _____ before mak-

   ing a will.

3. Karin's sister (arrive) _____ about ten minutes after

   Karin (leave) _____.

4. Philip (plan) _____ a formal dinner party for his father's

   fiftieth birthday until his mother (suggest) _____

   that his father might prefer a backyard barbecue.

5. By the time Kim (work) _____ the night shift for

   three months, she (think) _____ she would never

   have a social life again.

6. We (look) _____ forward to our vacation for months

   when my wife (get) _____ a promotion, and we (have)

   _____ to cancel our plans.

7. If I (know) _____ how difficult this course (be)

   _____, I would have signed up for something else.

8. When he (retire) _____, Professor Green (teach)

   _____ creative writing for twenty years.

9. We (decide) _____ to sell our condominium, but we

   (change) _____ our minds when the real estate agent

   (tell) _____ us the price we could expect to get.

10. I never (realize) _____ how difficult Ms. Wright was

to work for, although I (hear) _____ she was a very de-

manding supervisor.

III. Tenses that Express Future Time

The idea of future time can be expressed in several ways, depending on the meaning the writer intends to convey. To begin with, consider these sentences, all of which mean subtly different things:

It *will rain*. (sometime in the future)

It *is going to rain*. (very soon)

I am going for a run when the rain stops. (an indefinite point in the future)

A. Simple Future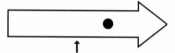

The **simple future** tense has an alternate form, the **present progressive of *go***. Both indicate an action or event that has not yet taken place.

1. *will*[4] + *the base form* is the simple future. This form is often used to express an activity that will occur at some unknown time in the future or if certain conditions are fulfilled.

I *will stop* smoking. (I don't know when.)

Marina *will take* over the driving if Kheeran gets tired. (Marina's driving depends on something else happening.)

We *will care* for our neighbour's children when she goes back to work. (Our babysitting depends on a particular set of circumstances.)

---

[4] Traditionally, grammarians have taught that the simple future tense is formed with *shall* for first-person subjects (e.g., I/We *shall* be happy when this review of tenses is finished) and *will* with second- and third-person subjects (e.g., You *will* be pleased to move on to articles, and they *will* be thrilled to turn to prepositions and plurals.) In Canada and the U.S., however, *will* is commonly used with first-person as well as with second- and third-person subjects. *Shall* is normally reserved for use in documents written in formal-level language.

2. *(be) going to + the base form* of the verb is used to express actions or events that you expect to happen very soon or that are definitely planned, intended, or decided on.

> I *am going to* quit smoking. ("Soon" is implied.)

> Marina *is going to* drive. (Marina intends or plans to drive.)

> We *are going to care* for my neighbour's children while she is at work. (The child care arrangements have been decided on.)

When you are predicting a future action, event, or state of being, you may use either form:

> The Ottawa Senators *will win* the Stanley Cup this year.

> The Ottawa Senators *are going to win* the Stanley Cup this year.

These two statements mean the same thing.

EXERCISE 27.6

Fill in the blanks with the appropriate form of the future: *will + base form* or *(be) going to + base form* of the verbs given in parentheses. Then compare your answers with ours on p. 380.

1. Elie (work) _____ on his car tomorrow, and I

   (help) _____ him.

2. Jean-Marc's parents (arrive) _____ sometime next

   week, and we (meet) _____ them at the airport.

3. I (buy) _____ a daytimer because my counsellor has

   assured me it (help) _____ me put some order in the

   chaos of my life.

4. According to this memo, the college (offer) _____ a

   course on teaching techniques next spring. We can only hope that Pro-

   fessor Green (be) _____ the first to sign up.

5. Until Yasmin's grades improve, her parents (not let) _____

_____ her get a part-time job, but, as soon as she can, Yasmin

(look) _____ for work in the fashion industry.

6. Since you (take) _____ an elective this semester, I sug-

gest you sign up for political science. You (enjoy) _____

Professor Singh's sense of humour.

7. We've got everything planned: we (go) _____ skiing

tomorrow, but if there is no snow, we (play) _____

cards instead.

8. Our neighbours (build) _____ an addition onto their

home. I hope we (be) _____ on vacation when the

construction begins.

9. If the weather is fine, the annual Canada Day celebration (be held)

_____ on Parliament Hill, but if it rains, we (move)

_____ into the mall.

10. When the general and his staff arrive, the troops (stand) _____

_____ at attention and salute. They (hold) _____

this position until the general has left the field; then they (stand)

_____ at ease.

B. Future Progressive

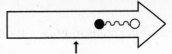

The future progressive tense (*will* + *be* + *present participle*) indicates a future action or condition that will continue over a period of time.

> We *will be working* on this experiment all afternoon.

> When Ali arrives, his whole family *will be waiting* for him.

> Biff has had a lot to drink, so I hope he *will* not *be driving* home.

EXERCISE 27.7

Use the appropriate verb form—future or future progressive—to fill in the blanks in these sentences.

1. About half-way through August, parents begin to wonder what their

   children (do) _____ to fill in the time until school

   starts.

2. I've no idea where I (work) _____ next week. I (let)

   _____ you know as soon as I find out.

3. This term I (write) _____ eight final exams. I'm not

   worried, though, because my grandmother (pray) _____

   for me.

4. My fiancée insists that I buy her a diamond ring before she (marry)

   _____ me, so I (buy) _____ a lot of

   lottery tickets.

5. Since Yuxiang (work) _____ in Calgary next year, he

   (sell) _____ his apartment in St. John.

6. If you call this afternoon, I (not answer) _____ the

   phone because I (cook) _____ a traditional dinner for

   fourteen people.

7. If you call after 10:00, the children (do) _____ the

dishes, and I (be) _____ free to talk with you.

8. Ranjan is going to Bombay where she (stay) _____

with her family for two months. They (be) _____

surprised to find how much she has changed in the last year.

9. If he passes this year, Ivo (go) _____ to school in

Fredericton for his final year. He should enjoy it, if only because he

(live) _____ with his girlfriend.

10. I (reorganize) _____ my office as soon as the term is over.

When you come to see me next year, I (work) _____

in a neat and tidy space. At the very least, I (able) _____

to find my telephone.

C. Using Present Tenses to Indicate Future Time

1. Both the present and the present progressive can be used to express an action that will take place in the future, especially when there is a time word or phrase (such as *when, before, as soon as, until, while*) or a specific date included in the sentence. Consider these examples:

As soon as this class *is* over, I'*m going* to lunch.

After Cécile *finishes* work, she *is meeting* us at the gym.

In March, we *are flying* to Florida.

Night school classes *begin* the second week of September.

2. A subordinate "*if*" clause requires a verb in the simple present tense; the main clause requires the simple future or the present progressive tense.

If the snow *continues*, the president *will close* the college.

Kwomo *is going to drop* this course if he *fails* the next quiz.

EXERCISE 27.8
Fill in the blanks with the correct form of the verb given in parentheses.

1. As soon as Val (graduate) _____, he (leave)

   _____ for Africa.

2. If Mrs. Mandell (have) _____ twins, she (plan)

   _____ to name them Gabrielle and Danielle.

3. Sophie (answer) _____ the phones while Ravi (be)

   _____ away on vacation.

4. If the weather (be) _____ bad, we (hold)_____

   _____ the convocation in the gym.

5. Please let me know when you (hear) _____ from

   Amrik. I (worry) _____ about him until I (know)

   _____ he is safe.

D. Future Perfect and Future Perfect Progressive

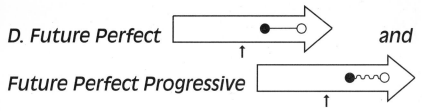

Both the **future perfect** (*will have + past participle*) and the **future perfect progressive** (*will have been + present participle*) are used to express actions that will be completed sometime in the future, either before a specified time or before another event occurs.

   We show the connection between two future events by expressing the one that will happen *first* in the future perfect or future perfect progressive, and the one that will occur *second* in the present tense or in a time phrase. The difference between these two tenses is, as you may have guessed, a matter of emphasis. If the event is a single, completed action, you use the perfect. If the event is one that will take place over a period of time and you want to stress the length of time involved, you use the progressive form. For example:

When we *get* home, the bread *will have finished* rising.
   2 (present tense)   *1* (future perfect)

<u>In June</u>, my parents *will have been renovating* their house for two years.

  2 (time phrase)   *1* (future perfect progressive)

EXERCISE 27.9

Choose the correct form—future perfect, future perfect progressive, simple present, present progressive—of the verbs in parentheses. More than one correct answer is possible in some of these sentences.

1. If she (continue) _____ to produce litters at the pre-

   sent pace, my cat (give) _____ birth to 68 kittens by

   the time she is ten years old.

2. Today is my husband's birthday, and before he (get) _____

   home, I (prepare) _____ his favourite dinner: stuffed

   cabbage.

3. We (finish) _____ this course by the time Eugene

   (figure) _____ out the difference between an affir-

   mative statement and a negation.

4. I (go) _____ with Josef to the Cowboy Junkies con-

   cert next month because by then he (earn) _____

   enough to pay for his share of the tickets and transportation.

5. If the Liberals (win) _____ again, they (be)

   _____ in office more than half my life.

6. By the time our college president's term (be) _____

   over, she (destroy) _____ the curriculum with her

   cutbacks.

7. By 2010, I (teach) _____ at this college for thirty

years, so I (consider) _____ early retirement.

8. By the time Michelle (be) _____ ready to leave,

William (drink) _____ beer all evening, so she (plan)

_____ to drive.

9. Daniel (work) _____ for more than half his life on

his next birthday, and I (be) _____ a student for

twenty years by the time I graduate.

10. We (go) _____ to be late. By the time we (get)

_____ to the station, the bus (arrive) _____

_____, and our friends will be waiting impatiently for us.

EXERCISE 27.10

Read this paragraph through carefully, then fill in each blank with the most
appropriate tense of the verb given in parentheses. The tenses you will require are the simple and progressive forms of the present, past, and future.

When we (have) _____ a bad day and it (seem)

_____ that we (be) _____ unable to do any-

thing right, we should pause and remember some of the mistakes that others

have made in the past, mistakes so big that they (make) _____

our small errors seem insignificant by comparison. Before long, you (laugh)

_____ when you (realize) _____ how terribly

wrong some otherwise brilliant people have been. For example, in 1962,

executives at the Decca recording company (debate) _____

whether or not to sign a contract with a new band. Their manager insisted,

"This group (be) _____ BIG!", but at the time they

(appear) _____ only in local clubs. The Decca executives

(respond) _____ by saying, "We don't like their sound;

guitar music is on the way out," and they (reject)_____

the contract. Those gentlemen (regret) _____ their decision

even now, because the group they (turn) _____ down be-

came known as The Beatles.

EXERCISE 27.11

As you read through the following paragraph, assume that the writer wants
to emphasize the *duration* of the events reported. Fill in the blanks using
the progressive forms of the present, past, and future tenses.

Many of us (study) _____ computers as part of our college

programs. In fact, computer skills have become essential for success in al-

most all of the jobs we (do) _____ in the next decade.

Most North Americans take the presence of a computer in the home, at

work, and at school for granted. It is astonishing, therefore, to reflect that

only a few years ago, many people (treat) _____ comput-

ers as a fad. During the forties, for example, *Popular Mechanics* magazine

(predict) _____ that computers in the future would weigh

approximately one and a half tons. In the same decade, the chairman of

IBM told his company, "We (not lose) _____ sleep over

these machines." He thought there would be a world market for "maybe

five computers." A decade later, an editor at Prentice-Hall (reassure)

_____ his employees that data processing was a fad that

would not last a year. In 1977, the founder, chairman, and president of Digital Equipment Corporation (tell) _____ the company's shareholders that there was no reason anyone would want a computer in the home.

Everyone who (use) _____ a computer today knows about Bill Gates, president of Microsoft. In the decades to come, his company (produce) _____ many of the amazing programs and applications that will become the standard of the future, using hundreds of gigabytes of memory. It is interesting to note, therefore, that in 1981, Bill Gates (tell) _____ anyone who would listen, "640K ought to be enough for anybody."

EXERCISE 27.12

Now go through the passage in Exercise 27.11 again. This time, assume that the writer wishes to emphasize the events themselves, not the time over which they took place. Fill in the blanks with the appropriate tenses, choosing from the simple and perfect forms. Avoid using any progressives. When you have finished, compare your two paragraphs. Which one do you prefer? Why?

EXERCISE 27.13

To test your mastery of verb tenses, try the following exercise. Fill in the blanks with the most appropriate verb form, choosing from the twelve tenses you have reviewed. No answers are given for this exercise.

Just when I (begin) _____ to consider starting a family,

my sister (arrive) _____ from the west coast with her two

young boys. I (intend) _____ to spend a quiet couple of

weeks with my sister and my nephews, getting to know them after a long time apart. My husband and I (renovate) _____ the house

to provide a private space for them during their stay. Within minutes of their

arrival, the younger boy (knock) _____ over the coffee

table because the older one (encourage) _____ him to

grab the plates of sandwiches and cookies that (lie) _____

on the table. By the time we (clean) _____ up that mess,

Damien, the older one, (manage) _____ to pour honey all

over the cat, while Daryl (set) _____ my husband's treasured

collection of baseball cards on fire, using our best brandy as a fire starter.

It was as if they (save) _____ all their energy for months

in order to run wild in my house. Both boys (see) _____

a doctor for treatment of their hyperactive conditions, and I (hope)

_____ that their behaviour would have shown some im-

provement. You (gather) _____ by now that this was not

the case.

    Today is the third day of their visit, and for the past two nights my

husband (sleep) _____ in his office. I suspect he (prepare)

_____ divorce papers. I (not see) _____

him since he (leave) _____. I (call) _____ him

tomorrow because, by then, I (evict) _____ my dear sister

and her two little monsters. The goldfish are all dead, the cat (have)

_____ most of her fur torn out, two windows have been

broken, and the police (come) _____ twice: once after

my neighbour's call and once after mine. My sister is a saint. She (want)

_____ a family for many years before Damien was born,

and now that she (have) _____ the two boys, she (seem)

_____willing to put up with anything they do. I don't know

how she (stand) _____ it. With luck, by the time they

come for their next visit, I (be) _____ childless for many,

many years; the cat's hair (grow) _____ back; and my hus-

band and I (book) _____ a room in a hotel for the entire

time they (be) _____ here.

EXERCISE 27.14

Write a short paragraph about an experience you had in the recent past.
Choose your verbs carefully to convey as precisely as you can the time of the
events you describe. Use the progressive forms only when you want to emphasize duration more than the events themselves.

EXERCISE 27.15

Write a short paragraph about something you are planning to do in the near
future. Use the simple future, present progressive, and future progressive
tenses, as appropriate, and include at least one sentence with a future perfect or future perfect progressive verb. Conclude with a sentence in the present tense expressing how you feel about your plan.

CHAPTER 28

More About Verbs (For Those Who Need It)

Using Modals

Modal verbs, a type of auxiliary or helping verb, are verb forms that cannot be located precisely in time. They are unusual because their form never changes. They do not add *-s* in the third-person singular, and they have no past or participial forms. The eight modal verbs are *can, could, may, might, will, would, should,* and *must.* (*Shall* is also a modal, but, as we have seen, its use is limited to formal writing.) These modals are used in combination with another verb or verbs to express present, past, or future action:

For example:

present	We *can* leave. We *must* leave. We *may* be leaving.
past	We *could* have left. We *could* have been leaving by now.
future	We *will* leave. We *might* leave.

Modals are used in two ways: to express possibility, necessity, or condition; and to make polite requests.

1. Expressing Possible, Necessary or Advisable, and Conditional Actions

1. **possible action:**   I *can* go; I *could* go, *could* have gone; *may* go; *might* go, *might* have gone

2. **necessary or advisable action:**   I *must* go,[1] *must* have gone; *should* go, *should* have gone[2]

3. **conditional action:**   I *would* go, *would* have gone; I *will* go

Study these examples closely.

Everyone **must pass** (*necessary action*) a driving test before getting a license. I **might take** (*possible action*) a few defensive driving lessons to improve my chances of passing the test. If I **could have taken** (*conditional action*) the lessons before I tried the test the first time, I **might** not **have failed** (*possible action*).

You **should** never **leave** (*advisability*) your keys in the car, even for a few minutes, because someone **could steal** (*possibility*) it.

If she **would like** to see me (*condition*), I am going to visit my grandmother, even though I **should be studying** (*advisability*) for tomorrow's test.

EXERCISE 28.1

Fill in each blank with an appropriate modal verb. More than one answer is possible in some cases. When you've finished, compare your answers with our suggestions on p. 382.

---

[1] Note that the modal-like phrases *have to* and *have got to* mean much the same thing as *must*, but they are more informal expressions. *Must* is the preferred form in written standard English.

[2] *Ought to* and *had better* mean the same as *should*. All three verbs are used to indicate that the action is a good idea, but *should* is the form most frequently found in SWE. *Had better* is usually restricted to informal speech or dialogue.

1. Our supervisor thinks the new clerk _____ have difficulty with our local area network. I suppose I _____ help him learn it.

2. You _____ go back to the apartment and close the windows, for the rain _____ ruin our carpet and furniture.

3. Roberto _____ go to France next year, but that _____ annoy his mother, who wants him to come home to Uruguay.

4. Jose _____ barely add or subtract. If he hopes to pass calculus, he _____ find someone to tutor him in math.

5. I don't know what's wrong with my car: the battery _____ be dead, or I _____ be out of gas. In any case, I _____ get it fixed tomorrow.

6. I know I _____ not feel envious, but I _____ not help being jealous of someone with her looks, brains, and boyfriend.

7. Giorgio _____ show up on time for class today; he certainly _____, since he's been late every day this week.

8. I think Margit _____ apply for the new marketing position. It pays much more than her current job, and she _____ certainly do with the extra money.

9. Nicholas _____ not come to the conference; in fact, he told me he _____ miss it entirely if he _____.

10. I wonder if I _____ telephone the police. I thought I heard

someone scream, but it _____ just be the children playing

next door, and I _____ not want to annoy my neighbours.

CONTRARY-TO-FACT CONDITIONALS

Modals that are used to express conditional circumstances are more complicated than those used to indicate possibility, advisability, or necessity. Conditional sentences consist of two clauses: a subordinate "if" clause and a main "then" or result clause. The subordinate clause is always introduced by *if*. In the main clause, *then* is more often implied than stated, but it always expresses the result that is expected. We've already dealt with conditional sentences that talk about what WILL happen in the future (see p. 260). Now let's look at conditional sentences that express actions that MIGHT have taken place but in fact DID NOT take place. These sentences are technically known as **hypothetical** or **contrary-to-fact** conditionals.

A.   Present or future contrary-to-fact conditionals

IF CLAUSE (simple past tense)	*THEN* CLAUSE (*would/could + base form of verb*)
If I *had* a job,	(then) I *would ask* you to marry me.
If you *wanted* to,	you *could support* us.
If we *were*[3] married,	we *would live* happily every after.

The subordinate clause need not come first; e.g., I *would ask* you to marry me if I had a job.

---

[3] In SWE, when the verb in the "if" clause is (*be*), it is ALWAYS in the subjunctive form (*were*), even when the subject is in the first- or third-person singular. E.g., *If Ravi **were** in better shape, he would have more energy.* In speech or dialogue, however, the simple past tense is often used: *"If Ravi **was** in better shape, he'd have more energy."*

B.   Past contrary-to-fact conditionals

IF CLAUSE	*THEN* CLAUSE
(*had + past participle*)	(*would have/could have + past participle*)

If I *had had* a job, (then) I *would have asked* you to marry me.
If you *had wanted* to, you *could have supported* us.
If we *had been* married, we *would have lived* happily ever after.

Now try your hand at forming conditional sentences.

E X E R C I S E   28.2

The statements below are all hypothetical or contrary-to-fact. Fill in the blanks with the correct forms of the verbs given in parentheses. In some of these sentences, you can choose either past or present tense.

1. If Waldemar (have) _____ to live abroad, he

   (choose) _____ to live in Prague.

2. Eili's marks (improve) _____ if she (be)

   _____ more careful about her spelling and

   punctuation.

3. If Desmond (realize) _____ how important the

   assignment was to Martha, he (give) _____ it to

   her.

4. René (finish) _____ cutting the lawn if it (not begin)

   _____ to rain.

5. If André (spend) _____ as much time on his

   homework as he does on his band, he (graduate) _____

   by now.

6. If the cookies (not be) _____ in the jar, I (not eat)

   _____ them.

7. If he (see) _____ the condition Luisa's car was in,

   William (lend) _____ her his car to go camping.

8. Your cat (not run) _____ away if you (not give)

   _____ it a bath.

9. I (skip) _____ class today if I (not be)

   _____ afraid of what Professor Gradgrind might

   do to me.

10. Ivo's family (not survive) _____ if they (not leave)

    _____ Bosnia when they did.

2. Making Polite Requests

In English, modal verbs replace the courtesy forms of address found in other languages such as French and Spanish. Consider the following sentences:

> I *want* to speak to Sohil.
>
> I *would like* to speak to Sohil.
>
> *Could* (or *may* or *can*) I speak to Sohil?

These sentences all communicate the same idea: the speaker wants to talk to Sohil. However, the impression they convey is very different. "I *want*" is a demand; "I *would like*" expresses a courteous request; "*could* I" is a request for permission. (*Could* is the most courteous of the three possible verbs in this sentence. *May* is more formal and is the form you should use when you write. *Can* is most often used in informal speech.)

Other polite expressions you can use to soften a request and achieve a favourable response are "*Would* you *mind* if. . . ?" and "*Could* you please *tell* me. . . ?"

EXERCISE 28.3

The sentences that follow are all requests, but they sound more like demands. Using modal verbs, express each request in a more courteous form. In most cases, more than one answer is possible. When you have completed the exercise, compare your answers with our suggestions on p. 382.

1. I want a muffin.
2. Tell me what time it is.
3. Can I use your phone?
4. Close the window.
5. I want to see the manager.
6. Check the oil, too.
7. Give me a bowl of soup and a sandwich.
8. Send the applicant in.
9. Can you cash a cheque?
10. Move your car so I can get past.

Forming Negations

In English, we can change an affirmative statement to a negative statement in two ways:

1. Add *not* (or *n't*) immediately after a modal, an auxiliary verb, or *(be)* + *present/past participle*.

AFFIRMATIVE	NEGATIVE	EXAMPLE
may need	*may*[4] *not* need	You *may not* need this information.
can see	*cannot/can't* see	I *cannot (can't)* see you right now.
is coming	*is not/isn't* coming	She *is not (isn't)* coming today.
are finished	*are not/aren't* finished	We *are not (aren't)* finished yet.

2. When the verb in the main clause is NOT a modal, an auxiliary verb, or *(be)*, add *do + not* (*don't, doesn't, didn't*) to its base form.

AFFIRMATIVE	NEGATIVE
Caesar came.	Caesar did not (didn't) come.
Caesar saw.	Caesar did not (didn't) see.
Caesar conquered.	Caesar did not (didn't) conquer.

---

[4] *May* is the only modal that cannot be combined with *n't*. We do not write or say *"mayn't."*

EXERCISE 28.4

In the following paragraph, rewrite the sentences containing **boldface verbs** as negations. (In a couple of places, it is more idiomatic to change the adjective from positive to negative than it is to change the verb. E.g., *I am happy* can be negated by rewriting the sentence either as *I am not happy* or *I am unhappy*. Where there is a choice, try both and choose the one that sounds better.) Compare your answer with ours on p. 382.

I **enjoy** the many crows that fly around my neighbourhood. Their loud cries **are** welcome, especially in the spring when the flocks grow in size and activity. I **think** they are very friendly birds; they call to one another in loud voices and argumentative tones. Crows **seem** to be popular with less noisy and aggressive species of birds. Seagulls and pigeons, for example, **are** often found in the same vicinity as crows. You **may be** aware that a flock of crows is technically called a "murder." This word, along with "clowder," which refers to cats, and "pride," which refers to lions, **is** a widely known English noun. "A murder of crows" **calls** to mind a very pleasant image: a group of crows getting together to assault the neighbourhood with their cries. **Could** they **be plotting** to harm some innocent creature? Certainly, they **can be counted on** to leave my newly planted corn and beans in peace.

EXERCISE 28.5

The following paragraph will make sense if you rewrite it in the negative. (Leave the quotation as it is.) In some sentences, you may wish to change the form of an adjective or adverb rather than the verb itself.

Inventions are always warmly welcomed by the general population. Innovation, however practical, normally receives immediate approval from the public. The early experimenters in aviation, for example, quickly became famous. They would have been surprised to have been told, "If God wanted humans to fly, He would have given them wings." Orville and Wilbur, the Wright brothers, certainly expected large crowds to assemble and cheer them on as they took their first historic flight in 1903. They had an idea that their flight at Kitty Hawk would result in fame and glory. Their desire for fame was what drove them to experiment with the powered flight of a heavier-than-air, hand-built aircraft. But the public took them seriously. Those who thought the Wright brothers were fools thought they were sane. Today, thanks to the persistence of the Wright brothers, we have to spend ten days crossing the Atlantic by boat.

EXERCISE 28.6

Change the following affirmative sentences to negative ones; make any negative clauses affirmative. No answers are provided for this exercise.

1. Mohamed and Ali have enjoyed the winters in Canada.
2. I certainly do want to see you.
3. Romesh has found a conveniently located dentist.
4. We managed to find our way to the lost-and-found department.
5. Most of the class attended the president's reception for international students.
6. The Vancouver Grizzlies succeeded in winning many new fans in their first season.
7. Solaya always wants to come to the movies with us, even when we don't want her to.
8. Irving planned to skip class and go skiing last week.
9. Irving's math professor gave out a major assignment last week.
10. Fortunately, Irving changed his mind and did not go skiing after all.

CHAPTER 29

Solving Plural Problems

Most of the time, forming plurals in English is easy. In this chapter, we'll look at how to pluralize three classes of nouns: regular countable nouns, irregular countable nouns, and noncountable nouns. But first, let's distinguish between the two kinds of nouns.

As their name suggests, **countable nouns** identify persons, places, or things that can be counted. They name individual, separate, distinct items: e.g., *city, college, immigrant, job, meal, student.* **Noncountable** nouns name things that cannot be counted because they are abstractions (e.g., *anger, courage, fun, health, information, prejudice*), or substances made up of components too numerous to count (e.g., *clothing, salt, sugar*), or items that cannot be cut into parts (e.g., *furniture, poetry, water*). Also in the noncountable category are the names of many sports (e.g., *tennis, football, hockey*), foods (e.g., *baklava, butter, corn, tofu*), illnesses (e.g., *arthritis, flu, diabetes*), and subjects of study (e.g., *biology, chemistry, literature*).

The rules for pluralizing nouns are simple to remember and apply. As usual, however, there are exceptions, and the exceptions can cause problems. Let's consider each class of nouns in turn.

A. Regular Countable Nouns

> To form the plural of most regular, countable nouns, you add -*s* to the singular form.

Examples:

friend	friends	requirement	requirements
idea	ideas	source	sources
piano	pianos	text	texts

There are three exceptions to this simple rule. In the first two, the plural endings are spelled the way they sound, so they are easy to remember. The third exception is a bit more complicated.

> 1. When a noun ends in *s, z, x, sh,* or *ch,* add *-es.*

Examples:

kiss	kisses	lash	lashes
buzz	buzzes	church	churches
box	boxes		

> 2. For nouns ending in *-f* or *-fe,* be guided by the pronunciation of the plural form. If the plural is pronounced with a *v* sound, change the *f* to *v* and add *-es.*

If the *f* sound doesn't change, neither does the spelling; just add *s*.

Examples:

half	halves	BUT	proof	proofs
knife	knives		belief	beliefs
calf	calves		chef	chefs

> 3. For nouns ending in a *consonant + y,* change the *y* to *i* and add *-es.*

Examples:

dictionary	dictionaries
penny	pennies
reply	replies

Note: For nouns ending in a *vowel + y,* there is no spelling change. Form the plural in the regular way by adding *s*.

Examples:

boy	boys
delay	delays
key	keys

EXERCISE 29.1

In the spaces provided, insert the correct plural forms of the nouns given in the margin. Then check your answers on p. 383. (*Tip:* phrases beginning with "one of the(se) _____" ALWAYS end with a plural noun. E.g., The answer is in one of these books.)

cigarette, match   1.   Since I quit smoking, I never carry either

_____ or _____.

mushroom, berry   2.   Please eat one of these _____ and

some of the _____ , so we can tell

if they are poisonous.

tree, leaf   3.   It is difficult to identify _____ by

their bark, but it's easy if you have one of their

_____.

quiz, course   4.   We are lucky to have only three _____

because in some _____ there are

seven.

activity, study   5.   Marcel has so many after-school _____

that he has no time left for his _____.

library, wolf   6.   Tomas has been to four _____ in

search of information about _____.

city, community   7.   Most Canadian _____ contain a

number of different ethnic _____.

inquiry, reply   8.   Denis mailed out a dozen _____,

but he received only six _____.

knife, fork   9.   Are there enough _____ and

_____ for everyone at the table?

ninety, attorney   10.   When my grandfather was in his

_____, he hired a couple of

_____ to manage his business for

him.

B. Irregular Countable Nouns

There are five classes of irregular countable nouns you need to be aware of.

1. Nouns ending in -o that form the plural by adding -es. There is no rule governing these nouns, so if you aren't sure whether *-s* or *-es* is required, check your dictionary. Here are some common *-o* nouns that require *-es* in the plural:

hero	heroes	potato	potatoes
echo	echoes	tomato	tomatoes
veto	vetoes		

2. Nouns that form the plural by changing their spelling. Some irregular plurals are old forms of common English nouns that have resisted becoming regularized. Here are some of the most familiar ones:

child	children	mouse	mice
foot	feet	ox	oxen
goose	geese	tooth	teeth
man	men	woman	women

3. Nouns that are found only in plural form. There are two groups of English nouns that are plural in form but singular in meaning. One group includes the names of common items that are in two parts but thought of as a single unit. Some examples are tools such as *pliers, scissors, shears,* and articles of clothing such as *jeans*, *pants*, *pyjamas*, *shorts*, *trousers*, and *glasses*. These nouns are normally treated as plurals. When used as subjects, they require plural verbs. When used as antecedents, they require plural pronouns. For example, even though a pair of jeans is a single garment and a pair of scissors is a single tool, we use plural pronouns to refer to them:

> I have only one clean pair of jeans, and *they're* full of holes.

> Have you seen my scissors? I can't find *them* anywhere.

Another group of plural-only nouns names academic courses or disciplines: for example, *economics*, *linguistics*, *physics*, *mathematics*, and *statistics*. These nouns are normally treated as if they were singular. As subjects, they take singular verbs, and as antecedents, they take singular pronoun referents.

> <u>Economics</u> <u>is known</u> as "the dismal science," and I hate *it*.

Two of the nouns in this group, *mathematics* and *statistics*, can be used as plurals. When they are used as plurals, they require plural verbs and pronoun referents. Consider these examples:

> The <u>mathematics</u> of this experiment <u>are</u> highly theoretical, and only a few scientists have mastered *them*.

> The <u>statistics</u> on poverty in Canada <u>are</u> horrifying; all citizens should be concerned about *them*.

4. ***Nouns that are found only in singular form.*** The names of many fish and a few animals are irregular in that they do not change form in the plural. For example:

bass	salmon	perch
moose	sheep	trout

> We screeched to a halt to avoid hitting two female moose and their calves crossing the road.

> The Hell's Gate dam caused a 90 per cent drop in the number of salmon in the Fraser River.

5. ***Foreign language nouns that have retained their original plural forms.*** A large number of words borrowed from foreign languages have resisted regularization and have kept their original plurals. Most of these words are technical or theoretical terms used in the sciences. For example:

SINGULAR	PLURAL	SINGULAR	PLURAL
analysis	analyses	larva	larvae
criterion	criteria	nucleus	nuclei
fungus	fungi	phenomenon	phenomena
hypothesis	hypotheses	stimulus	stimuli

Some borrowed nouns have acquired regular plural forms (e.g., *appendixes, indexes, formulas, stadiums*), and some—e.g., *data, broccoli*—are regularly used as singular nouns despite their technically plural endings.

> The most recent <u>data</u> <u>does</u> not support your conclusion.

> Our <u>broccoli</u> <u>has</u> been in the fridge so long it has turned yellow.

Now test your ability to pluralize irregular countable nouns by doing the following exercise and checking your answers on p. 383.

EXERCISE 29.2
Fill in the blanks with the correct plural form of the words given in parentheses.

1. It is my experience that only (child) _____ can

   figure out how to operate child-proof lighters. They defeat ordinary (man)

   _____ and (woman) _____ every

   time.

2. With so many provinces demanding (veto) _____, it's

   not likely there will be many (change) _____ made to

   Canada's constitution.

3. The chairperson presented the committee's (analysis) _____

   of the most recent (statistics) _____ on poverty and

   crime.

4. The (echo) _____ of their (hoof) _____

   lingered long after the herd had disappeared.

5. Your teacher has asked you to prepare (yourself) _____

   for a test on John Steinbeck's novel, *Of (Mouse)* _____

   and *(Man)* _____ .

6. Three (fish) _____ whose names change form

   in the plural are (anchovy) _____, (guppy)

   _____, and (sardine) _____ .

7. A dozen (sheep) _____, a flock of (goose) _____

   and four (ox) _____ can supply the needs of our

   little community.

8. My (goldfish) _____ prefer live (larva)

   _____ to packaged fish food.

9. You don't see (hero) _____ in western (movie)

   _____ being sent out for (tomato) _____,

   (onion) _____, (potato) _____, and

   other (grocery) _____ .

10. My dentist has two (criterion) _____ for a successful

    office visit: I keep all my (tooth) _____, and she takes

    all my money.

C. Noncountable Nouns

Noncountable nouns do not normally change form in the plural. To indicate a particular amount or quantity of a noncountable noun, we add a modifier. Consider these examples:

Wrong: I still have *homeworks* to do.
Right: I still have some *homework* to do.

Wrong: Conrad Black has made a great deal of *moneys* from pub-
          lishing newspapers.
Right: Conrad Black has made a great deal of *money* from publish-
          ing newspapers.

Wrong: Children should drink *milks* each day.
Right: Children should drink three glasses of *milk* each day.

Some nouns can be either countable or uncountable, depending on how they are used. If the meaning is intended to be general, the noun is non-countable and has no plural form. If the meaning is intended to be specific, the noun is countable and requires a plural ending. Study these examples:

Exercise (general) promotes good health, and aerobic *exercises* (specific) are particularly beneficial.

When I found two *hairs* (specific) in my salad, I asked our waiter, a young man with beautiful black *hair* (general), to bring me ice cream instead.

My girlfriend is so fond of *chocolates* (specific) that I can believe *choco-late* (general) is an addictive substance.

EXERCISE 29.3

Correct the noncountable noun errors in the following sentences. Make sure your subjects and verbs agree, and that your pronouns agree with their antecedents. Note that you must change some of the modifiers to ones that are appropriate to your corrections.

1. Where can we get informations on how to work these machineries?

2. My hairs have become thin from too many stresses, but your stomach
   has become fat from too many sweets.

3. My children won't drink milks with their meals, but they drink several
   milks while doing their homeworks.

4. We arrived at the airport, collected our luggages, and passed through
   customs where we were required to pay duty on the liquors we had
   bought in Grand Cayman.

5. I would be able to get to work on time if it weren't for the rush-hour traffics that cause me many angers and frustrations as well as many reprimands from my supervisor.

6. You can have many funs in sports, but the enjoyments disappear if you play too many hockeys or footballs.

7. This winter I caught three flus, but my family's healths were good.

8. There are many literatures on the subject of love, and other popular themes include quests for justices, the pursuit of wealths, and the search for happiness.

9. Young students often do not have the same appreciations of their educations as mature students because many of them take learnings for granted.

10. Many of Suniti's poetries contain sensitive descriptions of the courages her family showed on their long journey from India and expressions of the happinesses they have found in Canada.

The following exercises will give you practice in solving all three kinds of plural problems.

EXERCISE 29.4

Correct the errors in the following paragraph. Look for incorrect spellings, singular forms used as plurals, and plural forms used where the singular is required.

The Internet is a technological phenomena that has opened up a world of learnings for today's students. On the Net, they can connect with librarys to look up datas, studys, and analysises written by student and researcher all over the world. They can communicate with people in other countrys and discuss everything from politic to chess match to the price of potato. Foreign student find the Internet especially appealing because they can keep in touch with their familys without paying postages or long-distance charge. Some students are taking course on the Internet, conducting researches, getting homeworks from their teachers, and even taking testes on line. Before long, some clever student will probably figure out how to hold partys on the Net!

EXERCISE 29.5

Rewrite the following paragraph, changing the appropriate nouns from singular to plural. (We've done the first sentence for you as a guide.) Don't forget to make your verbs and pronouns agree with your plural nouns!

A Canadian who enjoys winter is a strange person. (*Canadians* who enjoy winter are strange *people*.) With his nose red and his fingers frozen, he actually seems to take pleasure in shovelling the huge mound of snow in his driveway. He doesn't mind when his cold water pipe freezes or his car doesn't start. With a smile on his face, he bundles up in thermal underwear, flannel shirt, sweater, down jacket, scarf, boots, and woollen toque. Then this peculiar creature goes out into the bitter cold and howling wind to engage in an activity that leaves a normal person completely baffled. He looks for a rink, or a trail, or a hill on which to skate or ski. While a sensible person stays indoors, huddles close to the stove, and warms himself with a hot drink, the winter-loving Canadian is outside behaving like a child with a new toy. I can't decide whether such a person is to be admired or pitied.

EXERCISE 29.6

Correct all errors in plural form in this paragraph. No answers are given for this exercise.

Many people think that moonlights influence the lifes of human, animal, and even plant. Police surveyes show that more criminal activitys occur when the moon is full. People who like to fish are convinced that the fishes bite better during the full moon. Some newspaper publish datas on the phases of the moon, showing the best times to catch various species. I know I always catch more pikes, basses, and trouts when the moon is full than at any other time. On the other hand, many gardener will not plant anything during a full moon, believing that crop such as tomatos, corns, and bean will not grow properly if they do. We know that mushroom and other fungus grow faster when the moon is new. Finally, in many societys we find legend of werewolfs: man and woman who turn into wolfs when the moon is full. Are these storys true? Probably not. But only we ourselfs know what influence the moon has on us as individual.

CHAPTER 30

Using Articles Accurately

How do you know when to write "*a* computer" and when to write "*the* computer"? "*An* architect" or "*the* architect"? "Beer and pizza" or "*the* beer and pizza"? To answer these questions you need to know the rules governing the use of **articles**. Some languages have complex systems of articles that vary according to person, gender, number, and case. In English, fortunately, we have only two forms to deal with: the **definite article**, *the*, and the **indefinite article**, *a* or *an*.

You won't find instruction on how to use articles in books written for native English speakers because they know from long experience when, where, and which articles to use. As a foreign-language learner, however, you will probably find that articles cause you difficulty. This is because you are trying to learn quickly a complex system that native speakers have spent their entire lives using. Some second-language learners eventually develop an "ear" for articles. They learn by the sound which nouns need an article and whether the definite or the indefinite article is the one required. Others of us are not so fortunate. Like tone-deaf people learning to play an instrument, we can, with practise, learn to execute compositions accurately, but only by keeping the notes (or rules) in front of us while we play (or write).

Here are a few rules to guide you in using articles accurately:

1. Use the *definite article* with common, concrete, specific nouns. The noun can be singular or plural ("the ticket," "the tickets"), countable or uncountable ("the bottles," "the beer"). If the noun is not specific, we use either the indefinite article (if the noun refers to any member of a group) or no article at all (if the noun refers to a group or concept in general).

Tip: If *this* or *these* can be substituted for the article without changing the meaning of the sentence, then the definite article is the one you need. For example, we do not write "I enjoyed reading book." We write "I enjoyed reading *the* (or *this*) book." We don't write, "*The* (or *this*) college education benefits us both professionally and personally." We write, "College education benefits us both professionally and personally."

Study these examples carefully:

The tree my grandfather planted for my sixteenth birthday is now 3 metres tall.(The tree—this tree—is specific. No other tree could fit this description.)

Tanya bags groceries at *the* corner store. (Groceries in general, not *these*, specific, groceries, at *this* store.)

The women students on our floor bought *the* beer for *the* dorm party. (*These* students bought *this* beer for *this* party.)

Pet ownership is often important to young adolescents. (*Pet ownership* is a concept, so it is used without an article. *Young adolescents* are a general, not a specific, group, so this phrase requires no article.)

The definite article is always used with some proper names, such as those of mountain ranges, rivers, oceans (but not lakes, islands, or waterfalls), and a few countries and cities:

the Philippines	the Mackenzie River
the Vatican	the Baltic Sea
the United States	the Mediterranean Sea
the Hague	the Straits of Juan de Fuca
the Laurentians	Lake Suprior
the Rockies	Bowron Lake
the St. Lawrence River	Vancouver Island
the Seine	Iguassu Falls

Note that the names of most countries and cities do not require an article: Poland, North Korea, Canada, India; Rome, Halifax, Whitehorse, Changsha, Saint-Louis-du-Ha! Ha! (It's in Quebec.)

2. The *indefinite article* is used to identify a common noun in a general, indefinite way, or to refer to any member of a group. *A* and *an* are generally used with singular, countable nouns. They are less often used with uncountable nouns, and they are never used with plural nouns. Plural nouns used in a general, indefinite way are normally used with no article.

Study these examples:

> *A* tree in the backyard would provide us with shade. (Here we mean any tree, not a specific, identifiable one, such as the one grandfather planted.)

> On average, *a* woman can expect to live longer than *a* man. ("*A* woman" refers to any member of the group, *women*; "*a* man" refers to any member of the group, *men*.)

> Jean-Luc often annoys his teachers by reading magazines in class; in fact, he is reading *a* magazine now. ("*A* magazine" is the singular form of a countable noun.)

> I have difficulty finding time for homework. (*Difficulty* and *homework* are uncountable nouns.)

> On average, women live longer than men. (Indefinite articles are never used with plural nouns.)

> 2.1 Use *an* before vowel sounds (*a, e, i, o, u*), however spelled: *an* Albertan, *an* honour, *an* MP
>
> Use *a* before consonant sounds and the semi-vowel *y* or any variant spelling that sounds like *y* (*a* European, *a* UN official, *a* eulogy)

3. Usually, when an *indefinite noun* is mentioned for the first time in a sentence or paragraph, it is preceded by an *indefinite article*. But when the same noun is mentioned again, the writer assumes the reader now knows which particular person, place, or thing is being referred to, and so uses the definite article.

Consider the placement of definite and indefinite articles in the following paragraph. Then re-read the paragraph, substituting definite for indefinite articles, and vice versa. Does the paragraph still make sense?

> *A* police car was following *a* white van that was driving very slowly through *a* dark neighbourhood late at night. *The* van slowed, turned suddenly, and parked in *a* driveway. *The* police car pulled into *the* driveway and parked behind *the* van. Both drivers got out of their vehicles. *The* van driver was holding *a* map in her hand. She was using *the* map to try to find her way in *an* unfamiliar part of *the* city. *The* police officer, who had been patrolling *the* area for years, was happy to help her find *the* address she was looking for.

In the following sentences, fill in each space with *a, an,* or *the,* or leave it blank. Answers begin on p. 384.

EXERCISE 30.1

1. What is _____ name of _____ student you were talking to this morning?

2. I saw _____ young woman who looked very much like your daughter in _____ laundry room this morning.

3. _____ kind of vacation I enjoy most is _____ long train ride.

4. I don't need _____ special destination when I board _____ train; for me, _____ important thing is _____ journey.

5. Today it is not difficult for _____ woman to succeed as _____ lawyer; fifty years ago, however, _____ women who entered law school faced many obstacles.

6. Thinking it would enhance his image as _____ supersalesman, A. J. longed for _____ big, flashy car. _____ compact car his company provided was _____ big disappointment.

7. In North America, if not elsewhere, _____ sports stars and _____ journalists need each other to survive.

8. In Canada, _____ college students begin school in _____ September, and _____ school year ends in _____ April.

9. It is generally believed that _____ men enjoy playing _____ violent, competitive sports more than _____ women do; however, _____

women on my hockey team are even more aggressive and competitive

than _____ men.

10. Oscar Wilde, _____ English writer known for his wry wit, wrote that

_____ Niagara Falls was every bride's second-biggest disappointment.

EXERCISE 30.2

1. Can you recommend _____ movie that is enjoyable without being

full of _____ violence and _____ bloodshed? We'd like to see

_____ good, old-fashioned comedy.

2. _____ students who will be graduating this year will pay special _____

fee if they choose to attend _____ convocation ceremony.

3. _____ movie industry agrees that 1995 was _____ hundredth an-

niversary of _____ birth of cinema, but there are _____ conflicting

claims about who is actually responsible for _____ first movie.

4. _____ fastest-growing segment of _____ Internet over _____ past

few years has been _____ World Wide Web.

5. _____ recent public opinion poll conducted in _____ United King-

dom showed that _____ higher proportion of the general public want

their police officers to be armed than _____ police officers themselves

think is desirable.

6. Marisa, one of _____ few employees at our store who work part-time,

claims that _____ fact she is working without _____ contract or

_____ benefits doesn't really bother her.

7. _____ Earthquakes happen occasionally in B. C., but almost never

in _____ prairie provinces, _____ central Canada, or _____

Maritimes.

8. Many of _____ geographical names in Canada are derived from

_____ languages of aboriginal peoples who lived here for thousands

of years before _____ first European settlers arrived.

9. For example, in _____ Lake Huron there is _____ huge island called

_____ Manitoulin, whose name was given to it long ago by _____

native peoples.

10. _____ Saskatchewan, _____ Ontario, _____ Magnetawan River,

_____ Lake Huron, and even _____ name "Canada" itself are just

_____ few examples of _____ aboriginal influence on _____

contemporary place names.

EXERCISE 30.3

Read through the following paragraph and decide where and what kind of
articles are needed. Fill in each space with a definite or an indefinite article, or leave the space blank, as appropriate.

You can tell all you need to know about _____ person from _____

shoes he or she wears. Our economics teacher, for example, wears _____

worn-out, old brown leather loafers. From this, I know that he doesn't care

about _____ appearances, that he likes to save _____ money, that he

enjoys _____ comfort, and that he does not have _____ wife who

checks his appearance in _____ mornings when he leaves for

_____ work. On _____ other hand, our computer instructor is _____ fashionably-dressed woman who wears _____ different pair of shoes al-most every day. My favourites are her black patent leather pumps with _____ gold buckles on _____ toes. Such _____ stylish selection of _____ shoes tells me that she is _____ clothes-conscious person who cares what _____ others think of her appearance. She appreciates quality and is willing to spend _____ money necessary to buy it. If my theory about _____ relationship between _____ character and _____ footwear is valid, I would be interested in _____ analysis of my English instructor, who wears _____ black army boots one day, _____ white running shoes _____ next day, _____ pair of cowboy boots one day and _____ pair of platform sandals another.

In the following paragraphs, correct any misused or missing articles.

EXERCISE 30.4

While Josée was visiting her sister Marie, a cat walked into room where they were sitting. It seemed like the friendly animal, but Josée was surprised because she knew Marie hated the cats. So Josée asked her sister what cat was doing there, and Marie explained that cat had been lent to her by a neighbour to control the mice in her apartment. Cat had been with Marie for two weeks now, and there was not the mouse left in the apartment. In fact, Marie and cat had become good friends. Josée quickly came to con-clusion that neighbour may need to get new cat.

EXERCISE 30.5

Ramon was searching a supermarket shelves for box of detergent when he noticed sugar spilling from broken bag in his shopping cart. He put broken bag of sugar back on shelf and put a new bag in cart. Then, as he went up and down the aisles of supermarket, he added the coffee, the orange juice, the jar of jam, and some fruit to his cart. After selecting bunch of grapes and basket of peaches, Ramon went to vegetable counter where he chose broccoli, beans, grapes and kilo of field tomatoes. Finally, he added package of cookies and made his way to the line-up at cash register. Only after he had paid for his purchases and left store did he realize that he had forgotten a detergent.

EXERCISE 30.6

I love the travelling and have been to many interesting places around world. My favourite places are the China and the Morocco because, of all places I have been, they are most different from the Canada in the culture, the language, the architecture, and the cuisine. When I go to United States or the Great Britain or even Australia, I find experience much like that of home, but in the exotic countries, I am always conscious that I am far away from a home. In the Morocco, I sampled the couscous, which is very popular dish in North Africa. In markets, people were dressed in the long, flowing robes and traditional turbans, or tasselled red caps, called fez. In streets, the buildings were all made of the pink clay, and many of cities were surrounded by the large walls. China, too, is fascinating to the Canadians because it is so foreign, especially in countryside. There, the oxen are still used to plow fields, and the bicycles are more common than the cars. Food is very spicy in some areas, and visitor will be surprised by variety of foods in different regions. China is not country like Canada, where, everywhere you go, food, culture, dress, and architecture are pretty much same. Travel is wonderful way to learn about the world and discover the other countries and the other people.

EXERCISE 30.7

Correct any misused articles and supply any missing articles in the following paragraph. No answers are given for this exercise.

The goldfish make the terrific pets. I bought three goldfish at local pet store for $3.99, a price that wouldn't even buy the collar for dog. They're also easy to care for. I change water in their bowl once the week, throw the pinch of food in bowl twice a day, and they seem happy and healthy. Furthermore, goldfish are endlessly interesting. I can spend the hours watching them cruise around their little world, occasionally nuzzling or fighting each other. The goldfish may not bark at the intruders or rub against my leg when I come home, but, for me, they are as close to perfect as the pets can get.

CHAPTER 31

Practising with Prepositions

Choosing the correct preposition to use in a phrase can be a challenge. English uses dozens of prepositions in combination with other words to convey specific meanings. Some words can be used with two or more prepositions, and the meaning changes with each one. For example, if you *put up* a friend for the weekend, you offer her accommodation. But if you *put up with* a friend, you tolerate her annoying behaviour. We *stick by* our friends when they are in trouble, but *stick to* a task until it is completed.

Two kinds of error can result from careless use of prepositions:

1. Sometimes the construction does not mean what you intended:

    Wrong: After working *in* my essay all evening, I was happy to set it *apart*.

    Right: After working *on* my essay all evening, I was happy to set it *aside*.

2. Sometimes the construction is simply incorrect:

    Wrong: I am bored *of* doing homework; let's go *in* a movie.

    Right: I am bored *with* doing homework; let's go *to* a movie.

When you are not sure which preposition to use with a particular word, look up the word—not the preposition—in the dictionary. Be sure to read through all the meanings given. You'll be surprised to find how many different meanings a prepositional phrase can have. Notice, too, that many common English verbs (and a few nouns and adjectives) can be used with several prepositions.

Let's look at an example. Here are ten sentences illustrating the use of some of the prepositions that can follow the verb *look*:

1. Cécile looks *after* her sister's children while their mother works.
2. It seems that few people these days look *back on* a happy childhood.
3. Ceaucescu was a dictator who looked *down on* those who were subject to his rule.
4. My boss sent me to look *for* the missing visitor.
5. After ten months of winter, the people of Inuvik look *forward to* spring.
6. The dean agreed to look *into* the students' complaints about the bookstore's pricing policies.
7. I was told to go to the main entrance and look *out for* a tall woman wearing glasses and a backpack.
8. Ivo asked the tutor if she would look *over* the first draft of his paper.
9. My mother looked *through* her cookbooks to find the recipe for Nanaimo bars.
10. In my country, everyone looks *up to* the elders.

Below is a list of common English verbs together with some of the prepositions that can follow them. Go over the list carefully, highlighting the ones you are not familiar with. You need to be able to use these phrases accurately in your writing. Remember: many of these phrases have multiple meanings. The meaning will depend on the context in which the phrase is used: you can *back up* a van; you can *back up* an opinion; you can *back up* a friend; you can *back up* a short distance; and, if your car stalls, you can *back up* traffic. *Back up* means something different in each case.

admit (someone) *to* (something); admit *to* (someone) or (something)
agree *to* (something); agree *with* (someone) or *with* what (someone) says
be angry *at* or *about* (something); be angry *with* (someone)
apply *for* (something); apply *to* (someone)
approve *of* (someone) or (something)
argue *about* (something) *with* (someone)
arrange (something) *with* (someone)
arrive *at* a place or *in* a city (exception: arrive home)

back *away from* (someone) or (something); back *down from* (something);
   back *out of* (something) or some place; back *up* (someone) or (something)
break (something) *down* or *in*; break *off* or *through* (something)
bring (something) *forward* or *up*

care *about* (someone) or (something); care *for* (someone)
call (someone) *back*; call *for* (someone) or (something); call (something)
   off; call *on* (someone)

carry (something) *forward, to,* or *through*; carry *on with* (something)
check *in to* (someplace); check *out* (someone) or (something); check *out of* (someplace)
combine (something) *with* (something) else
come *down with* (something) (usually an illness)
compare (someone) or (something) *with* another
be composed *of* persons or things
conform *to* (something)
count *on* (someone) or (something)
congratulate (someone) *on* (something)

do *away with* (something)
draw (something) *up*

face *up to* (someone) or (something)
be fed *up with* (someone) or (something)
figure (something) *out*
find (something) *out*; find *out about* (someone) or (something)
find fault *with* (someone) or (something)
follow *through with* (something); follow *up on* (something)

get (something) *across to* (someone); get *ahead of* (someone) or (something); get *around* (something) or (someone); get *around to* doing (something); get *away with* (something); get *back at* (someone)
give (something) or (someone) *away*; give *in to* (someone); give (something) *up*
get *around to* doing (something)
go *into* or *over* or *through* (something) *with* (someone); go *with* or *without* (something)
go *back on* (something)
grow *out of* (something)

hand (something) *down* or *in* or *to* or *over to* (someone)
hang (something) *up*; hang *up* (the telephone)
hold (someone) or (something) *back,* or *off,* or *over,* or *up*; hold *on to* (someone) or (something)

impose (something) *on* (someone)
introduce (someone) *to* (someone) else

laugh (something) *off*
be laughed *at*
lay (something) *aside* or *down*; lay (someone) *off*
live *up to* (something)

look *after* (someone) or (something); look *back on* (something); look *down on* (someone) or (something); look *for* (someone) or (something); look *forward to* (something); look *into* (something); look *out for* (someone) or (something); look *over* or *through* (something); look *up to* (someone) or (something)

make *fun of* (someone)
make (something) *out* or *up*; make *up for* (something)

object *to* (someone) or (something)

point *out* (someone) or (something) *to* (someone)
prefer (someone) or (something) *to* another
put (something) *aside* or *away* or *down* or *on* or *out* or *together*; put (someone) *down* or *off* or *out*; put (someone) *up*; put *up with* (someone) or (something)

read (something) *over*; read *through* (something)
refer *to* (someone) or (something); refer (someone) *to* (someone) or (something)
rule *out* (something)
run *into* (someone); run *out*; run *out of* (something)
see *about* (something); see (someone) *off*; see *through* (someone) or (something); see *to* (something)
sell (something) *out*
send *for* (someone) or (something); send (someone) or (something) *in* or *off* or *out*; send *out for* (something)
set (someone) or (something) *aside* or *back* or *off*; set (something) *up*
settle *for* or *on* (something); settle *in* (someplace)
show (something) *off*; show up; show *up with* (someone) or (something)
shut (something) *off*; shut (someone) or (something) *out*
stand *by* (someone) or (something); stand *for* (something); stand *up for* (someone) or (something); stand up to (someone) or (something)
stick *by* (someone); stick *to* (something); (people) stick *together*; stick *up* for (someone) or (something)
succeed *in* doing (something)

take (something) *apart* or *back* or *out* or *over*; take *to* (someone); take *up* (something); take (something) *out on* (someone)
take care *of* (someone) or (something)
talk *back to* or *down to* (someone); talk (someone) *into* or *out of* (something); talk (something) *over* or *through*
think *of* or *up* (something); think (something) *out* or *over* or *through*; think *back on* (someone) or (something)

try (something) *on*; try *out for* (something)
turn (someone) or (something) *around* or *away* or *back* or *down*

wait *for* (someone) or (something); wait *on* (someone)
work *at* or *on* (something); work (something) *out*
worry *about* (someone) or (something)

The following sentences contain misused or missing prepositions. After you have finished correcting each set, check your answers beginning on p. 386.

EXERCISE 31.1

1. We all congratulated Harjinder for her speech.
2. After putting aside my winter clothes too soon, I came down for a cold.
3. Ovie's girlfriend promised to hand his assignment for him.
4. Sons often find it difficult to live to their fathers' ambitions for them.
5. Most children in this world have to wear their clothes long after they have grown from them.
6. Whenever my supervisor has to take care for her children, I have to fill for her.
7. Our company decided to do away DOS and settled in Windows 95 instead.
8. After a semester of trying to combine a full-time job to full-time study, Tung decided to give in his job.
9. I cannot agree about my supervisor's proposal to do away overtime pay.
10. My boss asked me to put apart the inventory check and work at the department's sales figures.

EXERCISE 31.2

1. You can count in me; I never go back from my word.
2. The pipes have frozen, so we need to shut out the water supply.
3. When my uncle came with pneumonia, we admitted him in the hospital for treatment.
4. Teenagers love checking in shopping malls to try out new clothes.
5. After arguing my friends for more than an hour, I got fed and left.
6. This book is not the one I was looking, so I shall take it again to the store.
7. The concert was sold, and the management had to turn off about 300 people.
8. It's time you faced to your limitations; since you hate people, you will never succeed with the restaurant business.
9. As soon as Sati arrived to Canada, she applied to a job as a bank clerk.
10. I wonder how I should introduce my new friends with my wife. She will never approve for them.

EXERCISE 31.3

1. I am angry at my brothers when they make fun with me.
2. René applied with the Director of Human Resources to the technologist's position.
3. My boss's English is so poor that he often finds fault in me because I cannot figure what he tells me to do.
4. The worst thing a teacher can do is talk down on his or her class.
5. After class, I went to the library to look out Aldo, who had promised to wait on me and drive me home.
6. Before she started college, Ruwaida arranged her sister to take care for her two children.
7. I do not agree about the college's rule that students may not carry cellular phones for class.
8. The Appeals Committee is composed from five students and three faculty members.
9. When Sadik's restaurant went bankrupt, his employees agreed to stick him.
10. Khai was so angry for being laughed that he went away to make fun his little brother just so he could take his anger out with someone.

EXERCISE 31.4
Correct the faulty prepositions in the following paragraph.

A good friend of mine recently introduced me for bowling. She said that she prefers bowling on any other game she has tried. Before long she had talked me onto checking up this sport. Many cultures have games similar with bowling, such as boules in France and bocce in Italy, and I looked forward on learning how to play. When we arrived in the arena, which is called a bowling alley, my friend tried to explain for me the system of keeping score. But all I wanted to do was figure up how to knock down the clubs. My friend laughed and told me the clubs were called bowling pins, but I pointed up that they didn't look anything like pins. Eventually, she gave away trying to teach me how to keep score, and we just threw the balls down the alley, knocking over as many pins as we could. I admit for

you that I had a wonderful time, and that I can't wait for my friend to call

me to set on another evening of bowling.

EXERCISE 31.5

Fill in the blanks with the appropriate prepositions.

I am working _____ a course in business writing that is offered by

computer. I found _____ about the course from a friend who had looked

_____ the possibility of taking it himself; however, since he does not own

a computer, he had to settle _____ a classroom course. I attended class

only once, to be introduced _____ the program that connects my com-

puter to the "electronic classroom." It is quite a simple program, and, after

I had looked _____ the manual, I succeeded _____ loading it on my

computer without difficulty. Each evening, I call up the program, and it

connects me to my course which comes from a college about 500 kilome-

tres away. The program gets the messages, lessons, and assignments that are

waiting for me and I read them _____when I feel like it. When I get

to doing my homework assignments, I send them _____ to my professor

by e-mail. I can put my work _____ any time and return to it when

I have time or am in the mood. I prefer this method of learning _____

regular classroom instruction because I don't have to show _____ at a

certain place at a certain time, and I can work _____ my course for

as long as I need to. This system will help me succeed _____ finishing my college diploma sooner than I would if I were attending classes in the

regular way.

EXERCISE 31.6
Write ten sentences using the verb *put* with different prepositions. Then exchange papers with a classmate and check each other's work.

EXERCISE 31.7
Use the following phrases in sentences of your own composition.

agree to	introduce to
call off	object to
count on	see about
go without	succeed in
hold up	think over

EXERCISE 31.8
Now try this mastery test. Fill in each blank with the preposition that most appropriately follows the given verb. No answers are given for this exercise.

1. I have given _____ trying to arrange a meeting with an astronaut, so

   you will have to settle _____ being introduced _____ a former

   baseball player instead.

2. May I point _____ that you admitted _____ being the one who

   laughed _____ me when I accidentally used hair remover instead of

   shampoo.

3. If Stefan shows _____, we will begin working _____ the new song

   that we looked _____ last week but didn't have time to rehearse.

4. I would settle _____ a car that didn't have to be worked _____

   twice a week and didn't need to be shut _____ by disconnecting the

   battery.

5. Ms. Iacono is looking forward _____ meeting her new co-workers and being introduced _____ the project manager. She wants to begin immediately to draw _____ a business plan.

6. I prefer a collie dog _____ a bloodhound for herding, because a collie can figure _____ exactly what the sheep are going to do next. More often than not, a collie will succeed _____ getting the sheep to do what the herder wants rather than what they want.

7. We're going to have to work _____ our presentation if we want people to come and check _____ our display without laughing _____ our feeble explanations of it.

8. Our landlady found _____ that Arnaud has admitted _____ coming in late and tearing the garage door off its hinges. She can't figure _____ how he did it since he didn't have the car.

9. Brigitte has agreed _____ point _____ our instructor that her tests are too hard, and we are fed _____ the marks we are getting.

10. Rudolf has thought _____ another brilliant scheme. Since a cat always lands on its feet, and buttered toast always lands buttered side down, Rudolf has figured _____ that by strapping a piece of buttered toast to the back of a cat, he can succeed _____ creating perpetual motion because the two will spin forever just inches off the ground.

CHAPTER 32

Understanding Idioms

A college student who was looking for summer employment went from door to door asking, "Could you please give me the works? I do strange jobs." Again and again, she was turned away. Finally, a sympathetic homeowner figured out that what the student meant was that she could do odd jobs and wanted work. There was nothing the matter with the student's grammar, but her lack of familiarity with English idioms cost her a great deal of time and frustration.

An idiom is a group of words that, when used together, has a different meaning from the one it would have if you took the meaning of each word individually. Idioms defy rules, and students of ESL often find them difficult to master. Only reading and practice will help you identify, understand, and use idioms correctly.

Most books on English idioms contain lists of time-worn expressions known as clichés. Phrases such as "on the ball," "rat race," and "playing with fire" are common in informal spoken English, but they are not appropriate in standard written English. Over time, you will learn to recognize these cliches and perhaps use them in conversation. For use in writing, however, you need to familiarize yourself with other kinds of idioms.

In this chapter you will find two sorts of idiomatic expressions. The first type, idiomatic words and phrases, is expressions you will encounter frequently in your reading. These are the ones you should set out to master. Your ability to use them correctly will contribute significantly to your fluency as a writer. The second type, proverbs and sayings, are traditional expressions that are common in both spoken and written English. They are brief metaphorical expressions that communicate age-old wisdom or advice. Your goal should not necessarily be to use these expressions in your writing, but you should be sufficiently familiar with them to recognize them when you hear or read them, even when—as often happens—only a part of the saying is used: e.g., "don't count your chickens," "a stitch in time," "too many cooks."

Idiomatic Words and Phrases

Read through the following list, highlighting the expressions you don't know. Look them up in your dictionary and jot a brief definition or sample usage beside each one.

after hours
all over
arm's length
around the clock
asking price
at loose ends

back street
bear in mind
behind someone's back
bad debt
ballpark figure
be *or* feel blue
blue-collar
boiling point
bottom line
brainstorm
break even
break one's word
break the news
brush up on
burnout
(have) butterflies in one's stomach

call it a day (*or* a night)
car pool
carrying charge
catch one's breath
catch sight of
change one's mind
change hands
check-up
a chip on one's shoulder

clear the air
clear cut
clear sailing
close call
come to one's senses
come to the point
common ground
cover-up
cross one's fingers
cut corners

daylight saving time
double park
draw the line at
drop out (verb); drop-out (noun)
dry run

elbow room
explain oneself

face-to-face
fact of life
fair play
fed up
fifty-fifty
find time

get along (with)
get the feel of
get on one's nerves
get to the point
get in touch with
get in the way

get together

give oneself up

give someone a hand

go along (with)

go broke

going strong

good deal

a good many

a good time

on hand (*also:* at hand, by hand,
   off hand)

hand in hand

hand out (verb)

handout (noun)

have grounds for

have in mind

have one's hands full

head-on

head start

heart-to-heart

heavy-duty

hit-and-run

hit-and-miss

hit the books

hold one's own

hold out

ill at ease

in the black

in common

in (*or* into) effect

in keeping

in line (with)

in the way (*or* in someone's way)

in the red

in spite of

in the long run (*or* in the short run)

jump (*or* leap) to a conclusion

just so

keep a straight face

keep an eye on

keep in mind

keep in touch with

keep (*or* lose) one's head

keep (*or* lose) one's temper

keep one's fingers crossed

keep one's word

keep track (of)

kill time

know the ropes

last straw

lend a hand

let slide (*or* let slip)

let well enough alone

long shot

lose heart

lose one's head (*or* shirt *or* temper)

lose track

a lost cause

make believe

make certain

make a difference

make do

make ends meet

make an example of

make fun of

make the best of (*or* make the
   most of)

make up (verb); makeup (noun)

make up one's mind

make time for

make way

a matter of fact

a matter of opinion

meet (someone) halfway

men's room

middle ground

narrow-minded

no way

no wonder

of age

off the ground

on average

on the contrary

on deposit

on the dot
on edge
on hold
on one hand . . . on the other hand
on one's hands
on one's mind
on purpose
on the record
on the safe side
on schedule
on (the) track (of)
on the whole
on target
on trial
once in a while
out of hand (*or* out of control)
out of date
out of luck
out of order
out of place
out of practice
out of the question

pay one's way
play (it) safe
pull oneself together

rain check
rear-end
red herring
resign oneself
rest room
right away
road test
run short

save face
save one's breath
second thought(s)
see eye to eye
serve the purpose
serve someone right
set one's heart on
settle for
so many (*e.g.,* The room will hold
    only so many.)

so much (*e.g.,* so much to do; so
    much time)
spend time
stand a chance
stand for
standard time
step by step
stick together
straight answer

tailgate (verb)
take advantage (of)
take after
take care (of)
take charge (of)
take exception (to)
take for granted
take it easy
take hold (of)
take into account
talk shop
tell apart
think a great deal of
time out
to order
touch and go
trade-in

under the circumstances
under the table
under the weather
up to date

waste one's breath
wear thin
wear well
weather the storm
weigh the pros and cons
what if
what's what
workout
world war
waiting list
warm-up

year in, year out

EXERCISE 32.1

Below are five pairs of sentences using common English idioms. Only one sentence in each pair uses the idioms correctly, so only one sentence makes sense. Identify the meaningful sentence in each pair by circling either a) or b). You'll find answers to this exercise on p. 388.

1. a) If you feel *ill at ease*, you are feeling sick even though you are resting.
   b) If you feel *ill at ease*, you are feeling anxious or worried about something.
2. a) To compromise means *to meet someone halfway* rather than *head-on*.
   b) To compromise means *to meet someone head-on* rather than *halfway*.
3. a) The *asking price* is the approximate amount a vendor is willing to settle for when selling an item, and a *ballpark figure* is the price he or she wants to get.
   b) The *asking price* is the price vendors want for an item and a *ballpark figure* is the approximate amount they are willing to settle for.
4. a) If you want to succeed in college, you must *hit the books* as soon as the term starts. To *make a difference* to your grades, you must treat schoolwork as a *fact of life* rather than a *lost cause*.
   b) If you want to *make a difference* in college, you must recognize that homework is a *fact of life* and that *hitting the books* is a *lost cause*.
5. a) When people suffer from *burnout*, they need to *draw the line* at taking on more work so that they can pause, *catch their breath*, and *get in touch with* their feelings about their job.
   b) When people need to *get in touch with* their feelings, they should *catch their breath*, *draw the line* at work, and consider the advantages of *burnout*.

In the following sentences, substitute an idiomatic expression for the word or words that are printed in italics. (You'll find a list of idioms to choose from at the end of each exercise.) You may need to make grammar or syntax changes to accommodate the idioms. When you've finished each exercise, compare your answers with our suggestions on p. 388.

EXERCISE 32.2

1. Two days before Tony and Ramona's wedding day, Ramona *altered her decision*.

2. She knew she had to *communicate the information* to her fiancé *without delay*.

3. Ramona felt bad about *not fulfilling her promise*, but she knew she couldn't spend the rest of her life with someone who *made her an object of humour* to his friends.

4. Ramona decided it would be best to speak with Tony *directly and in person*.

5. She asked him to meet her in their favourite coffee shop at 6:00 *punctually*.

6. As she waited for Tony, Ramona *experienced evidence of nervousness in her abdomen*.

7. When Tony arrived, he was *anxious and irritable*.

8. When Ramona delivered the bad news, he *went into an uncontrollable rage*.

9. Tony's shouts and threats were *the final event in a series of unacceptable actions*.

10. His behaviour convinced Ramona that their relationship *had no chance of succeeding* and that a reconciliation was *not feasible*.

on the dot	on edge	at arm's length
the last straw	out of the question	lost his temper
lost cause	spend time	weathered the storm
right away	lost heart	made fun of
breaking even	break the news	changed her mind
face-to-face	breaking her word	got butterflies in her stomach

EXERCISE 32.3

1. Instead of obeying the detective's order that he *surrender to the police*, the suspect made his escape through the *streets far away from the main thoroughfares*.

2. After *carefully considering the advantages and disadvantages* of continuing to chase the suspect, the police decided to *consider their work for the night done*.

3. *Given this particular state of affairs*, it is hardly surprising that Brigitte believes she *has reason and justification for* suing her eleventh husband for divorce.

4. Anton seemed to be *embarrassed and uncomfortable* when the boss told him it was his responsibility to *maintain accurate and up-to-date information with respect to* the department's budget.

5. I could hardly believe that Tony would *fabricate* such a lie, and so I asked him to *give an account of himself.*

6. When you are *overwhelmed by feelings of sadness*, it is not helpful to have your friends tell you *to consider the positive aspects of the situation.*

7. Drivers who *fail to maintain a safe distance between their car and mine* really *exasperate* me.

8. To a driver fighting her way home in rush-hour traffic, a car that is *parked beside another at the side of the road* may well be the *last in a series of unpleasant events that makes her feel she cannot tolerate the situation any longer.*

9. Most gang leaders share two characteristics: they *have an enormous grudge against the world* and they *are well familiar with the routines that govern street life.*

10. When a gang's behaviour gets completely *beyond tolerable limits*, the police must *refuse to ignore or condone it;* otherwise, they will be unable to *make themselves look good* in the community.

has grounds for	tailgate	make the best of
make up	explain himself	know the ropes
double parked	feeling blue	back streets
elbow room	give himself up	car pool
keep track of	out of hand	a chip on their shoulders
draw the line	has grounds for	under the circumstances
save face	call it a night	last straw
get on my nerves	ill at ease	weighing the pros and cons

In the paragraphs below, the italicized phrases are inappropriate because they are too formal for their context (the topic, audience, and level of language of the rest of the paragraph). From the list of idiomatic expressions that follows each paragraph, choose phrases that are appropriate substitutes for the phrases given in italics.

EXERCISE 32.4

Soon after the term began, my roommate, Ganesh, and I got into the habit of *restaurant dining* almost daily. Not surprisingly, we soon *found ourselves without funds*. This problem forced us to *regain a reasonable perspective*. We decided to begin cooking our own meals, sharing the responsibility *perfectly equitably*. Last night was Ganesh's turn; he cooked a delicious curry while I *pursued my studies*. Tonight, it was my turn in the kitchen. I decided to *take a cautious approach* and make Kraft Dinner. But it soon became clear that even that simple dish was too difficult for someone so *lacking in habitual experience* in the kitchen as I was. I cut my finger trying to open the package while the water in the pot reached the *vaporization point* and spilled all over the stove. My screams of frustration caused Ganesh to *consider anew the wisdom of our decision*. Taking pity on me, he suggested that we order a pizza. Only by paying for the pizza with my credit card was I able to *preserve my dignity*. Now I am *on the debit side of my balance sheet*. Tomorrow I will *atone* for tonight's disaster by cooking a masterpiece, even if it takes me all day.

save face	hit the books	went broke
play it safe	save face	have second thoughts
in the black	boiling point	out of the question
got together	eating out	out of practice
fifty-fifty	in the red	come to our senses
make up		

EXERCISE 32.5

If I were *in physical and cardiovascular condition*, I'd ride my bicycle to work every day. Many of my co-workers bike to work, and they claim they enjoy the *concentrated period of physical exercise*. I, *in marked contrast*, feel *distinctly uncomfortable* with the idea of my colleagues *enjoying themselves at my expense* as I stagger, exhausted, through the front door and down the hall to the *room reserved for male employees to perform their ablutions*. Driving the car to work is not the answer, either. There are no legal parking spaces near my work site, so I often have to *accommodate myself in* an illegal spot. This means that, *as a precautionary measure*, I must leave my desk every few hours and move my car. I admit that I enjoy cycling and that I would benefit from the daily *regular physical exercise*. However, after having had *a careful reconsideration of the matter*, I've decided to *set aside a suitable time allocation* for exercise on the weekends. For me, *arriving at an appropriate allotment of time* during the week is a *futile endeavour*.

finding time	in shape	workout
ill at ease	men's room	to be on the safe side
make do with	lost cause	making fun of me
make time for	think nothing of	on the other hand
double park	second thoughts	have my hands full
last straw		

Common English Proverbs and Sayings

Below are three sets of well-known English proverbs and sayings. Read each one carefully and discuss its meaning with a partner or in a group. Then test your understanding of these sayings by doing the exercise that follows each set.

1. a) Beggars can't be choosers.
    b) Birds of a feather flock together.
    c) A stitch in time saves nine.
    d) A bird in the hand is worth two in the bush.
    e) Blood is thicker than water.
    f) Don't count your chickens before they are hatched.
    g) It is no use crying over spilt milk.
    h) The early bird catches the worm.
    i) Don't put all your eggs in one basket.
    j) All that glitters is not gold.

EXERCISE 32.6

The following sentences "translate" into modern English the meanings of the sayings in the list above. In the space beside each sentence, place the letter of the proverb or saying that means the same thing.

1. _____ Correcting a fault early prevents much time and trouble later.

2. _____ Family relationships are more important and reliable than any other.

3. _____ A person who acts quickly is more likely to be successful than one who delays.

4. _____ It isn't wise to count on a single project or venture to fulfill all your hopes.

5. _____ Don't risk what you already have in the hope of getting more.

6. _____ We must be satisfied with what we can afford.

7. _____ There is no point in regretting a mistake or worrying about a misfortune when it is too late to do anything about it.

8. _____ Don't make or act on assumptions; wait until you are sure the results are what you expected.

9. _____ People with similar interests and opinions tend to associate with one another.

10. _____ Things are not always what they appear to be at first glance.

2. a) People who live in glass houses shouldn't throw stones.
   b) Beauty is in the eye of the beholder.
   c) Necessity is the mother of invention.
   d) Every cloud has a silver lining.
   e) You can't have your cake and eat it too.
   f) You can lead a horse to water, but you can't make it drink.
   g) Strike while the iron is hot.
   h) A rolling stone gathers no moss.
   i) Many a true word is spoken in jest.
   j) Half a loaf is better than none.

EXERCISE 32.7

In the space beside each sentence below, write the letter of the proverb or saying from list 2 that means the same thing.

1. _____ Even though we may not have everything we want, we should be grateful for what we do have and not waste time wishing for more.

2. _____ There's always some good to be found in a difficult or unpleasant situation.

3. _____ You will have best success if you act quickly, when the time is right.

4. _____ People who move frequently, from place to place or job to job, tend not to acquire friends or property.

5. _____ Remarks that are made in fun, without serious intention, often contain some truth.

6. _____ If two things are incompatible, you cannot enjoy them both.

7. _____ People's judgments about what is aesthetically pleasing are subjective.

8. _____ Don't criticize others for a fault you yourself have.

9. _____ When a problem is urgent, a solution is often found.

10. _____ You can encourage someone to do what you want, but you can't force cooperation.

3. a) Still waters run deep.
   b) Make hay while the sun shines.
   c) Too many cooks spoil the broth.
   d) You can't make an omelette without breaking eggs.
   e) It never rains but it pours.
   f) Let sleeping dogs lie.
   g) A watched pot never boils.
   h) There's many a slip between the cup and the lip.
   i) Two heads are better than one.
   j) It's an ill wind that blows nobody any good.

EXERCISE 32.8

In the space beside each sentence below, write the letter of the proverb or saying from list 3 that means the same thing.

1. _____ Some things are impossible to accomplish without causing difficulty or even harm.

2. _____ People who say little often think a great deal.

3. _____ All sorts of things can go wrong between having an idea and putting it into practice.

4. _____ What is a misfortune to one person may benefit someone else.

5. _____ It's a good idea to get advice or help from others rather than face difficulties alone.

6. _____ Waiting attentively for something to happen makes it seem to take longer.

7. _____ Don't disturb or call attention to a potentially troublesome problem if it isn't causing any difficulty right now.

8. _____ Troubles tend to come in large numbers or in quick succession.

9. _____ Sometimes the more people who are involved in doing a task, the less efficiently the work gets done.

10. _____ Take advantage of favourable circumstances to achieve your goal or to enjoy yourself.

EXERCISE 32.9

Proverbs and familiar sayings occur in all languages. Around the world, similar ideas are expressed in different ways, depending on the local cultural context. Review the proverbs and sayings we've listed above, and, for as many as possible, think of sayings in your own language that convey similar meanings. For example the Spanish expression *Dígame con quién andas y te diré quién eres* ("Tell me who you spend your time with, and I will tell you who you are") means essentially the same thing as "Birds of a feather flock together."

EXERCISE 32.10

Consider this old English saying:

> A son is a son till he gets him a wife,
> But a daughter's a daughter all of her life.

Does your language have a saying that conveys a similar meaning? Or perhaps an opposite meaning? Write a paragraph in which you consider the cultural implications of either the English verse or a comparable one from your native language.

APPENDIXES

Readings

Writing a Good Business Letter

Brian Green

1   A good business letter is one that gets results. The best way to get results is to develop a letter that, in its appearance, style, and content, conveys information efficiently. To perform this function, a business letter should be concise, clear, and courteous.

2   The business letter must be concise. Little introduction or preliminary chat is necessary. Get to the point, make the point, and leave it. It is safe to assume that your letter is being read by a very busy person with all kinds of paper to deal with. Such a person does not want to spend time on a newsy letter about your ski trip or medical problem. Hone and refine your message until the words and sentences you have used are precise. Revision and rereading take time but are a necessary part of writing a good letter. A short business letter that makes its point quickly has much more impact on a reader than a long-winded, rambling exercise in creative writing. This does not mean that there is no place for style or even, on occasion, humour in the business letter. While it conveys a message in its contents, the letter also provides the reader with an impression of you, its author. Your style is part of the message.

3   The business letter must be clear. You should have a firm idea of what you want to say, and you should let the reader know it. Use the structure of the letter—the paragraphs, topic sentences, and transitions—to guide the reader point by point from your introduction, through your reasoning, to your conclusion. Paragraph often, to break up the page and to provide visual cues to the organization of your letter. Use an accepted business-letter format. There are several, and they can be found in any book of business English. Reread what you have written from the point of view of someone who is seeing it for the first time, and revise to be sure that all

necessary information is provided (including reference numbers, dates, and other identification) and that all explanations are clear. A clear message, clearly delivered, is the essence of business communication.

4   The business letter must be courteous. Sarcasm and insults are ineffective and can often work against you. If you are sure you are right, point out the fact as politely as possible, explain why you are right, and outline what you expect the reader to do. Always put yourself in the place of the person to whom you are writing. What sort of letter would you respond to? How effective would sarcasm and threats be in making you fulfill a request? Another form of courtesy is taking care in your writing or typing. Grammatical and spelling errors (even if you call them typing errors) tell a reader that you don't think enough of him or her to be careful. Such mistakes can lower the reader's opinion of you faster than anything you say, no matter how idiotic. There are excuses for ignorance; there are no excuses for sloppiness.

5   The business letter is your custom-made representative. It speaks for you and is a permanent record of your message. It can pay big dividends on the time you invest in giving it a concise message, a clear structure, and a courteous tone.

What I Have Lived For

Bertrand Russell

1   Three passions, simple but overwhelmingly strong, have governed my life: the longing for love, the search for knowledge, and unbearable pity for the suffering of mankind. These passions, like great winds, have blown me hither and thither, in a wayward course, over a deep ocean of anguish, reaching to the very verge of despair.

2   I have sought love, first, because it brings ecstasy—ecstasy so great that I would often have sacrificed all the rest of life for a few hours of this joy. I have sought it, next, because it relieves loneliness—that terrible loneliness in which one shivering consciousness looks over the rim of the world into the cold unfathomable lifeless abyss. I have sought it, finally, because in the union of love I have seen, in a mystic miniature, the prefiguring vision of the heaven that saints and poets have imagined. This is what I sought, and though it might seem too good for human life, this is what—at last— I have found.

3   With equal passion I have sought knowledge. I have wished to under- stand the hearts of men. I have wished to know why the stars shine. And I have tried to apprehend the Pythagorean power by which number holds sway above the flux. A little of this, but not much, I have achieved.

4   Love and knowledge, so far as they were possible, led upward toward the heavens. But always pity brought me back to earth. Echoes of cries of pain reverberate in my heart. Children in famine, victims tortured by op- pressors, helpless old people a hated burden to their sons, and the whole world of loneliness, poverty, and pain make a mockery of what human life should be. I long to alleviate the evil, but I cannot, and I too suffer.

5   This has been my life. I have found it worth living, and would gladly live it again if the chance were offered me.

From Bertrand Russell, *The Autobiography of Bertrand Russell*. Reprinted with permission of Routledge, on behalf of Bertrand Russell Peace Foundation.

Flunking with Style

Nell Waldman

1   People often remark that succeeding in school takes plenty of hard work. The remark implies that failure is a product of general idleness and zero motivation. This is an opinion I'd like to challenge. My long and checkered past in numerous educational institutions has taught me that to fail grandly, to fail extravagantly, to go down in truly blazing splendour, requires effort and imagination. To fail your year in the grand style, you must antagonize your teachers, disdain your studies, and cheat on your work. Keep the following guidelines in mind.

2   The first step, antagonizing your teachers, isn't difficult if you keep in mind what it is that teachers like: intelligent, interested, even enthusiastic faces in front row centre. Show that you're bored before the class begins by slouching in a desk at the back of the room. Wear your Walkman, and don't forget to turn up the volume when the teacher starts to talk. Carry on running conversations with your seatmates. Aim an occasional snort or snicker in the teacher's direction when she's putting a complex point on the board. Above all, never volunteer an answer and respond sullenly with an "I dunno" if the teacher has the nerve to ask you a question. Before long, you'll have that teacher bouncing chalk stubs off your head. Once you've earned the loathing of your instructors, you'll be well on your way to a truly memorable failure.

3   The second step, disdaining your studies, is easy to master. They're probably B-O-R-I-N-G anyway. First, don't buy your books until close to midterm and keep them in their original condition; don't open, read, or note anything in them. Better yet, don't buy your texts at all. Second, never attempt to take notes in class. Third, stop going to class completely, but have lots of creative excuses for missed assignments: "My friend's aunt died"; "My gerbil's in a coma"; "My boyfriend was in another car wreck"; "My dog ate the lab report"; "I've got mono." You can bet your teachers will be really amused by these old standbys. By now you are well on your way to disaster.

4   The third step, cheating, will deliver the *coup de grâce* to your academic career. Should an instructor be so sadistic as to assign a research paper, just copy something out of a book that the librarian will be happy to find for you. Your instructor will be astonished at the difference between the book's polished professional prose and your usual halting scrawls; you're guaranteed a zero. During your exams, sit at the back and crane your neck to read your classmate's paper. Roll up your shirtsleeves to reveal the answers you've tattooed all over your forearms. Ask to be excused three or four times during the test so you can consult the notes you've stashed in the hall or the washroom. Be bold! Dig out your old wood-burning kit and emblazon cheat

notes on the desk. If you want to ensure not just failure but actual expulsion, send in a ringer—a look-alike—to write the exam for you!

5   If you follow these guidelines, you will be guaranteed to flunk your year. Actively courting failure with verve, with flair, and with a sense of drama will not only ensure your status as an academic washout but will also immortalize you in the memories of teachers and classmates alike. The challenge is yours. Become a legend—pick up the torch and fall with it!

From Sarah Norton and Nell Waldman, eds., *Canadian Content* (Toronto: Holt, 1988).

Surviving Your Daughter's Adolescence

Janet Read

1   Living with a teenage daughter can cause friction in an otherwise peaceful home. To survive the years of turbulence, you may find it helpful to observe three basic rules: never criticize, never say "No," and never argue. Observing these rules does not mean the teen will always get her own way, but the right words in the right place can turn a potential confrontation into a calm discussion.

2   For a loving mother, the first rule can be extremely difficult. When your beautiful daughter appears at the breakfast table looking as if she were going into combat instead of into class, it will not be easy for you to offer a compliment. Take a deep breath, count to three, and tell her in a convincing tone how much you like her sporty new outfit. A compliment may make her wonder if battle gear is really the look she wants to achieve. After all, if Mom likes it, how can her friends be expected to approve? Don't be surprised if she leaves for school looking almost presentable. In any event, you can be sure that three-quarters of the student population looks just like your child. If all else fails, remember your class picture of 1966.

3   When you are trying to keep peace, the next rule is never to give a negative reply. This simply means that you never say an outright "No." Her request may seem preposterous to you, but not to a fourteen-year-old. During this period in your child's life, peer pressure is the most difficult thing for her to deal with. Often the request—to go to the dance club, for instance—is coming indirectly from her friends. Instead of immediately blurting out the N-word, try to find out her reasons for feeling her life will be over if she can't attend this one event. The strategy may turn your basement into a substitute Palace Pier for an evening, but it will give you peace of mind.

4   Finally we come to the hardest rule for a parent to follow: don't, under any circumstances, argue. Females between the ages of thirteen and eighteen are world-class debaters. They can argue black is white, rain is snow, or bitter is sweet. The most hazardous time is the period when your baby of a few short years ago is learning to drive. She will become, after only two driving lessons, an authority on rules of the road. We have all coped with back-seat drivers, but nothing will have prepared you for this experience. The teenager feels a learner's permit is a licence to tell her parents how to drive. There are a few useful phrases you can employ to reduce the risk of argument: "Yes, dear." "Is that right?" "How astute of you to notice that!" These simple phrases can forestall an argument that would entertain your entire neighbourhood.

5   I am not trying to give the impression that faithful observance of these three rules will mean your daughter's teenage years will be clear sailing all the time. They can, however, make the waters of adolescence a lot calmer.

Student Janet Read wrote this essay in her first term of college.

An Immigrant's Split Personality

Sun-Kyung Yi

1   I am Korean-Canadian. But the hyphen often snaps in two, obliging me to choose to act as either a Korean or a Canadian, depending on where I am and who I'm with.

2   When I was younger, toying with the idea of entertaining two separate identities was a real treat, like a secret game for which no one knew the rules but me. I was known as Angela to the outside world, and as Sun-Kyung at home. I ate bologna sandwiches in the school lunch room and rice and kim-chee for dinner. I chatted about teen idols and giggled with my girlfriends during my classes, and ambitiously practiced piano and studied in the evenings, planning to become a doctor when I grew up. I waved hellos and goodbyes to my teachers, but bowed to my parents' friends visiting our home. I could also look straight in the eyes of my teachers and friends and talk frankly with them instead of staring at my feet with my mouth shut when Koreans talked to me. Going outside the home meant I was able to relax from the constraints of my cultural conditioning, until I walked back in the door and had to return to being an obedient and submissive daughter.

3   The game soon ended when I realized that it had become a way of life, that I couldn't change the rules without disappointing my parents and questioning all the cultural implications and consequences that came with being a hyphenated Canadian.

4   Many have tried to convince me that I am a Canadian, like all other im-migrants in the country, but those same people also ask me which coun-try I came from with great curiosity, following with questions about the type of food I ate and the language I spoke. It's difficult to feel a sense of belonging and acceptance when you are regarded as "one of them." "Those Koreans, they work hard. . . . You must be fantastic at math and science." (No.) "Do your parents own a corner store?" (No.)

5   Koreans and Canadians just can't seem to merge into "us" and "we."

6   Some people advised me that I should just take the best of both worlds and disregard the rest. That's ideal, but unrealistic when my old culture demands a complete conformity with very little room to manoeuvre for new and different ideas.

7   After a lifetime of practice, I thought I could change faces and become Korean on demand with grace and perfection. But working with a small Korean company in Toronto proved me wrong. I quickly became estranged from my own people. My parents were ecstatic at the thought of their daughter finally finding her roots and having a working opportunity to speak my native tongue and absorb the culture. For me, it was the most painful and frustrating 2½ months of my life.

8   When the president of the company boasted that he "operated little Korea," he meant it literally. A Canadianized Korean was not tolerated. I looked like a Korean; therefore, I had to talk, act, and think like one, too.

Being accepted meant a total surrender to ancient codes of behaviour rooted in Confucian thought, while leaving the "Canadian" part of me out in the parking lot with my '86 Buick. In the first few days at work, I was bombarded with inquiries about my marital status. When I told them I was single, they spent the following days trying to match me up with available bachelors in the company and the community. I was expected to accept my inferior position as a woman and had to behave accordingly. It was not a place to practice my feminist views, or be an individual without being condemned. Little Korea is a place for men (who filled all the senior positions) and women don't dare speak up or disagree with their male counterparts. The president (all employees bow to him and call him Mr. President) asked me to act more like a lady and smile. I was openly scorned by a senior employee because I spoke more fluent English than Korean. The cook in the kitchen shook her head in disbelief upon discovering that my cooking skills were limited to boiling a package of instant noodles. "You want a good husband, learn to cook," she advised me.

9   In less than a week I became an outsider because I refused to conform and blindly nod my head in agreement to what my elders (which happened to be everybody else in the company) said. A month later, I was demoted because "members of the workplace and the Korean community" had complained that I just wasn't "Korean enough," and I had "too much power for a single woman." My father suggested that "when in Rome do as the Romans." But that's exactly what I was doing. I am in Canada so I was freely acting like a Canadian, and it cost me my job.

10   My father also said, "It doesn't matter how Canadian you think you are, just look in the mirror and it'll tell you who you *really* are." But what he didn't realize is that an immigrant has to embrace the new culture to enjoy and benefit from what it has to offer. Of course, I will always be Korean by virtue of my appearance and early conditioning, but I am also happily Canadian and want to take full advantage of all that such citizenship confers. But for now I remain slightly distant from both cultures, accepted fully by neither. The hyphenated Canadian personifies the ideal of multiculturalism, but unless the host culture and the immigrant cultures can find ways to merge their distinct identities, sharing the best of both, this cultural schizophrenia will continue.

Sun-Kyung Yi, "An Immigrant's Split Personality," *The Globe and Mail*, 12 April 1992. Reprinted with permission of the author. Sun-Kyung Yi is a writer-broadcaster in Toronto. Her documentaries about immigration and multiculturalism have been broadcast on CBC television and radio.

The Myth of Canadian Diversity

1   Canadians cling to three myths about their country. The first is that it is young. In fact, Canada is well advanced into middle age. At 127, it has existed as a unified state for longer than either Italy (unified in 1870) or Germany (1871). Less than a third of the 180-odd nations now belonging to the United Nations existed in 1945, when Canada was already a mature 78. We were 51 when Iraq and Austria—two countries many think of as old—came into being.

2   The second myth is that, in everything but geography, Canada is a small country—small in population, small in economic heft. In fact, our population of 27 million is a fair size by international standards, bigger than that of Austria, Hungary, Sweden, Norway, Finland, Romania, Greece, Algeria, Peru and Venezuela, to name only a few. Our economy, by traditional measures, is the seventh-largest in the world.

3   But the most important myth about Canada—the one that distorts our self-image, warps our politics and may one day tear us apart—is the myth of Canadian diversity. Almost any Canadian will tell you that his Canada is a remarkably varied place. "Canada, with its regional, linguistic and cultural diversity, has never been easy to govern," wrote *The Globe and Mail* when Jean Chrétien became Prime Minister last fall. Provincial politicians routinely parrot this myth to push for greater regional powers; federal politicians repeat it to let people know what a hard job they have.

4   In fact, Canada is one of the most homogeneous countries in the world. A foreign visitor can travel from Vancouver in the West to Kingston in the centre without finding any significant difference in accent, in dress, in cuisine or even, in a broad sense, in values. A highschool student in Winnipeg talks, looks and acts much like his counterpart in Prince George. Where they do exist, our regional differences are no match for those of most other countries.

5   Canada may have a few regional accents in its English-speaking parts— the salty dialect of Newfoundland, the rural tones of the Ottawa Valley— but these are nothing compared with the dozens in the United States or Britain. It may have two official languages, but that is unlikely to impress India, which has 14.

6   To be certain, we have our French–English divide, two "nations" living under one roof. That hardly makes us unique either. Spain has the Catalans and the Basques. Russia has the Tatars, Ukrainians, Belarussians, Chechens, Moldavians, Udmurts, Kazakhs, Avars and Armenians. And, although few would dispute that francophone Quebec is indeed a distinct society, the differences between Quebec and the rest of Canada are diminishing over time. As Lucien Bouchard himself has noted, we share a host of common attitudes—an attachment to the Canadian social system, tolerance of minorities, a respect for government and law.

7   Even our much-discussed ethnic differences are overstated. Although Canada is an immigrant nation and Canadians spring from a variety of backgrounds, a recent study from the C.D. Howe Institute says that the idea of a "Canadian mosaic"—as distinct from the American "melting pot"—is a fallacy. In *The Illusion of Difference*, University of Toronto sociologists Jeffrey Reitz and Raymond Breton show that immigrants to Canada assimilate as quickly into the mainstream society as immigrants to the United States do. In fact, Canadians are less likely than Americans to favour holding on to cultural differences based on ethnic background. If you don't believe Mr. Reitz and Mr. Breton, visit any big-city highschool, where the speech and behaviour of immigrant students just a few years in Canada is indistinguishable from that of any fifth-generation classmate.

8   This is not to say that Canada is a nation of cookie-cutter people. The differences among our regions, and between our two main language groups, are real. But in recent years we have elevated those differences into a cult. For all our disputes about language and ethnicity and regional rifts, our differences shrink beside our similarities, and the things that unite us dwarf those that divide us.

"The Myth of Canadian Diversity," *The Globe and Mail*, 13 June 1994, A12. Reprinted with permission of *The Globe and Mail*.

List of Grammatical Terms

adjective   a word that modifies (describes, restricts, relates to, makes more precise) a noun or pronoun. Adjectives answer the questions **What kind? How many? Which?**—e.g., the *competent* student; *five* home runs; my *last* class.

adverb   a word that modifies a verb, adjective, or other adverb. Adverbs answer the questions **When? How? Where? Why? How much?**—e.g., Nino talks *fast* (*fast* modifies the verb *talks*); he is a *very* fast talker (*very* modifies the adjective *fast*); he talks *really* fast (*really* modifies the adverb *fast*). Adverbs often—but not always—end in *-ly.*

antecedent   the word that a pronoun refers to or stands for. Literally, it means "coming before, preceding." The antecedent usually comes before the pronoun that refers to it—e.g., *Karen* believes *she* is possessed. (*Karen* is the antecedent to which the pronoun *she* refers.)

clause   a group of words that contains a subject and a verb. If the group of words can stand by itself and makes complete sense, it is called an **independent clause** (or **principal clause** or **main clause**). If the group of words does not make complete sense on its own but is linked to another clause (depends on the other clause for its meaning), it is called a **dependent** or **subordinate clause.** Here's an example: *The porch collapsed.* This group of words can stand by itself, so it is called an independent clause.

Now consider: ***When Kalim removed the railing with his tractor.*** This group of words has a subject, ***Kalim,*** and a verb, ***removed,*** but it does not make complete sense on its own. It depends for its meaning on ***the porch collapsed;*** therefore, it is a dependent clause.

colloquialism   a word or phrase that we use in casual conversation or in informal writing.

> Steve *flunked* his accounting exam.
> ***Did*** you *get* what the teacher said about job placement?
> I can't believe that *guy* is serious about learning.

comma splice   the error that results when the writer joins two independent clauses with a comma—e.g., ***The comma splice is an error, it is a kind of run-on sentence.*** (See Chapter 7.)

dependent-clause cue   a word or phrase that introduces a dependent clause—e.g., ***when, because, in order that, as soon as.*** See p. 52.

modifier   a word or group of words that adds information about another word (or phrase or clause) in a sentence. See ***adjective, adverb, dependent clause,*** and Chapter 8.

noun   a word that names a person, place, or thing and that has the grammatical capability of being possessive. There are concrete nouns that are **proper** (*Calgary, Beijing, Gaza, January, Sharon*); **common** (*woman, man, city, car, animal*); and **collective** (*group, audience, swarm, jury, committee*). There are also **abstract** nouns (*truth, softness, pride, confidence*). Unlike their concrete cousins, abstract nouns refer to concepts, ideas, characteristics—things we know or experience through our intellect rather than through our senses.

object   the "receiving" part of a sentence. The **direct object** is a noun or noun substitute (pronoun, phrase, or clause) that is the target or receiver of the action expressed by the verb. It answers the question **what?** or **whom?**—e.g., John threw the *ball.* (John threw *what?*)

> He wondered *where the money went.* (He wondered *what?*)
> Munira loves *Abdul.* (Munira loves *whom?*)

The **indirect object** is a noun or pronoun that is the indirect target or receiver of the action expressed by the verb in a sentence. It is *always* placed in front of the direct object. It answers the question **to whom?** or **to what?**

> Doug threw *me* the ball. (Doug threw *to whom?*)
> Lisa forgot to give *her* essay a title. (Give *to what?*)

The **object of a preposition** is a noun or noun substitute (pronoun, phrase, or clause) that follows a preposition—e.g., after the *storm* (*storm* is a noun, object of the preposition *after*); before *signing* the lease (*signing the lease* is a phrase, object of the preposition *before*); he thought about *what he wanted to do* (*what he wanted to do* is a clause, object of the preposition *about*). Notice that what follows a preposition is always its object; that is why the subject of a sentence or clause can never be found in a prepositional phrase.

participle   the form of a verb that can be used as an adjective (the *completed* work, the *weeping* willows) or as part of a verb phrase (am *succeeding,* have *rented*).

> The **present participle** of a verb ends in **-ing.**
> The **past participle** of a **regular verb** ends in **-d** or in **-ed.** For a list of **irregular verbs,** see pp. 100-103.

person   a category of pronouns and verbs. **First person** refers to the person who is speaking (*I, we*). **Second person** refers to the person being spoken to (*you*). **Third person** is the person or thing being spoken about (*he, she, it, they*). Verb forms remain constant except in the present tense third person singular, which ends in *s.*

phrase   a group of meaning-related words that acts as a noun, a verb, an adjective, or an adverb within a sentence. Phrases do not make complete sense on their own because they do not contain both a subject and a verb.

> Please order *legal-size manila file folders.* (phrase acting as noun)
> I *must have been sleeping* when you called. (verb phrase)
> *Sightseeing in Ottawa,* we photographed the monuments on *Parliament Hill.* (phrases acting as adjectives)
> Portaging a canoe *in this weather* is no fun. (phrase acting as adverb)

prefix   a meaningful letter or group of letters added to the beginning of a word either (1) to change its meaning or (2) to change its word class.

> 1. **a** + moral = amoral
>   **bi** + sexual = bisexual
>   **contra** + indication = contraindication
>   **dys** + functional = dysfunctional
> 2. **a** + board (noun) = aboard (adverb, preposition)
>   **con** + temporary (adjective) = contemporary (noun, adjective)
>   **de** + nude (noun, adjective) = denude (verb)
>   **in** + put (verb) = input (noun)

Some prefixes require a hyphen, as here:

> **all**-Canadian
> **de**-emphasize
> **mid**-morning

preposition   a word that connects a noun, pronoun, or phrase to some other word(s) in a sentence. The noun, pronoun, or phrase is the **object** of the preposition.

> I prepared the minutes *of the union meeting.* (*of* relates *meeting* to *minutes*)
> One *of the parents* checks the children every half hour. (**of** relates *parents* to *One*)

prepositional phrase	a group of grammatically related words having the function of a noun, adjective, or adverb and beginning with a preposition. See the list on p. 44.
pronoun	a word that is noun-like. Pronouns usually substitute for nouns, but sometimes they substitute for other pronouns.

> *He* will promote *anything that* brings in money.
> *Everyone* must earn *her* badges.

There are several kinds of pronouns:

> **personal:** *I, we; you; he, she, it, they; me, us; him, her, them*
> **possessive:** *my, our; your; his, her, its, their*
> **demonstrative:** *this, these; that, those*
> **relative:** *who, whom, whose; which, that*
> **interrogative:** *who? whose? whom? which? what?*
> **indefinite:** all *-one, -thing, -body* pronouns, such as *everyone, something,* and *anybody; each; neither; either; few; none; several*

subject	in a sentence, the person, thing, or concept that the sentence is about—the topic of the sentence (see Chapter 12). In an essay, what the paper is about—the topic of the paper (see Chapter 22).
suffix	a letter or group of letters that is added to the end of a word (1) to change its meaning, (2) to change its grammatical function, or (3) to change its word class.

1. king + *dom* = kingdom
   few + *er* = fewer
   tooth + *less* = toothless
2. buy (base form) + *s* = buys (third person singular, present tense)
   eat (base form) + *en* = eaten (past participle)
   instructor + *s* = instructors (plural)
   instructor + *'s* = instructor's (possessive singular)
3. your (adjective) + *s* = yours (pronoun)
   act (verb) + *ive* = active (adjective)
   active (adjective) + *ly* = actively (adverb)
   ventilate (verb) + *tion* = ventilation (noun)

Some words add two or more prefixes and/or suffixes to the base form. Look at *antidisestablishmentarianism,* for example. How many prefixes and suffixes can you identify?

tense	The different forms of the verb used to indicate past, present, or future time are called **tenses.** The verb ending (e.g., play*s,* play*ed*) and any helping verbs associated with the main verb (*is* playing, *will* play, *has* played, *had* played, *will have* played) indicate the tense of the verb.

There are simple tenses:	**present:** *ask, asks*
	past: *asked*
	future: *will ask*
and perfect tenses:	**present:** *have (has) asked*
	past: *had asked*
	future: *will (shall) have asked*

The simple and perfect tenses can also be **progressive:** *am asking, have been asking,* etc.

transition   a word or phrase that helps readers to follow the text smoothly from one sentence to the next or from one paragraph to another. See Chapter 25.

verb   a word or phrase that says something about a person, place, or thing and whose form may be changed to indicate tense. Verbs may make a statement, ask a question, or give commands. They may express action (physical or mental), occurrence, or condition (state of being).

> Wesley *hit* an inside curve for a home run. (physical action)
> Laurence *believed* the Blue Jays would win. (mental action)
> Father's Day *falls* on the first Sunday of June. (occurrence)
> Reva eventually *became* interested in English. (condition)

Some verbs are called **linking verbs:** they help to make a statement by linking the subject to a word or phrase that describes it.

> William Hubbard *was* Toronto's first Black mayor. (*was* links *William Hubbard* to *mayor*)
> Mohammed *looks* tired. (*looks* links *Mohammed* and *tired*)

In addition to *am, is, are, was, were,* and *been,* some common linking verbs are *appear, become, feel, grow, look, taste, remain, seem, smell, sound.*

Another class of verbs is called **auxiliary** or **helping verbs.** They show the time of a verb as future or past (*will* go, *has* gone), or as a continuing action (*is* reading). They also show the passive voice (*is* completed, *have been* submitted).

voice   verbs may be **active** or **passive,** depending on whether the subject of the verb is *acting* (active voice) or *being acted upon* (passive voice).

> In 1995, the Liberal government *introduced* another set of tax reforms. (active)
> Another set of tax reforms *was introduced* in 1995. (passive)

Answers to Exercises

Answers for Chapter 1: Three Suggestions for Quick Improvement (Pages 3 to 11)

Exercise 1.1
1. *blonde.* No, they are not interchangeable. A *blond* is a male; a *blonde* is a female.
2. *humor.* You must use the root *humor* when adding an ending: e.g., *humorous.*
3. The word is spelled *tattoo* and can be used both as a noun and as a verb.
4. *Ketchup* is the preferred spelling of the word, which can also be spelled *catchup* and *catsup.*
5. *program, theater, center, medieval, judgment.* The preferred spellings are *program, theatre, centre, medieval,* and *judgment.*

Exercise 1.2
1. echoes
2. ratios
3. criteria
4. ghettos
5. personnel
6. crises
7. data (the singular is datum)
8. phenomena
9. nuclei (*or* nucleuses)
10. appendixes (*or* appendices)

Exercise 1.4
1. boring
2. movement
3. scarcely
4. unusable
5. careful
6. advertisement
7. excusable
8. providing
9. sensible
10. improvement

Exercise 1.5
1. safety
2. ranging
3. reducible
4. balancing
5. entirely
6. insurance
7. definitely
8. careless
9. responsible
10. distancing

Exercise 1.6
1. suffering
2. quizzed
3. permitting
4. stripped
5. meeting
6. compelling
7. cropped
8. tipping
9. allotting
10. quartered

Exercise 1.7
1. overlapped
2. expelling
3. barred
4. acquitted
5. focusing
6. excelling
7. developed
8. transferred
9. paralleled
10. rebelling

Exercise 1.8
1. occurrence
2. existence
3. coherence
4. concurring
5. interfering
6. subsistence
7. difference
8. dependence
9. recurrence
10. insistence

Exercise 1.9
1. chow mein, stein
2. Neither, Geiger counter
3. neighbour, niece
4. beige, leisure
5. conceivable, either

Answers for Chapter 2: Sound-Alikes, Look-Alikes, and Spoilers (Pages 12 to 22)

Exercise 2.1
1. It's, women
2. later, except
3. there, peace, our
4. than, morals
5. Where, we're
6. hear, you're, chose, course
7. whose, advice
8. advice, personal, it's
9. their, moral
10. principal, peace, minor

Exercise 2.2
1. are, conscious
2. affected, personal
3. then, excepted
4. loose, accept
5. it's, principle
6. minors, they're, they're
7. chose, dining
8. than, our
9. too, coarse, to
10. hear, your

Exercise 2.3
  Led by my desire to watch more television **than** the six or seven hours a day I normally viewed, I decided to subscribe to satellite TV. The **effect** of this move

was **later** to prove detrimental to my health and my wealth. First, I did not know that **there** is a monthly subscription fee in addition to the initial purchase price of almost $1000 for the "unobtrusive pizza-sized **stationary** dish antenna." Second, I was **quite** surprised to find that I was able to get many "pay-per-view" programs in addition to the basic 40 available stations. I was even more surprised to discover how fast I was running up a bill by **choosing** to view these optional programs. To restore my **peace** of mind, not to mention my bank balance, I telephoned the satellite service **personnel** to request that they limit my monthly spending for pay-per-view programs. Seven hockey games, four basketball games, **two** movies, six music specials, and an award ceremony **later**, my TV screen informed me that I had reached my spending limit. I'm afraid I responded with a few **coarse** expressions, since I was all set to see a new fine **dining** show on exotic **desserts** featuring papaya as the **principal** ingredient. Then, my TV screen informed me I could override my limit simply by pressing "star." I did, and went on watching with a clear **conscience** since, after all, I had limited my spending. In addition to **its effect** on my budget, satellite service caused me to **lose** what little muscle tone I had left, since the only times I left the couch were to go **forth** to the kitchen for more food. The **moral** of my sad story is that **you're** probably better off with less choice and poorer quality on **your** TV than in **your** life.

Answers for Chapter 3: Capital Letters (Pages 23 to 26)

Exercise 3.1
1. **D**iana always wanted to be a **p**rincess when she grew up.
2. It amazes me that anyone could think *Beavis and Butthead* is funny.
3. Beatrix, queen of **T**he **N**etherlands, visited Canada last **w**inter.
4. The **R**otary **C**lub of Halifax sponsors a scholarship to **D**alhousie University.
5. Gina tries hard, but she'll never be as good at **d**ata **p**rocessing as Ravi.
6. *Black Robe* was a Canadian-made film that featured international stars as well as young **C**anadian actors.
7. I should be looking for a sensible **s**edan, but I'm tempted by the **s**ports **m**odels every time I visit the GM, **F**ord, or **H**onda dealer.
8. I wonder how the **c**ollege gets away with requiring us students to take English and mathematics in addition to our **m**ajor subjects.
9. We were late for **P**rofessor Chan's lecture on **t**ime **m**anagement.
10. Stock is running low, so if you need **X**erox paper or toner, you'd better see Carla in **O**ffice **S**upplies right away.

Exercise 3.2
1. My **m**other and **f**ather drive **s**outh each **f**all to look at the leaves.
2. Ali went with his **E**nglish class to the Calgary **S**tampede and then to the West **E**dmonton **M**all.
3. Alain took a **G**reyhound bus to the **c**oast and then a ferry to Prince Edward Island.
4. Her parents thought they were seeing Gina off to **u**niversity, but in fact she spent the **w**inter in Mexico.
5. I've always wanted to be a **p**ope, but, unfortunately, I am not **I**talian, **C**atholic, or male.
6. Luc went to Paris last **s**ummer to study **F**rench, art history, and gourmet cooking.
7. Although I am generally fairly **c**onservative, I consider myself a **l**iberal on matters such as abortion and gun control.
8. Clement works for **B**ell **C**anada, which has an office on Bayview **A**venue.

9. After the **b**aseball and **h**ockey seasons were cancelled, Sabina became a **b**asketball fan and now is devoted to the **R**aptors.
10. A letter to the **e**ditor in today's *Globe and Mail* says Jean Chrétien's claim to fame is that "he is the only Canadian **p**rime **m**inister to have mastered neither of the country's two **o**fficial **l**anguages."

Exercise 3.3
1. Since you have yet to pass a single **p**hysics or **m**ath course, I suggest you reconsider your decision to be an **e**ngineer.
2. As the official representative of **Q**ueen Elizabeth, Canada's **g**overnor **g**eneral opens each new session of **p**arliament.
3. During the **s**pring break, Saieed drove down to **F**lorida, where he toured **W**alt **D**isney **W**orld, the **E**pcot **C**enter, and Busch **G**ardens.
4. The Quebec **p**remier influences not only the policies of his own **p**rovince, but also those of the rest of Canada.
5. After Clive missed the meeting, the **p**resident told him angrily, "**T**hat, young **m**an, was what is called a CLM: a career-limiting move."
6. Visitors to Canada are sometimes surprised to find they cannot see the **R**ockies, Niagara **F**alls, Newfoundland, and the arctic **t**undra all in one week.
7. We stopped at **S**afeway for the basics: spaghetti, milk, a box of **K**ellogg's cornflakes, and a tube of **C**rest.
8. Canada's **I**mmigration **A**ct sets out the policies that govern the conditions for entry into the **c**ountry by immigrants from all over the **w**orld.
9. We went to see Atom Egoyan's film *Exotica*, which was playing at the **C**apitol theatre.
10. Among Canada's great waterways, the St. Lawrence **R**iver, the Mackenzie **R**iver, the Fraser **R**iver, and the **R**ed **R**iver are the most interesting to me because of the role each played in developing our **n**ation.

Answers for Chapter 4: The Apostrophe (Pages 27 to 34)

Exercise 4.1
1. you're
2. we'd
3. they'll
4. can't
5. I'll
6. didn't
7. shouldn't
8. could've
9. who'd
10. everybody's

Exercise 4.2
1. can't
2. she'd
3. didn't
4. let's
5. she'll
6. wouldn't
7. we'd
8. they're
9. won't
10. he'll

Exercise 4.3
1. **We'll** have to postpone the meeting because **they're** still not here.
2. If Krystal finds out **what's** been going on, **she'll** be furious.
3. **It's** been a long time since **we've** had a break, **hasn't** it?
4. **We're** still about 10 km away from where **they'd** planned to meet us.
5. **It's** a tough decision, but **somebody's** got to make it, or **we'll** never get out of here.

6. Hockey is Canada's most popular game, so **I'm** surprised to learn **it's** not our official national sport.
7. **Everyone's** welcome, but if **you're** all coming, **we'd** better buy another keg.
8. **He's** offered to drive all those **who're** going to the game.
9. **Let's** first find out **who's** coming; then **we'll** know if **we've** bought enough to go around.
10. **You'll** have to wait until **he's** sure you **haven't** brought along someone **who's** under age.

Exercise 4.4
1. woman's
2. technicians'
3. the Simpsons'
4. management's
5. workers'
6. someone's
7. Iguassu Falls' (or Iguassu Falls's)
8. memo's
9. babies'
10. Dennis's (or Dennis')

Exercise 4.5
1. **Biff's** favourite pastime is spending his **girlfriend's** money.
2. **Whose** fault is it that the **car's** tank is empty?
3. After about one **second's** hesitation, I accepted a **week's** pay instead of time off.
4. **Bikers'** equipment is on special at **Leather Larry's**.
5. Virtue may be **its** own reward, but I won't refuse **your** offer of cash.
6. Our college aims to meet its **students'** social needs as well as **their** academic goals.
7. To **no one's** surprise, the **children's** scores were higher than ours on every game we tried.
8. The traditional male dominance in medicine and law is disappearing as **women's** acceptance into these programs now exceeds **men's**.
9. The **college's** climate survey revealed that most **students'** opinion of their program is positive.
10. **The United States'** vast wealth makes some Canadians wonder whether it is worth maintaining our **country's** independence.

Exercise 4.6
1. **Mei-ling's** paper got a better grade than **Louis's**.
2. **Gordie Howe's** record may eventually fall, but his **career's** achievements will never be surpassed.
3. Alicia gave one **month's** notice before leaving her position as **children's** wear buyer for **Eaton's**.
4. After the **union's** strike threat, the **owners'** solution was to lock out the players for the rest of the season.
5. One of **Toronto's** landmarks is **Honest Ed's** store at the corner of Bloor and Bathurst.
6. Canadian **authors'** works are increasingly recommended by the **Ministry of Education's** curriculum planners.
7. **Cassandra's** fate was probably more miserable than **anyone's**, including **Achilles'**.
8. Our **group's** presentation was on **Davies'** *Fifth Business,* while **theirs** was on **Yeats's** early poetry.
9. The **survey's** results were not surprising: more than half the voters surveyed were unhappy with **their MP's** performance.

10. **Dorothy Parker's** solution to boredom was to hang a sign on her office door reading "**Men's** Room."

Exercise 4.7

1. **Today's** popular music is returning to the sounds and themes of its roots in the sixties.
2. Our government is not serious about solving its financial problems; in fact, **it's** getting deeper and deeper into debt.
3. **Charles's** feelings about **Diana's** book are well-known, but who knows what **Camilla's** thoughts are?
4. A **patient's** fears can be eased by a sensitive **nurse's** attention.
5. The girls won the **cheater's** money in **Luisa's father's** poker game.
6. The **speaker's** topic was well beyond our **class's** ability to understand.
7. We were told to read Northrop **Frye's** essay, "**Don't** You Think **It's** Time to Start Thinking?" for **tomorrow's** class.
8. In the paper today, **there's** a short article entitled, "**It's** Clear the **Apostrophe's** Days are Numbered, **Isn't** It?"
9. At her **wits'** end, the angry mother turned to her daughter and shouted, "**Who're** you to tell me what **you'll** do and **won't** do?"
10. **The Crash Test Dummies'** first major hit was the off-beat "**Superman's** Song"; in contrast, their award-winning *God Shuffled His Feet* features Brad **Roberts'** songs, which are rich in symbolism and insight.

Answers for Chapter 5: Cracking the Sentence Code (Pages 37 to 47)

Exercise 5.1

1. <u>Algy</u> <u>met</u>
2. <u>bear</u> <u>met</u>
3. <u>bear</u> <u>was</u>
4. <u>bulge</u> <u>was</u>
5. <u>Grizzlies</u> <u>are</u>

6. <u>Meeting</u> . . . <u>is</u>
7. <u>bears</u> . . . <u>run</u>
8. (<u>You</u>) <u>take</u> it from me. <u>They</u> <u>do</u>.
9. <u>Females</u> . . . <u>are known</u>
10. <u>Defending</u> . . . <u>presents</u>

Exercise 5.2

1. <u>Change</u> <u>is</u> the only constant in life.
2. <u>Information</u> <u>doubles</u> every 18 months.
3. Our <u>survival</u> <u>depends</u> on our ability to adapt to change.
4. Today, effective <u>planning</u> <u>means</u> training for change.
5. Otherwise, <u>we</u> <u>risk</u> becoming roadkill on the highway of life.
6. <u>Learning</u> to adapt to change <u>is</u>, therefore, everyone's challenge.
7. <u>Silicon</u>, a form of sand, <u>is</u> a computer chip's main component.
8. To get ahead in the 90s, <u>people</u> <u>need</u> knowledge from many fields.
9. Soon, a single <u>crystal</u> <u>will hold</u> the entire Library of Congress catalogue.
10. Ironically, high <u>technology</u> <u>is</u> now our forests' best friend.

Exercise 5.3

1. <u>Canada</u> <u>is</u>
2. <u>word</u> . . . <u>means</u>
3. <u>Newfoundland</u> <u>is</u>
4. <u>Are</u> <u>you</u>
5. <u>is</u> . . . <u>CN Tower</u>

6. <u>Money</u> . . . <u>does</u>
7. <u>are</u> . . . <u>steps</u>
8. <u>Flin Flon</u> <u>is named</u>
9. <u>idea</u> <u>was</u>
10. (<u>You</u>) <u>drive</u>

Exercise 5.4
1. <u>Doing</u> . . . <u>is</u>
2. <u>Were</u> <u>they</u>
3. <u>were</u> . . . <u>children</u>
4. <u>Are</u> <u>you</u>
5. <u>Stampede</u> <u>is held</u>
6. <u>(You)</u> . . . <u>stop</u>
7. <u>address</u> <u>is</u>
8. <u>Have</u> <u>you</u> <u>finished</u>
9. <u>lives</u> . . . <u>family</u>
10. <u>lived</u> . . . <u>tribe</u>

Exercise 5.5
1. <u>Dwight</u> <u>is sleeping</u>
2. <u>You</u> <u>should have been paying</u>
3. <u>Should</u> <u>we</u> <u>conclude</u>
4. <u>fall</u> <u>arrives</u>
5. <u>did</u> <u>you</u> <u>get</u>
6. <u>We</u> <u>do</u> . . . <u>want</u>
7. <u>are</u> <u>we</u> <u>meeting</u>
8. <u>old</u> <u>will</u> . . . <u>think</u>
9. <u>coach</u> <u>has</u> . . . <u>begun</u>
10. <u>swam</u> . . . <u>shark</u>

Exercise 5.6
1. <u>country</u> <u>is covered</u>
2. <u>would</u> <u>anyone</u> <u>want</u>
3. <u>Canadians</u> <u>should be</u>
4. <u>will</u> <u>I</u> <u>agree</u>
5. <u>person</u> <u>may forgive</u>
6. <u>have been</u> . . . <u>players</u>
7. <u>You</u> <u>can become</u>
8. <u>did</u> . . . <u>you</u> <u>stay</u>
9. <u>Have</u> <u>you</u> . . . <u>been</u>
10. <u>has</u> . . . <u>coach</u> <u>become interested</u>

Exercise 5.7
1. A <u>bird</u> ~~in the hand~~ <u>is</u> worth two ~~in the bush~~.
2. Only a <u>few</u> ~~of us~~ <u>have done</u> our homework.
3. <u>Most</u> ~~of your answers~~ <u>are</u> entertaining but wrong.
4. More than a dozen <u>brands</u> ~~of video recorders~~ <u>are</u> now ~~on the market~~.
5. <u>(You)</u> <u>meet</u> me ~~at six~~ ~~at the corner~~ of Robson and Granville.
6. A <u>couple</u> ~~of hamburgers~~ <u>should be</u> enough ~~for each of us~~.
7. <u>Do</u> <u>you</u> <u>know</u> anything ~~about the latest rumours~~ ~~in the government~~?
8. There <u>is</u> a <u>show</u> ~~about laser technology~~ ~~on television~~ tonight.
9. ~~After eight hours~~ ~~of classes~~, the <u>thought</u> ~~of collapsing~~ ~~in front of the TV set~~ <u>is</u> very appealing.
10. One <u>episode</u> ~~of *Geraldo*~~ <u>was</u> more than enough for me.

Exercise 5.8
1. The <u>verb</u> ~~in this sentence~~ <u>is</u> "is."
2. ~~For many students~~, <u>lack</u> ~~of money~~ <u>is</u> probably the most serious problem.
3. ~~In the middle~~ ~~of May, after the end~~ ~~of term~~, the <u>Intercollegiate Arm-Wrestling Championships</u> <u>will be held</u>.
4. One <u>strand</u> ~~of fibre optics~~ <u>can carry</u> both telephone and television signals.
5. ~~During the second week~~ ~~of term~~, the <u>class</u> <u>will be taken</u> ~~on a tour~~ ~~of the resource centre~~.
6. ~~Contrary to your expectations~~, and ~~despite the rumours~~, your <u>instructor</u> <u>does</u> not <u>bite</u>.
7. ~~On Callisto~~, one ~~of Jupiter's thirteen moons~~, <u>snow</u> <u>"falls"</u> up, not down.
8. ~~On the eastern shore~~ ~~of Vancouver Island~~, <u>you</u> <u>can find</u> both oysters and clams.
9. <u>One</u> ~~of the most entertaining comedies of the 1990s~~ <u>was</u> *Wayne's World*.
10. ~~In similar circumstances~~, <u>most</u> ~~of us~~ <u>would</u> probably <u>have taken</u> the money.

Exercise 5.10
1. <u>Maple sugar</u>, <u>wild rice</u> <u>are</u>
2. <u>Kim</u>, <u>Avi</u> <u>will go</u>

3. Professor Singh <u>handed</u>, <u>wished</u>
4. <u>I</u> <u>tried</u>, <u>tried</u>, <u>did</u> (not) <u>succeed</u>
5. <u>canoeists</u>, <u>dog</u> <u>were missing</u>
6. <u>Point</u>, <u>Click</u> . . . <u>are sleeping</u>
7. <u>Point</u>, <u>Click</u> . . . <u>killed</u>, <u>slaughtered</u>
8. <u>Timothy Findley</u> <u>farms</u>, <u>writes</u>, <u>lectures</u>
9. <u>(you)</u> <u>wait</u>, <u>call</u>
10. <u>Shooting</u>, <u>scoring</u> <u>are</u>

Exercise 5.11
1. <u>Misspellings</u> <u>can create</u>, <u>(can)</u> <u>cause</u>
2. <u>*Durham County Review*</u> <u>printed</u>
3. <u>soldier</u> <u>was praised</u>, <u>was described</u>
4. <u>soldier</u> <u>called</u>, <u>demanded</u>
5. <u>writer</u>, <u>editor</u> <u>soothed</u>, <u>promised</u>
6. <u>paper</u> <u>apologized</u>, <u>explained</u>
7. <u>(you)</u> <u>drive</u>, <u>see</u>; <u>(you)</u> <u>drive</u>, <u>see</u>
8. <u>drivers</u> <u>obey</u>, <u>lose</u>
9. <u>(you)</u> <u>drink</u>, <u>you</u> <u>want</u>, <u>(you)</u> <u>drive</u>, <u>you</u> <u>do</u>
10. <u>Come-by-Chance</u>, <u>Blow-Me-Down</u>, <u>Run-by-Guess</u>, <u>Jerry's Nose</u> <u>are</u>

Answers, for Chapter 6: Solving Sentence-Fragment Problems (Pages 48 to 56)

We have made the sentence fragments into complete sentences for the first set, to give you an idea of how the sentences might be formed. Many different sentences can be made out of the fragments given; just be sure each of your sentences has a subject and a verb.

Exercise 6.1
1. F   This <u>chapter</u> <u>is</u> about sentence fragments.
2. F   <u>We</u> <u>have</u> to go to the wall.
3. F   <u>I'll</u> <u>be</u> glad to do it for you.
4. F   <u>She</u> <u>keeps falling asleep</u> in class, after working all night.
5. F   The Doom <u>players</u> <u>are meeting</u> in the upper lounge.
6. S
7. F   <u>Watching</u> television <u>is</u> a cheap form of entertainment.
8. F   <u>I am hoping</u> to hear from you soon.
9. F   <u>We</u> <u>were</u> saved by the bell.
10. S

Exercise 6.2
1. F	6. F
2. F	7. S
3. F	8. F
4. F	9. F
5. F	10. S

Exercise 6.3 (suggested answers)

___F___ The fact <u>is</u> that I have to hold down at least one part-time job to go to school. ___F___ The <u>cost</u> of tuition, books, rent, food, and other living expenses, not to mention clothing and a little money for entertainment <u>is</u> too high. ___S___ I can't survive without working. ___F___ I <u>don't</u> <u>mind</u> getting the minimum wage for work that is heavy, dirty, or boring. ___F___ I <u>have held</u> jobs such as dishwasher, stock clerk, warehouser, cleaner, and short-order cook throughout my college years. __F__ There __is__ one __thing__ [t]hat I do find upsetting, though. __F__ Some __teachers__ __do__ not __understand__ that I work out of necessity, not out of choice. __S__ I wish I did have the luxury of concentrating on nothing but school work. __F__ Instead, I __must__ __deal__ with problems such as class schedules that conflict with my work schedule [F] or assignments that are due with less than a week's notice. __F__ The inescapable fact, however, __is__ that I can't attend all my classes and hand in all my assignments on time because I'm too busy working to pay for the education I'm not getting!

Exercise 6.4

1. F	who	6. F	when
2. F	that	7. F	Whether
3. S		8. F	whichever
4. S		9. F	until
5. F	Where	10. F	that

Exercise 6.5

1. S		6. S	
2. F	Though, who	7. F	If
3. F	that	8. F	Because
4. S		9. F	Until, as long as, whichever
5. S		10. F	When, where, that

Exercise 6.7

Although spring is my favourite season, and I look forward eagerly to its arrival after the long winter, there are some things about the season **that** I could do without. **When** the warm weather begins, I am always tempted to buy new, fashionable shoes **which** are ruined in the wet muck **that** is everywhere. **Unless** I act quickly, my dog also becomes a problem in the spring. She delights in tracking mud from the backyard into the house. **After** she creates a mess that Mr. Clean would need steroids to tackle, she will go back outside and find something sticky and smelly to roll in. **Until** the warm weather dries up the mud and my dog loses the annual urge to coat herself with disgusting substances, my joy at the arrival of spring is always a little restrained.

Answers for Chapter 7: Solving Run-On Sentence Problems (Pages 57 to 65)

Exercise 7.1

1. I hate computers; they're always making mistakes.
2. correct
3. Stop me if you've heard this one. **T**here was this cab driver on her first day at work.
4. Rudolf is bone lazy; Dwight isn't much better.
5. Chocolate is Ninik's weakness; she cannot resist a Toblerone bar.
6. I'll probably be going out tonight, **since** Gretta offered to take me to a movie.
7. Efficiency is what most consumers look for in a new car. **H**igh performance isn't as important as it used to be.
8. I have a 3000-word assignment due tomorrow; if it weren't for that, I'd love to teach you to play solitaire.
9. It bothers me to see Krystal and Sparkle playing cards all the time; they could easily fail the term.
10. Anand was transformed. **O**vernight he had changed from a normal-looking student into a fashion plate.

Exercise 7.2
1. A fine mess this is; I'll never forgive you for getting me into this situation.
2. Let's take the shortcut. **W**e need to get there as quickly as possible.
3. No one in the department supports her, **because** she's both arrogant and indolent.
4. I want to play the banjo; the only thing stopping me is a complete lack of musical talent.
5. Of course, it would also help if I owned a banjo.
6. I'd rather be lucky than good; on the other hand, I'd rather be good than unlucky.
7. Many environmentally aware people are heating their homes with woodstoves nowadays; the result is "ecologists' smog."
8. The snow is turning into freezing rain. **W**e'll be lucky to get home before dawn if these conditions persist.
9. When you are looking for a new car, there are many factors to consider, **but** the most important is probably price.
10. Many good films are made in both Canada and the United States. **I** wish I could tell which ones they were before paying my admission to a movie theatre.

Exercise 7.3
1. The largest dog in the world is the Irish Wolfhound; the strongest dog in the world is the Newfoundland; the stupidest dog in the world is my Afghan.
2. Please go to the door and see who's there. **I**'m on the phone.
3. Early Canadian settlers saw the Americans as a constant menace. **E**ven Ottawa—miles from anywhere and hardly a threat to anyone—was not considered safe.
4. They can crawl on their knees and beg. **T**hat's the only way they'll ever get any more money from me!
5. Think carefully before you answer; a great deal depends on what you decide.
6. Cooking is my favourite pastime, **but** I don't enjoy it nearly so much when I have to do it as when I choose to do it.
7. correct
8. My chiropractor has given me a sheet of exercises that he says will make my back stronger, **and** he has convinced me that if I do these exercises daily, my pain will disappear.
9. Karin was given the choice of joining her father's firm as a driver or continuing her education at college. **K**nowing Karin, I think she's sure to take the job.
10. There are two students in this class named Xan; one is from China, the other from Russia. **T**he latter's name is a nickname. **I**t is a short form of Alexandra.

Exercise 7.4

An acquaintance of mine recently became a Canadian citizen. **W**hen she told me about her citizenship hearing, however, I couldn't bring myself to offer her the congratulations she was obviously expecting. In preparation for the hearing, she had been told to study a small book containing basic facts about Canada, its government, history, and people. **S**he was told the judge who interviewed her would ask questions based on the information in this book, **but** she neglected to study, or even to read the book.

At the hearing, the judge asked her to identify the name of the current governor general, to explain some of the advantages of being a Canadian citizen, and to tell him whether health care was a federal or a provincial responsibility. Unable to answer any of these questions, my friend just giggled and shrugged; then she listened while the judge gave her the answers. She expected to be told to come back when she had learned more about her adopted country, **so** she was astonished when the judge congratulated her for successfully completing the interview and set a date to confirm her citizenship.

I find the judge's decision appalling for three reasons. **F**irst, my friend's failure even to open the book she was given suggests she doesn't have much respect for Canadian citizenship. **S**econd, her low opinion of our citizenship process was reinforced when the judge passed her. **T**hird, I can't help but feel that she was passed because she is an attractive blonde woman, a university professor, and speaks with a polished, upper-class English accent. If she had been a man or woman of colour, or spoken little or no English, or had a less impressive job, I cannot help but think she would have been rejected, **as** she deserved to be.

Exercise 7.5
1. Special effects have been the focus of sci-fi movies since Stanley Kubrick made a computer and a space ship the stars of *2001: A Space Odyssey*. George Lucas continued the trend with the *Star Wars* trilogy, and movie makers ever since have been employing increasingly powerful computers to generate increasingly spectacular effects.
2. A great many films have been made about Count Dracula. **F**rom *Buffy the Vampire Slayer* to *Nosferatu*, Dracula has been portrayed as a depraved monster, a legendary warrior, and even a misunderstood social outcast. **S**o many versions of his story have been told that fact and fiction are now inseparable.
3. For more than thirty years, Clint Eastwood has held the Hollywood record for successful films. **W**hile others have had longer careers, no one has equalled his record in producing box-office winners. **F**urthermore, he is internationally acclaimed as a director as well as an actor.
4. An annual poll is taken among film critics to determine the best movies ever made. **E**very year one film ranks first, and this movie didn't even win the Academy Award as best picture for its year. Shot in black and white, it is the story of a newspaperman who is driven to succeed. **M**ade in 1941, this film is *Citizen Kane*.
5. Some of the worst movies ever made have become big money-makers, thanks to the industry's practice of describing all movies as "the best," "the biggest," and "not-to-be-missed," no matter how mediocre or even downright bad they may be. **A** good example is the work of Edward D. Wood, Jr., the man known as the world's worst director. **I**f you want to see a couple of sensationally dreadful films, check your local video store for Wood's *Bride of the Monster* and *Plan 9 from Outer Space*.

Answers for Chapter 8: Solving Modifier Problems (Pages 66 to 75)

Exercise 8.1
1. Fernando has insulted almost everyone he's gone out with.
2. On Friday, the boss told me I was being let go.
3. They decided to pay me nearly $350 a week.
4. correct
5. My sister could only pray to win the lottery.
6. I hate parties where the food is served on tiny paper plates to the guests who are all standing around.
7. Elmo bought a cigarette lighter costing $29.95 for his girlfriend.
8. In a rage, the angry hippo chased me toward the exit.
9. Most pet owners don't bother having their dogs professionally groomed unless they are poodles or terriers.
10. I appreciate a car with an air bag and soft seat designed for the safety and comfort of the driver.

Exercise 8.2
1. People who shoplift get caught frequently.
2. Stan watched television almost all night.
3. Dolly enthusiastically tried to convince the members of her fan club to wear two or three sets of false eyelashes.
4. In a saucepan, stir the sifted flour into the melted butter.
5. correct
6. No one except petrochemical company executives is allowed to dump any pollutants into the river.
7. With an old black-powder rifle, he took a stand against a tree while waiting for the bear.
8. Walking to school, Rosa passed the security guard and two workmen.
9. Here in Petawawa, I am pleased to meet with student representatives from all of our colleges.
10. Perhaps you're on your own in Vancouver, with a sparkling city to explore and a couple of tickets in your pocket to an event at the covered stadium.

Exercise 8.3
1. As a college English teacher, I am annoyed by dangling modifiers.
2. When writing, you will find that your best friend is your dictionary.
3. Driving recklessly, Sula was stopped at a roadblock by the police.
4. Our neighbours love their Cornish Rex cats because they don't shed their hair.
5. Before applying the varnish, sand the surface smooth.
6. Upon entering, I saw the store was empty.
7. Attempting to hotwire a '95 Mercedes 318, a suspect was arrested by the police.
8. Having rotted in storage, the grain could not be sold for the profit the farmers were counting on.
9. In very cold weather, you should warm up the engine thoroughly before attempting to drive.
10. Driving through the desert, we found that our mouths became drier and drier.

Exercise 8.4
1. After changing the tire, you should release the jack.
2. Having decided on pizza, we should decide next whether to order beer or wine.
3. After waiting for you for an hour, I knew the evening was ruined.
4. Jogging through Stanley Park, I saw a cluster of totem poles.
5. After spending nine dollars on them, I have lost most of the spare keys.
6. Having set the microwave on automatic, I quickly cooked the turkey to perfection.
7. Having completed the beginning, we will turn to the ending, the second most important part of the essay.
8. Convicted of aggravated assault, she was sentenced to two years in Kingston.
9. After scoring the goal in overtime, the team led a huge victory parade through the city.
10. It was a great moment: after making the speech of a lifetime, he was elected to the leader's office.

Exercise 8.5
1. Since I am a college English teacher, dangling modifiers annoy me.
2. When you are writing, you will find that your best friend is your dictionary.
3. Because she was driving recklessly, the police stopped Sula at a roadblock.
4. Because Cornish Rex cats don't shed their hair, our neighbours love them.
5. The surface must be sanded smooth before you apply the varnish.

6. When I entered, the store was empty.
7. While he attempted to hotwire a '95 Mercedes 318, a suspect was arrested by the police.
8. Because the grain had rotted in storage, the farmers could not sell it for the profit they were counting on.
9. In very cold weather, the engine should be thoroughly warmed up before you attempt to drive.
10. As we drove through the desert, our mouths became drier and drier.

Exercise 8.6
1. After you change the tire, release the jack.
2. The next question is whether to order beer or wine, now that we have decided on the pizza.
3. After I had waited for you for an hour, the evening was ruined.
4. As I jogged through Stanley Park, a cluster of totem poles came into view.
5. Most of the spare keys, after I spent nine dollars on them, have been lost.
6. After I set the microwave on automatic, the turkey quickly cooked to perfection.
7. After you have completed the beginning, the ending is the second most important part of the essay.
8. After she was convicted of aggravated assault, the judge sentenced her to two years in Kingston.
9. After the team scored the goal in overtime, a huge victory parade wound through the city.
10. It was a great moment: after he had made the speech of a lifetime, the election put him in the leader's office.

Exercise 8.7
1. Although he lives more than 50 km away, he manages to come to nearly every class.
2. The sign said that only students are admitted to the pub.
3. The lion was recaptured by the trainer before anyone was mauled or bitten.
4. While asleep, the child kicked the blankets off the bed.
5. Through a plate-glass window, I saw the Queen and her entourage arrive.
6. Having ruled out the other two Japanese imports, we chose the Mazda.
7. Swimming isn't a good idea if the water is polluted.
8. The man wore a hideous hat on his head.
9. In last week's letter, I learned about Joan's having a baby.
10. The counsellor who recently admitted he was not familiar with the college's harassment policy has alienated the students.

Exercise 8.8
1. Joe found his dog gnawing on a bone.
2. He said we would have a test on Tuesday. *Or:* On Tuesday, he said we would have a test.
3. Our guests didn't find the food, which was left over from last week's party, very appetizing.
4. Employees who are frequently late are dismissed without notice. *Or:* Employees who are late are frequently dismissed without notice.
5. Since Jim forgot twice this week to pick me up, I'm quitting his car pool.
6. Maria turned the badly bruised avocados into great guacamole.
7. Before going to bed, you should set the alarm for 6:00 A.M.
8. Though they drink it daily, many people don't trust Lake Ontario water.

9. It is a tradition to pay one's respects in a funeral parlour to friends and relatives after they have died.
10. After completing the study of staffing requirements, the personnel manager will hire an assistant.

Answers for Chapter 9: The Parallelism Principle (Pages 76 to 83)

Exercise 9.1
1. The three main kinds of speech are demonstrative, informative, and persuasive.
2. . . . Two of the most difficult are supporting her household and being sole parent to her child.
3. She advised me to take two aspirins and call her in the morning.
4. Books provide us with information, education, and entertainment.
5. To make your court appearance as painless as possible, prepare your case thoroughly and maintain a pleasant, positive attitude.
6. The apostrophe is used for two purposes: contraction and possession.
7. Swiftly and skilfully the woman gutted and scaled the fish.
8. I am overworked and underpaid.
9. You need to develop skill, strategy, and agility to be a good tennis player.
10. The two main responsibilities of a corrections officer are security and control of the inmates.

Exercise 9.2
1. A part-time job can develop your decision-making skills, your sense of responsibility, your self-confidence, and your independence.
2. The three keys to improving your marks are study, hard work, and bribery.
3. I couldn't decide whether I should become a chef or a data processor.
4. . . . the widespread lack of strong religious beliefs and the absence of strict moral codes.
5. A course in logical reasoning will help us evaluate what we read and make sound decisions.
6. My supervisor told me that my performance was generally satisfactory but that my writing must improve.
7. Ms. Hencz assigns two hours of homework every night and an essay each week.
8. The two most important characteristics of a personal work space are how neat and well organized it looks and how private it is.
9. Playing with small construction toys is beneficial to young children because it develops their fine motor skills, encourages concentration and patience, and stimulates their creative imagination.
10. When you're buying a new car, you should look at more than just the size, style, and cost. The warranty, operating cost, and trade-in value should also be taken into consideration.

Exercise 9.3
1. The role of the health instructor is to teach preventive medicine, care of the sick, and rehabilitation of the injured.
2. The most common causes of snowmobile accidents are mechanical failure, poor weather conditions, and driver carelessness.
3. The portable classrooms are ill-equipped, poorly lighted, and inadequately heated.
4. The advantages of a thesis statement are that it limits your topic, clarifies the contents of your paper, and shows how your paper will be organized.

5. Unemployment deprives the individual of purchasing power and reduces the country's national output.
6. A good nurse is energetic, tolerant, sympathetic, and reliable.
7. The money spent on space exploration should be used to provide aid to under-developed countries and funding for medical research.
8. The best house cats are quiet, clean, affectionate, and elsewhere.
9. . . . : a new appreciation for the beauty of nature and a new admiration for members of the opposite sex.
10. You can conclude a paper with a summary of main points, a question, or a quotation.

Exercise 9.4
1. Our winter has not been very pleasant; we've had vicious ice storms, heavy snowfalls, and dangerous freezing rain.
2. Baseball is a game that requires a high level of skill and a large measure of natural talent.
3. Many foreigners see Canadians as conservative, patriotic, and orderly.
4. Patience and dexterity will make you a good piano player, meat cutter, or Lego builder.
5. Being a dutiful son, a loyal husband, and an affectionate father made Jason so stressed that he took up boxing as an outlet for his aggression.
6. There are some parents who think that rock music is dangerous and addictive.
7. Selena has three passions in her life: dancing with her boyfriend, listening to Charlie Major's music, and driving fast cars.
8. After this year at school, I intend to go into nursing or teaching.
9. After nine years of making up faulty sentences for students to fix, Brian can no longer write properly or express himself correctly.
10. Both managers and workers must make compromises if this joint committee is to succeed.

Exercise 9.5
   When they buy a car, most people consider a number of factors such as safety, style, **speed, reliability, and cost.** For some buyers, the most important consideration is the impression their new car will make on their relatives and **friends.** Unfortunately, these would-be buyers often make an unfavourable impression on their loans officer or **bank manager** by choosing a vehicle that is beyond their means. Another kind of car buyer will settle for nothing less than the loudest, flashiest, **most powerful** vehicle available. As I plug along in my aged, **rusty,** underpowered Ford, I console myself with the thought that people who drive flashy, **overpowered** sports cars are trying to make up for other inadequacies.

Answers for Chapter 10: Refining by Combining (Pages 84 to 96)

Exercise 10.1
1. Though it was a difficult decision, we made it. (*Or:* It was a difficult decision, but we made it.)
2. After the test was over, we went to the cafeteria. (*Or:* The test was over, so we went to the cafeteria.)
3. Since Maia works every night until 2:00, she is always tired. (*Or:* Maia works every night until 2:00, so she is always tired.)
4. correct
5. Even though you apologized, I am still angry with you. (*Or:* You have apologized, yet I am still angry with you.)

6. correct
7. Before I came to college, I worked as a nanny.
8. Because I want to see the dean today, I am prepared to wait all afternoon, if necessary. (*Or:* I want to see the dean today, so I am prepared to wait all afternoon, if necessary.)
9. correct
10. Though my mother has told me many times before, she will undoubtedly tell me again. (*Or:* My mother has told me many times before, and she will undoubtedly tell me again.)

Exercise 10.2
1. Matti has a friend whose locker was broken into.
2. Anna is wearing a ring that Rudi gave her.
3. The clerk in the Registrar's office who provided me with a new timetable was most helpful.
4. Co-op programs are popular among students who are enrolled in college full time.
5. Rene speaks often about his daughter, of whom he is very proud.
6. The professor still hasn't returned the homework that I handed in two weeks ago.
7. Today our class attended a lecture on financial management, which we knew nothing about.
8. The train station, which is in the centre of the city, is easy to find.
9. I enjoy talking with my classmates, from whom I have learned a great deal about other countries.
10. Some children who were eating a watermelon were having a seed-spitting contest.

Exercise 10.3
1. The picketers left the streets when the police arrived.
2. The angry bystanders knocked down the assassin and tore him limb from limb.
3. Maria is forty-one years old, but she looks about twenty.
4. He always quits just when you need him.
5. Politicians complain that newspapers distort facts.
6. Even though football is violent, North Americans love it.
7. Many people are not aware that television manipulates feelings.
8. Eazy-E was a gansta rapper who died of AIDS in 1994.
9. Although Vesna hates zucchini, she planted some anyway to please her husband.
10. Whereas scientists in the ancient world looked to the stars for guidance, modern scientists may travel to the stars.

Exercise 10.4
1. The rich, dark, chocolate sauce covered my dessert like a thick blanket.
2. Matthew stumbled down the stairs and was horrified by the sight of Sadik wrestling in the living room with two of his friends.
3. If I don't get there by noon, come looking for me because I may be in trouble.
4. Key glanced at first base, went into his windup, and then threw a curve ball that Murray hit over the right field wall.
5. Begging for mercy, the student who had been caught plagiarizing threw herself at her instructor's feet.
6. The moon was full, and we sat huddled in our warm sleeping bags for a long time before we finally fell asleep.

7. The old train station, which was once the hub of the city, is now the dilapidated refuge of rats.
   Or: The old train station, which is now the dilapidated refuge of rats, was once the hub of the city.
8. Sensing danger, the moose lifted its head, ready to explode into action at the slightest sound.
9. Lonely and miserable, Jamie stumbled into the classroom, her school books heavy in her hand.
10. Thinking it is a tough course, few students register for philosophy, but Philosophy 101 is Monika's favourite course.

Exercise 10.5
1. Each year more Canadians buy mutual funds because they diversify investment and make purchasers feel secure.
2. The city of Toronto boasts about its CN Tower which, at 555 metres high, holds the record as the world's tallest freestanding structure.
3. It was 10:15, and the concert was supposed to begin at 10:00. The band, whose van was stuck in traffic, had not arrived, and the audience was growing restless.
4. The patient, who thought she had broken her ankle, complained of pain. The young intern who examined her ordered X-rays.
5. A vegetarian diet is healthy. Since peas, beans, and lentils contain protein, and iron is found in spinach, people do not need to eat meat.
6. In the fall, which is Canada's most beautiful season, the leaves turn red, yellow and orange; the days are cold and sunny; and there are no mosquitoes or black flies.
7. When the mail carrier was walking up the path, the dog began to bark. After the carrier had pushed the letters through the mail slot, the dog grabbed the letters in his mouth and began shaking them.
8. Many people go to night school. Some go to learn a new skill, others to qualify for a promotion at work, and some just to socialize with other students.
9. Although they are both summer games, baseball and cricket are very different. For example, baseball is played with a round bat, cricket with a flat one; a baseball team has nine players, and a cricket team has eleven.
10. To most people, citizenship is an abstract term meaning loyalty, obedience, and conformity. To a few people, citizenship means thinking for themselves, acting independently, and taking control of their own lives.
11. Nursing is a discipline concerned with promoting the well-being of the individual. A good nurse respects the dignity, autonomy, and individuality of each human being.
12. All across Canada, we find some unusual place names. Saskatchewan has a particularly large number of peculiar place names, such as Cut Knife, Moose Jaw and, perhaps the most famous example, Climax.
13. Newfoundland, too, has some strange-sounding names, such as Jerry's Nose, Bumble Bee Bight, and Come-by-Chance, all of which sound amusing to people who don't live there.
14. The new Exclusiva, which is priced for the successful executive, is the ultimate in luxury automobiles. Engineered for safety, built for comfort, and powered by a state-of-the-art engine, the Exclusiva looks sleek and sophisticated.
15. Lawyers, doctors, and businesspeople are professionals who make up less than 10 percent of the Canadian workforce but occupy almost 75 percent of the seats in the House of Commons.
16. Blue-collar workers make up nearly 50 percent of Canada's population, but they hold less than 10 percent of the seats in the House of Commons. The fact

that blue-collar workers, together with women, native people, and minorities, are underrepresented in government calls into question our nation's commitment to democracy.

17. On May 13, 1989, in Beijing, China, 3000 students began a hunger strike in Tiananmen Square.
18. During their four-week demonstration, the students erected a homemade, 10m tall replica of the Statue of Liberty, which they called the Goddess of Democracy.
19. Thousands of armed troops descended on the square, firing off tracer bullets and tear gas. After using loudspeakers to urge the students to leave, the soldiers opened fire directly on the crowds and charged them with bayonets.
20. Hundreds of demonstrators were killed or wounded in the massacre on Sunday morning, June 4, 1989.

Answers for Chapter 11: Choosing the Correct Verb Form (Pages 99 to 114)

Exercise 11.1

1. wore, worn
2. built, built
3. laid, lay
4. blew, blown
5. bore, borne
6. hit, hit
7. ridden, rode
8. spent, spent
9. won, won
10. told, told

Exercise 11.2

1. wound, wound
2. tore, torn
3. lay, lain
4. bit, bitten
5. grew, grown
6. had, had
7. burst, burst
8. ran, run
9. made, made
10. brought, brought

Exercise 11.3

1. bid, bid
2. rung, rang
3. saw, seen
4. broken, broke
5. fought, fought
6. kept, kept
7. put, put
8. wrote, written
9. threw, thrown
10. taken, took

Exercise 11.4

1. thought, thought
2. begun, began
3. felt, felt
4. bought, bought
5. done, did
6. gave, given
7. paid, paid
8. lent, lent
9. gone, went
10. hurt, hurt

Exercise 11.6

1. exciting
2. embarrassed
3. exhausting
4. disappointed
5. confusing
6. amazed
7. boring
8. bored
9. satisfied
10. thrilled, disgusted

Exercise 11.8
1. Some Canadians call the two dollar coin a "toonie."
2. The scanner at the airport destroyed the magnetic strip on my Visa card.
3. During the summer, Lucienne and Marcel took their dog for long walks on the beach.
4. A panel of conservative thinkers recommended the legalization of all recreational drugs.
5. A Bavarian brewmaster living in Burnaby brewed this beer.
6. The Vancouver Grizzlies broke several records during their first season.
7. Returning graduates gave some of the most interesting talks at our college this term.
8. A graphics artist who is colour-blind designed our company's letterhead and business cards.
9. I told the police that a drunken pedestrian had hit my car.
10. That woman stole my wallet! Stop her!

Exercise 11.9
1. Muhsin drove his car over to Farida's place. (Active voice is more effective.)
2. My unique combination of brains, beauty, and talent overcame all obstacles in the way to my success. (Active is more effective.)
3. Someone had dragged the body for approximately 2 k before hiding it in the underbrush. (Passive voice is more effective because it puts the focus on the object affected by the action—the body—rather than on the unknown person who performed the action.)
4. An unknown horse with an unpronounceable name won the race in a photo finish. (Active is more effective.)
5. After a few minutes of panic, the bartender stopped Tina's nosebleed by applying an ice cube to her nose. (Active is more effective.)
6. Those of us who had waited until January to buy winter clothing took advantage of Sears 70% discount sale. (Active is more effective.)
7. A substitute teacher discovered that I had done no homework since the term began. (Passive is more effective because the discovery is more important than who made it.)
8. With only three seconds left in the overtime period, Felix scored the winning goal. (Active is more effective.)
9. After Aida filed the court order, no one ever saw it again. (The most effective version would be a combination of active and passive: "After Aida *filed* the court order, it *was* never *seen* again." This combination focusses, first, on who made the error and, second, on the result.)
10. Our translator made the telephone call, but she did not tell us what she and the other person agreed to. (Again, a combination would be most effective: "Our translator *made* the telephone call, but we *were* not *told* what *was agreed* to." Who made the call is more important than the call itself, and the agreement is more significant than the person(s) who made it.)

Answers for Chapter 12: Mastering Subject–Verb Agreement (Pages 115 to 125)

Exercise 12.1
1. Clothes **are** what Vinh spends most of his money on.
2. The only junk food Tim eats **is** Hostess Twinkies.
3. My least favourite meal **is** brown rice and tofu.
4. Strong leadership and more jobs **are** what Canada needs now.

5. Too many absences from class **were** the reason for Eugene's failure.
6. Computer games, especially *Doom* and *Myst*, **are** Vince's favourite pastime.
7. The cause of strikes **is** often disputes over wages and benefits.
8. The differences between the Chinese and the Canadian attitudes toward the elderly **are** what I find fascinating.
9. Political discussions **are** something Tanh always enjoys.
10. The only known protection against a vampire attack **is** garlic, a cross, and a stake through the heart.

Exercise 12.2
1. seems
2. is
3. is
4. are
5. are
6. is
7. were
8. cause
9. remain
10. know

Exercise 12.3
1. is
2. writes
3. is
4. is
5. remains
6. wants
7. is
8. is
9. expects
10. has

Exercise 12.4
1. was
2. was
3. believes
4. is
5. seems
6. is
7. is
8. dares
9. has
10. looks

Exercise 12.5
1. works
2. is
3. interests
4. hopes
5. is
6. is
7. was
8. has
9. answers
10. has

Exercise 12.6
1. is
2. seems
3. prides
4. fight
5. Has
6. was
7. gives
8. find
9. is
10. sits

Exercise 12.7
1. seems
2. seems
3. seems
4. is
5. is
6. was
7. is
8. is
9. goes
10. takes

Exercise 12.8
1. A group of unbiased students and faculty **is** . . .
2. Anybody who really **wants** to . . .
3. correct

4. Every one of the contestants **thinks** . . .
5. You'll find that not only ragweed but also cat hairs **make** . . .
6. If there **are** . . .
7. Neither Amelash nor I **am** . . .
8. The lack of things to write about **causes** . . .
9. Michael Jackson, along with his handlers, pets, and bodyguards, **has** . . .
10. The amount of money generated by rock stars on concert tours **is** . . .

Exercise 12.9

There **are** many good reasons for staying fit. The diminished strength, flexibility, and endurance that **result** from lack of exercise are very compelling factors, but everyone who joins the many health clubs in this city **has** individual reasons as well. The people I talked with **say** appearance or weight loss **is** their main motivation for working out. No one among the two hundred patrons of a local health club **was** there for the social life, according to my poll. Either weightlifting or daily aerobics was what they wanted from their club, and the intensity of the workouts **was** clear evidence that they were serious. The manager of the club, along with all the members of the staff, **was** careful to point out that supervised exercise is essential for best results, but neither she nor her staff **were** in favour of fad diets or sweat programs.

Exercise 12.10
1. singular
2. singular
3. plural
4. singular
5. singular

6. singular
7. singular
8. plural
9. singular
10. singular

**Answers for Chapter 13: Keeping Your Tenses Consistent
(Pages 126 to 130)**

Exercise 13.1
1. Allan went home and **told** Guljan what happened.
2. Kristi was so tired that, about ten minutes after class started, she **went** right to sleep.
3. The umpire stands there, rubbing his eyes, unable to believe what he **is** seeing.
4. correct
5. When I answered the phone, there **was** yet another person on the line soliciting a contribution to some worthy cause.
6. First, gently fry the onion, garlic, and seasonings; then **brown** the meat.
7. correct
8. My deadline is next Thursday, by which time I **have** to have an outline and a rough draft ready for my prof's inspection.
9. I drank a half-litre of milk, then I **ate** two protein- and veggie-stuffed sandwiches, and I **was** ready for anything.
10. When Roch Voisine came on stage, the crowd **went** crazy.

Exercise 13.2
1. First, backcomb your hair into spikes, then **coat** your head with glue.
2. The guard walked over and **punched** me in the stomach.
3. The Peter Principle states that every employee **rises** to his or her level of incompetence.

4. Amin and Mia go on their first date and it is a disaster; however, they **decide** to try again.
5. The couple living in the next apartment had a boa constrictor that **kept** getting loose.
7. Prejudice is learned and **is** hard to outgrow.
8. As usual, Professor Campbell began by asking a rhetorical question that he **proceeded** to answer without waiting for anyone in the class to attempt to respond.
9. Are you going to this week's game? **It's** sure to be the best one of the series.
10. Just as time runs out, Emir **launches** a shot at the basket from the centre line. It **misses** the rim by about two metres.

Exercise 13.3

As a boy, Ralph had a remarkable knack for making accurate predictions about the future. When he was 7, he **announced** to anyone who would listen that he would be a millionaire by the time he **was** old enough to vote. When he was 11, he **predicted** that he would star in a major motion picture by the time he **reached** the legal driving age. At the age of 14, he **prophesied** that he would be elected mayor before his twenty-third birthday. Incredibly, his predictions **came** to pass, one after the other. At 16, he **became** the youngest person ever to play James Bond in a movie, and this role **led** to other projects and a salary well into six figures. Good financial advice and careful investing **made** him a millionaire in two years. With all that money behind him, there **was** no stopping Ralph's campaign to **become**, at 22, the youngest mayor in Red Deer's history. However, his amazing early successes **were** not sustainable, and Ralph **became** a has-been by the time he **turned** 25.

Answers for Chapter 14: Choosing the Correct Pronoun Form (Pages 131 to 137)

Exercise 14.1
1. Those videotapes belong to Patrick and **me**.
2. I can't believe that the committee would choose Bennie along with **us**.
3. Neither **they** nor **we** deserve to be treated like this.
4. Danny and **he** think no one knows they smoke in the stairwell.
5. Just between you and **me**, the engagement between Yolande and **him** is off.
6. If I have to choose between **him** and you, I'm afraid it is **he** who will be going to the lake with me.
7. As devoted television watchers, **we** love it when **we** and the program producers share similar tastes.
8. It would be preferable for **them** to come here rather than for **us** to go there.
9. I can't believe Chandra would break up with me after **she** and **I** got matching tattoos and navel rings.
10. It is likely that **we** musicians would get more favourable reviews from the critics if we and **they** met socially more often.

Exercise 14.2
1. **She** and I have completely different tastes in music, though we agree on practically everything else.
2. There aren't many vegetarians besides Ettore and **me** who are so strict that they will not wear leather or wool.
3. It is not for you or **me** to decide whether they go to the game or stay home.

4. Iain and **she** are the best curlers on our team; if it weren't for **them**, we would be in last place.
5. **She** and Marie took the magazines before either Tom or **I** had had a chance to read them.
6. **We** and **they** were exhausted from studying all night, so we can't be blamed for the explosion.
7. Fate has put **us** two together and no matter what **she** or your father says, it is **we** who will live happily ever after at the end of the story.
8. Have you and **he** finally finished your project, or must **we** seniors do your work for you again?
9. It is up to you and **him** to piece together the clues and come up with the solution to the crime so that **we** innocent victims can be set free.
10. I don't need to see my doctor because I know that my chiropractor and **she** agree that I should not play in the championship game tonight, and they are both fans of **us** "Fighting Treefrogs."

Exercise 14.3
1. Nobody hates English more than **I**.
2. She is more frightened of being alone than **he** [is].
3. Everyone wanted to go to the movies except Yvon and **me**.
4. More than **I**, Yuxiang uses the computer to draft and revise his papers.
5. Only a few Mexican food fanatics can eat jalapeno peppers as well as **he** [can].
6. At last I have met someone who enjoys barbecued eel as much as **I** [do].
7. After our instructor handed out the papers, Rudolf and **I** got into a fight.
8. Since he had copied his essay from me, he shouldn't have got a better grade than **I** [did].
9. Rudolf's thinking is that since he is better looking than **I**, he deserves the higher mark.
10. I have a real problem with a teacher who gives good marks to **those** who are blessed with a winning smile and great hair.

Answers for Chapter 15: Mastering Pronoun–Antecedent Agreement (Pages 138 to 148)

Exercise 15.1
1. Clive is the only one **who** wants his picture hung in the board room.
2. Everyone **who** went to the party had a good time, though a few had more punch than was good for them.
3. Is this the dog **that** bit the mail carrier **who** carries a squirt gun?
4. The path led me past the home of a hermit **who** lives all alone in the forest **that** surrounds our town.
5. A filmmaker **who** stays within budget on every production will always have work, no matter how mediocre his movies might be.
6. The open-office concept is one **that** makes sense to anyone **who** has worked in a stuffy little cubicle all day.
7. One advantage of the open office is that it lets you see who is working hard and who is taking it easy. It also allows you to spot people **(whom)** you'd like to meet.
8. The four tests **that** we wrote today would have defeated anyone **who** wasn't prepared for them.
9. Sales clerks **who** want to make good commissions must have good people skills as well as knowledge of the products **(that)** they are selling.
10. The winning goal, **which** was made with only two seconds left in the game, was scored by a player **(whom)** I used to know in high school.

Exercise 15.2
1. herself
2. a
3. the
4. his or her
5. a
6. the
7. his or her
8. itself
9. his, their
10. who, his

Exercise 15.3
1. Every child is a product **of environment** as well as **heredity**. (*Or:* **Children are products** of their environment as well as their heredity.)
2. Anyone who would write a sentence like that last one should give up **the** computer.
3. The team agreed that everyone would have to show up for **the** practices.
4. Everybody must get in **place** for the game to begin. (*Or:* **All players** must get in their places for the game to begin.)
5. Anybody without a partner will have to try to find one approximately **the same** height.
6. Golf is a game that is good for anyone who wants to enjoy outdoor exercise without **getting sweaty or hurt**.
7. We have asked **all students with complaints to see their instructors**. (*Or:* We have asked every student with a complaint to see **his or her** instructor.)
8. Do you know whether anyone in your neighbourhood wants **a house-painter** or **a grass-cutter** this summer? (*Or:* Do you know whether **your neighbours** want their houses painted or their grass cut this summer?)
9. Few people I know **enjoy themselves** on a squash court, but they like to play tennis whenever they can.
10. We're looking for someone **with outstanding intelligence and creativity, who** can work unsupervised.

Exercise 15.4 (suggested answers)
1. Max is **good at skating,** which he practises daily. (*Or:* Max is a good skater, **and** he practises daily.)
2. He didn't hear her cry for help **because he was** wearing earplugs.
3. That **she** would be Betty's teacher never occurred to **Miss Grundy**. (*Or:* That Miss Grundy would be **her** teacher never occurred to **Betty**.)
4. Every time David looked at the dog, **it** barked.
5. **Biff cracked his ghetto blaster when he threw it on the floor** in a rage.
6. **"You're sure to get a job soon,"** Carla told her mother**.**
7. Whenever Rudolf and Biff met, **Rudolf** acted in a relaxed, friendly fashion so that no one would suspect he hated **Biff**.
8. Krystal told Sparkle **that Sparkle** was losing her looks.
9. At our college, the administration introduced a "no smoking" policy three years ago. (*Or:* Our college introduced a no-smoking policy three years ago.)
10. I am writing this letter in response to your ad for a waiter and bartender, male or female. **I have experience both waiting tables and tending bar,** so I wish to apply for the position.

Exercise 15.5
   Anyone **who** has competed in a triathlon (a three-part race consisting of swimming, cycling, and running) knows that proper training is an absolute necessity, not only to success, but also to survival. Swimming is one of the toughest contests, because it demands cardiovascular fitness as well as strength, and it makes demands on the whole body. While each of the three segments has **its** own challenges, the cycling part of the triathlon is the event **that** separates serious

athletes from part-time fitness buffs. Here, **the latter** will find **they** can't summon enough energy after **their** swim to stay close to **their opponents** if **their opponents have** trained harder [than **they**]. **Serious athletes** will begin to assert their dominance now, and by the end of the bike ride, **those who** have achieved a high level of physical efficiency through their training will still have a chance of a high placing. For the competitor in a triathlon, survival is often the primary goal. The body's reserves are called on, and only the dedicated, well-trained athlete will be able to **survive**. For most, reaching the finish line is a personal test, and the only competition is against one's previous finish times. **Those who** still have winning in mind after the swim, the cycle race, and the run **have** physical and mental reserves beyond the ordinary.

**Answers for Chapter 16: Maintaining Person Agreement
(Pages 149 to 154)**

Exercise 16.1

1. you want
2. she
3. you
4. you
5. we

6. you
7. You
8. we, we, our
9. you don't, your, you are
10. you know, you, you know

Exercise 16.2 (suggested answers)

1. A great worry is lifted from **your** mind when you learn your application has been accepted.
2. If only **I** had read the instructions carefully, I wouldn't have messed up the answer on the test.
3. If any of you are planning to go to the class party, **you** can pick up **your** tickets now.
4. Men who don't think women are their equals may have to get used to living on **their** own.
5. It has taken most Canadians far too long to recognize the seriousness of **their** debt and deficit problems.
6. If **you are** convicted on that charge, a fine is the least of your worries.
7. After we had driven about 400 km, the lack of sleep made it hard to keep **our** eyes open.
8. If you can't cope with the pressure, **you** must expect to be replaced by someone who can.
9. The penalties for plagiarism are severe, but one doesn't usually think about penalties until after **he or she is** caught. (*Or:* . . . **you don't** usually think about penalties until after you are caught.)
10. It's very difficult for **14-year-olds** to control **their** temper when **they** feel frustrated or angry.

Exercise 16.3

A woman who **enjoys** baseball may have difficulty explaining **her** passion to **someone** who **finds** the game boring. Each February, the serious **fan begins** to sharpen **her** watching and listening skills by tuning in to spring training games. If you have seen **one of** these fanatics (*or:* **a fanatic**) watch a game, you will have noticed the alertness and intensity with which **she follows** the play. It is this single-minded dedication that the **non-fan finds herself** unable to comprehend. How can **anyone** be so interested in a game that **she** can watch for three hours or more, only to see so little take place? How **can she** get excited by a no-hitter, which, by definition, means that nothing has happened during the game? **The**

baseball fan maintains that the game to which **she is** addicted **offers** many more pleasures than mere action. **She cites** fielding plays and the strategy of pitcher-versus-hitter matchups in defence of **her** game. To a **woman** who **finds** such detail meaningless, however, watching a baseball game is about as exciting as watching paint dry.

Answers for Chapter 17: The Comma (Pages 157 to 163)

Exercise 17.1
1. Does anyone remember John, Paul, George, and Ringo?
2. correct
3. Krystal thinks she wants to get married, but she can't decide whether Dwight, Rudolf, or Eugene should be the lucky man.
4. Fans of rock, folk**(,)** and ska all enjoyed the Days of You concert.
5. MacDonald, Laurier, Borden**(,)** and Pearson are four dissimilar men who have one thing in common.
6. Arnold is an all-round athlete; he enjoys skating, skiing, cycling, tobogganing**(,)** and showering.
7. Marieke has strong ambition, a cool head, good health**(,)** and an inquiring mind; everyone hates her.
8. Careful investment of time and money can lead to a luxurious lifestyle, international fame**(,)** and early retirement.
9. Mowing the lawn, shopping for groceries**(,)** and doing my teenagers' homework are my least favourite activities.
10. Most of the world sees Canada as a land where French is spoken, ice and snow are year-round hazards**(,)** and violent hockey is the natives' favourite pastime.

Exercise 17.2
1. My mother's favourite singer is Gordon Lightfoot, the former Elvis imitator from Orillia.
2. The winner of the 1994 Yorkton Film Festival Jury Award was Janis Lundman's documentary, *Lawn and Order.*
3. The underlying message of the film is that, whether you like it or not, your lawn says a lot about who you are.
4. correct
5. Despite her reputation as an air head, Leticia is, we have discovered, fairly bright.
6. To no one's surprise, Professor Lam, a popular mathematics instructor, won the distinguished teacher award again this year.
7. correct
8. In a radical departure from tradition, the bride wore a bright red gown and matching veil.
9. One of the wedding guests remarked, rather cattily I thought, that the bride looked like a Tomato Festival Queen.
10. Not surprisingly, a recent study of driver stress shows that aggressive behaviour, such as flashing high beams at other drivers, increases during high-congestion traffic.

Exercise 17.3
1. He and I are good friends, yet we often disagree.
2. We have a choice: we could try bribery, or we could resort to force.
3. We can't win this game, nor can we afford to lose it.
4. correct
5. Mona tried and tried to pass her driver's test, and her persistence finally paid off.

6. My wife and I would like to buy a house, but we don't have enough money for a down payment.
7. I'm bored and underpaid at work, so I'm going back to school next fall.
8. Ravi and Denis are travelling to Whitehorse this summer, and Sandy is going to St. John.
9. This is Bambi's last semester, so she's concentrating on school for a change.
10. Please pay close attention, for the instructions are a little complicated.

Exercise 17.4
1. In the end, quality is what counts.
2. Second, our department is required to cut costs by fifteen percent.
3. If there were any justice in this world, I'd have been rewarded for my performance.
4. Moved beyond words, the victorious candidate was able only to gesture his thanks to his supporters.
5. Carefully placing one foot in front of the other, she managed to walk along the white line for several metres.
6. Where a huge hardwood forest had once stood, only acres of tree stumps remained.
7. Finally, it is clear that we must make our decision today.
8. While Rudolf may be short on brain, he's long on brawn.
9. As her fortieth birthday approached, Drusilla met the challenge by trading in her sedan for a sports car and her husband for a boyfriend ten years her junior.
10. When the first robin heralds the return of spring, I begin to dream of lazy summer days lying beside the pool with a cool drink in my hand and a ball game on the radio.

Exercise 17.5
1. Despite some excellent action sequences, the movie was a failure because of the terrible script.
2. Your fall order, which we received last week, has been shipped.
3. These cold, wet(,) grey days are not good for the crops.
4. If starvation and lack of recognition made great artists, Canada would be a land of Picassos.
5. What you hear, what you read(,) and what you experience all help to form your cultural background.
6. A few days after we sailed, the boat sprang a leak.
7. Inside, the band was playing at full blast.
8. The letter of application is one of the most important documents you will ever write, yet you have spent only an hour composing it.
9. Despite some early problems, Ottawa's National Gallery has become the home of one of the most interesting collections in North America.
10. correct

Exercise 17.6
1. There is something wrong with this proposal, but I haven't yet figured out what it is.
2. Our hope, of course, is that the terrorists will be caught and punished.
3. George Washington, the first president of the United States, was an officer in the British army before he was engaged in the American Revolution.
4. Charlottetown, Quebec(,) and Kingston were the sites of the conferences that eventually led to Confederation in 1867.

5. If you can cope with overloaded logging trucks passing you at high speeds on narrow mountain roads, you'll enjoy the spectacularly scenic drive from Hope to Princeton.
6. correct
7. A good dictionary, consulted frequently, is probably the most important resource for any student who wishes to develop a mature vocabulary.
8. While I respect your opinion and your right to express it, that doesn't mean that I necessarily agree with you.
9. After our guests had gone home, we discovered that they had drunk all the beer but had left most of the food, so we'd be dining on leftovers for the next two weeks.
10. If there were any point in protesting the president's decision, I would have complained long ago, but I don't think anything will change her disastrous course of action.

Answers for Chapter 18: The Semicolon (Pages 164 to 169)

Exercise 18.1
1. correct
2. incorrect
3. correct
4. incorrect
5. incorrect
6. incorrect
7. incorrect
8. correct
9. correct
10. correct

Exercise 18.2
1. correct
2. incorrect
3. correct
4. correct
5. incorrect
6. correct
7. incorrect
8. correct
9. incorrect
10. incorrect

Exercise 18.3
2. He sat down near a refreshing stream, for he was very tired.
4. It's a beautiful day, just right for a long walk.
5. Six of the Indian nations joined together in a loose union; they were called Iroquois.
6. The lawn, a little ragged, needs to be cut; the hedge, shrubs, and ivy need to be trimmed; the flowers need to be watered; and, most important, the gardener needs to be paid.
7. I'd like to help; however, I'm supposed to rest all day.

Exercise 18.4
2. There are only a few who could catch him, and I'm sure she isn't one of them.
5. We'll have to go soon, for it's getting late.
7. If ever there were a time to act, it is now.
9. She disobeyed the rules, so she will have to be punished.
10. Krystal is always late; however, she's worth waiting for.

Exercise 18.5
1. There seems to be no end to the work that must be done; furthermore, there isn't enough time in which to do it.
2. There must be a way, or we're finished before we've even begun.
3. I can't afford a Porsche; therefore, I drive a Neon.

4. Jana is one of my favourite people; she can always cheer me up.
5. There will be ample opportunity to finish your homework, but right now I need your help.
6. The floor was knotty pine; the furniture and walls were designed and finished to complement it.
7. Brock was killed early in the morning, but the Americans were driven from Queenston Heights by nightfall.
8. Canada's history is not a very violent one; however, we've had several rebellions of note.
9. Jon has gone away to become a teacher; Marta now has twin baby girls; Kevin is unemployed; Julie is a lawyer or stockbroker (I forget which); and Pavel is, as usual, drifting from job to job.
10. When the rain started, they were trapped in the open; nevertheless, they stayed where they were until it let up and then made their way to the nearest shelter.

Exercise 18.6
1. Please leave dinner in the oven for a little while; I'll eat when I've finished this exercise.
2. Taking the corner at 90 kph, the police car swerved into the oncoming lane; fortunately, no one was coming.
3. The chair called the meeting to order; however, it quickly became apparent that none of us had done the background reading.
4. One of the products of the computer age is increased leisure; this, in turn, has led to increased opportunities for physical fitness.
5. A glance at the calendar will reveal that there are only 212 shopping days left until my birthday; that's just enough time for you to find the present I deserve.
6. Computers are marvellous tools; they are fast, efficient, and accurate, but they can't think. They remind me of a secretary I used to know; she's now my boss.
7. The Four Horsemen of the Apocalypse are Conquest, Slaughter, Famine(,) and Death.
8. Some Biblical figures are familiar to people from many different cultures; for example, the stories of Samson and Delilah and of David and Goliath are widely known.
9. We're unhappy about our instructor's evaluation procedures; in fact, we think they are irrational, arbitrary(,) and often unfair.
10. Every year at tax time, I am faced with the same problem: assembling my bills and receipts; figuring out my gas mileage; trying to recall which expenses were business-related and which were personal; finding my T4s, T5s, and other T forms; and organizing this mess so my accountant can attempt to keep me out of jail for another year.

Answers for Chapter 19: The Colon (Pages 170 to 173)

Exercise 19.1

1. correct	6. incorrect
2. incorrect	7. correct
3. correct	8. incorrect
4. incorrect	9. incorrect
5. correct	10. incorrect

Exercise 19.2

1. incorrect
2. incorrect
3. incorrect
4. correct
5. correct

6. incorrect
7. correct
8. incorrect
9. correct
10. correct

Exercise 19.3

2. Only one thing was missing: the boat.
4. On the list, we must include chips, mix, ice, and peanuts.
6. Three qualities of a good quarterback are leadership, intelligence, and physical strength.
8. The lake is deep and cold.
9. Dogs have many qualities that make them superior to cats: loyalty, intelligence, working ability, and friendliness.
10. Let me give you an example: Louis Riel.

Exercise 19.4

1. I'd like to help, but I can't.
2. I'll take the following volunteers: Marie, Susan, Ngoc, and Lewis.
3. We'll have to go back to get tent poles, matches, and paddles.
6. No one wants to go with him, for two very good reasons: money and time.
8. My boss is so mean she must be bitter or crazy.

Answers for Chapter 20: Quotation Marks (Pages 174 to 179)

Exercise 20.1

1. "Three thousand is a bargain for that coat," said Drusilla, eyeing the floor-length mink.
2. correct
3. "Put that gun down," shouted the officer, "or I'll shoot!"
4. "The time has come," the Walrus said, "to talk of many things."
5. Canada's national anthem, "O Canada," was written by Calixa Lavallée.
6. My father likes to remind me of John F. Kennedy's words: "Too often we enjoy the comfort of opinion without the discomfort of thought."
7. In his novel, *Generation X* (<u>Generation X</u>), Douglas Coupland warns, "Less is a possibility."
8. Two singles from Sheryl Crow's first album, *Tuesday Night Music Club* (<u>Tuesday Night Music Club</u>), became hits: "All I Wanna Do" and "Strong Enough."
9. *The Guinness Book of Records* (<u>The Guinness Book of Records</u>) claims that the world's most-married man is former Baptist minister Scotty Wolfe, who got married 27 times.
10. When asked how many children were born of these marriages, Mr. Wolfe replied, "I think I had 41."

Exercise 20.2

1. correct
2. After his best player suffered another injury, the coach pleaded with him, "Please, Marcel, wear a face mask!"
3. correct
4. Brian inquired, "When are we going to eat?"

5. "When you cook dinner," Val replied.
6. Marshall McLuhan's insight, "The medium is the message," appears in his most famous book, *Understanding Media* (<u>Understanding Media</u>).
7. The headline in today's *Winnipeg Free Press* (<u>Winnipeg Free Press</u>) is "Canada's dollar sinks to new low."
8. We've decided to rent a video this evening, but we can't decide between *The Lion King* (<u>The Lion King</u>) and *Priscilla, Queen of the Desert* (<u>Priscilla, Queen of the Desert</u>).
9. "This is the second time you've been thrown out of class," the dean told Biff. "I'm inclined to suspend you for a week."
10. "Say you love me," he pleaded. "OK," she replied, "You love me."

Answers for Chapter 21: Question Marks, Exclamation Marks, and Punctuation Review (Pages 180 to 186)

Exercise 21.1
1. What more could I possibly do to help?
2. Val asked Biff if he was absolutely positive he had paid the bill.
3. Why is there always a cop around when I'm speeding but never when I need help?
4. Have you checked the weather forecast to see when the weather is expected to clear?
5. I will always wonder if Rhonda handed in my essay.
6. Is it true that voters will act rationally only when all other possibilities have been exhausted?
7. Did the committee consider all the options carefully before making this decision?
8. I don't understand why sociology is so important in a business program.
9. Eugene is still asking the math teacher to raise his mark to at least a pass.
10. The question isn't whether or not there is intelligent life on Mars, it's whether there's intelligent life on earth.

Exercise 21.2
1. I'm not sure whether there is a game tonight or not.
2. Is there life after long days of boring classes, followed by long nights of homework?
3. If we can't complete the project on time, will we be penalized?
4. Our question was what to do after the boss had burst into tears and gone home.
5. What good will it do if I continue to be pleasant to people who take such delight in making me look foolish?
6. How can anyone just stand by while some innocent person is being attacked?
7. Whoever would have thought that the Canadian dollar would fall below the U.S. seventy-cents mark?
8. I am surprised and hurt that you would question my motives in asking you for help with my studying.
9. Please take a look at these tests and tell me whether you think these two students were cheating.
10. Why can't the sports fans who yell so loudly at players' mistakes try to put themselves in the same position as those they criticize and be a little more forgiving?

Exercise 21.3
1. Take that, you monster!
2. Ready, aim, fire!

3. I can't believe it! We've got the winning number!
4. That's the last straw. (*or* !) I quit!
5. There's a fly in my soup!
6. Run! It's right behind you!
7. "Slide!" The whole team was screaming in unison.
8. I can't believe it! The thing actually flies!
9. Turn the heat up. (*or* !) I'm freezing!
10. The girls descended on the mall waving their plastic and crying, "Charge!"

Exercise 21.4
1. The question was whether we would spend the night in Abbotsford or push on to Vancouver.
2. Just think! We have two glorious weeks free of English class! (*or* .)
3. Bruce thought he looked absolutely irresistible in his new leather pants.
4. If you think you're confused, just imagine how I must feel.
5. correct
6. Katy asked Ramon if he'd like to stay over.
7. correct
8. Today we read a poem by Irving Layton, who was born in Rumania, I think.
9. After seeing your test results, I wonder if you even bought the text, let alone read it.
10. Congratulations! You've just mastered end punctuation marks.

Exercise 21.6
1. "Enjoy the view," we called out as they left for the mountaintop; we had wisely decided to wait for them in a meadow halfway up.
2. To be a millionaire by the time you are thirty, you will have to take large risks, be lucky, and have creative ideas.
3. High school was, indeed, the best time of my life, because I met the friends there that I would continue to see for many years, and I learned the principles that were to guide me through later, more difficult years.
4. The question of whether evolution is a fact or a myth doesn't worry most of the people in my class; they're more concerned about whether there's a dance on Friday night.
5. "Why won't he listen?" Marsha whispered tearfully.
6. With the crowd chanting, "Out! Out!" the referee had a hard time justifying his decision: a ten-minute misconduct.
7. Typing as though his life depended on the completion of the assignment, Ted managed to get through the first chapter before supper. This left him with Chapter Two, "The Next Day," to complete before bedtime.
8. The rain looked as though it would never let up, so Gary and the two girls packed up to go home, their vacation plans ruined.
9. "Don't go," Angela fell to her knees and begged her friend to stay. "Why must you leave now," she asked, "just when we're about to succeed?"
10. You'll find he has just one fault, my friend: he snores.

Exercise 21.7
   All too often, it seems that the Canadian national pastime is complaining about the weather. Our summers are criticized because they're too hot, while our springs are too wet, our autumns too cool, and our winters too long. If the climate is so bad here, why does anyone live north of the U.S. border? Perhaps the problem is not that Canadians don't like living in Canada, but that they love to complain.
   Two of the most popular sports teams in Canada were at one time those with the worst records: the Argonauts and the Maple Leafs. Could this popularity be

due to the ample opportunity and scope they gave to their fans for complaint? Not only do we bemoan the record of such teams when they lose, but, when they win, we dwell with glee on the possibilities of disaster for next year.

The same syndrome can be seen in our attitude toward Canadian heroes. It has often been said that we are a nation without heroes, but I suspect that we have plenty of candidates. It's just that we enjoy complaining so much, we try to find fault wherever we can and prefer to focus on clay feet rather than great works. One cannot help but wonder how Canadians fare in heaven, where everything is perfect. I suspect they must be desperately unhappy!

Answers for Chapter 22: Finding Something to Write About (Pages 189 to 203)

Exercise 22.1
1. Not specific. It's too large a topic.
2. Not specific, nor is it supportable without a great deal of research.
3. Not significant. Every child knows what they are.
4. Not significant.
5. Not single. Choose one.
6. Not single or specific.
7. Not supportable. How can we know?
8. Not significant.
9. Not specific. Whole books have been written on this topic.
10. Not single.

Exercise 22.2
1. Not significant. It's a commonplace fact.
2. Not specific or significant. Again, it's a simple fact.
3. Not single or specific.
4. Not specific. Nor is it supportable, for most of us, without substantial research.
5. Not specific.
6. Not significant.
7. Not supportable.
8. Not specific.
9. Not significant.
10. Not specific.

Exercise 22.6
1. Alcohol (not a reason)
2. Large bakeries; saving money (these "points" are not part of the process)
3. Improved looks (overlaps with "improved appearance"); improved social life (not *directly* related to S)
4. White shark; hammerhead shark (these are species, not characteristics of sharks)
5. Make travel plans (overlaps with "plan a client's itinerary"); get a passport (client's responsibility)
6. May be dangerous; weight is often gained back (these points are not related to S: they are not fad diets)
7. Largely female audience (unrelated); quiz shows (overlaps with "game shows")
8. Surge in birth of children from 1947–1965 (unrelated: it's a definition of the postwar baby boom, not an effect)

Exercise 22.7

1. They are fun to play; Lottario, Lotto 6/49 (unrelated to S)
2. Practical training (offered in both); college students cannot smoke in the building (unrelated to S—students cannot smoke in high school either—and not significant)
3. The medical process by which a person learns to control autonomic body processes; autonomic responses are involuntary, self-regulating processes (these are definitions, not benefits)
4. Football requires helmets; football is more of a spectator sport (unrelated to S; these are contrasts, not comparisons)
5. Intensely active; cannot concentrate for long (unrelated to S; these are characteristics, not treatments)
6. Finding a job may take a while (unrelated to S); buy a suit (not significant)
7. In-laws; family breakdown (unrelated to S; these are not structures)
8. To ensure regular health checkups for prostitutes (overlaps with "to control spread of sexually transmitted diseases"); to decriminalize prostitution (not related; it means exactly the same thing as S)

Exercise 22.9

SUBJECT	ORDER	MAIN POINTS	
1. How to start a gas lawnmower	chronological	_2_	make sure there is enough gas in tank
		_3_	turn switch to start
		_1_	put lawnmower on flat ground
		_5_	when running, adjust to proper speed
		_4_	pull cord
		_6_	mow!
2. Differences between spoken and written language	climactic	_3_	speech is transitory; writing is permanent
		_2_	speech is direct and personal; writing isn't
		_1_	speech can't be revised; writing can
3. How to write a research paper	chronological	_3_	read and take notes on selected research sources
		_4_	draft the paper
		_2_	compile a working bibliography of research sources
		_1_	define the subject
		_7_	type and proofread paper
		_6_	prepare footnotes, if needed, and bibliography
		_5_	revise the paper

SUBJECT	ORDER	MAIN POINTS
4. How colleges benefit society	logical	_2_ they provide the individual with a higher level of general education _3_ society benefits from increased productivity and commitment of an educated populace _1_ they provide the individual with job skills
5. Some causes of World War II	chronological	_2_ World Depression in early 1930s _3_ Hitler's rise to power in 1933 _1_ heavy reparations demanded of Germany at end of World War I _4_ German aggression in Europe
6. Effects of malnutrition	logical	_3_ malnutrition affects the productivity and prosperity of nations as a whole _1_ malnutrition impedes the mental and physical development of children _2_ undernourished children become sickly adults unable to participate fully in their society
7. Why pornography should be banned	chronological	_1_ it degrades the people involved in making it _3_ it brutalizes society as a whole _2_ it desensitizes the people who view it

8. Decide on your own climactic arrangement for this question. Be sure you can explain your choice.

Answers for Chapter 23: Writing the Thesis Statement (Pages 204 to 213)

Exercise 23.1

1. There are three kinds of students whom teachers find difficult to teach: whiners, snoozers, and disrupters.

2. The most prolific producers of unnecessary jargon are politicians, sports writers, advertising-copy writers, and educators.

3. Dining in the cafeteria should be avoided if possible, (for) the food is high in cost, low in nutrition, and unappetizing in taste.
4. (Because) they lack basic skills, study skills, or motivation, some students run the risk of failure in college.
5. Pay television has faced challenges in Canada (because of) the relatively small market, the high monthly cost, and the stiff network competition.
6. Political violence has become ingrained in the social fabric of many Latin American countries (including) Nicaragua, El Salvador, Colombia, and Brazil.
7. The Canadian national character was shaped by early conflicts (such as) the battle for Quebec, the rebellion of 1837, and the Riel rebellion.
8. Canada is little more than an American satellite, (for) the United States influences our foreign policy, dominates our culture, and controls our economy.
9. The major improvements Western medical technology has made in impoverished parts of the world (consist of) widespread immunization, the availability of antibiotics, and improved sanitation.
10. Two cheers for democracy: one because it admits variety and two because it permits criticism. (E.M. Forster)

Exercise 23.2

1. d. packed up and headed for Rome
2. a. strong
3. c. ugly
4. b. intelligently
5. b. by boat
6. d. trusted by the media
7. c. watching less television
8. a. increase appetite
9. d. yacht in drydock
10. c. that fair-minded police are visible

Exercise 23.3

1. not parallel
2. not parallel
3. parallel
4. not parallel
5. not parallel
6. parallel
7. parallel
8. not parallel
9. parallel
10. not parallel

Exercise 23.4

1. His basement apartment was small, damp, cold, and dirty.
2. To be a good marriage counsellor, a person must have insight, patience, compassion, and experience.
3. correct
4. Too much coffee can give you nervous days, sleepless nights, and heart palpitations.
5. We require our employees to be honest, reliable, disciplined, and knowledgeable.
6. correct
7. correct
8. Inflation is down, interest rates are up, and unemployment is still high.
9. correct
10. Writing acceptable college-level prose involves applying the principles of organization, sentence structure, spelling, and punctuation.

Exercise 23.5
1. Do you know the difference between polygamy, bigamy, and monogamy?
2. Ahmad has given up not only on the Liberals but also on the Conservatives and on the New Reform Party.
3. Rudolf decided he'd rather be a plumber than a teacher.
4. A good coach must train, discipline, and motivate the team.
5. Two features of the semester system are flexibility and economy.
6. Going to college is good for broadening one's social life as well as for learning career skills.
7. Compared to those of ten years ago, today's cars are smaller, more efficient, and more expensive.
8. We find it's more interesting to explore the tide pools at the seashore than to lie in the sun all day.
9. Children who grow up in the city have a different outlook on life than those who grow up in the country.
10. Do Canadians really care if the United States dominates our economy, politics, and culture?

Exercise 23.6
1. The four kinds of prose writing are narration, description, exposition, and persuasion.
2. College fraternities and sororities have become less popular in the past twenty years because they are expensive, they are time-consuming, and they discriminate against some students.
3. Medical scientists are studying the link between weather and such diseases as colds, arthritis, and cancer.
4. If I could have three wishes, I would wish to be gorgeous, brilliant, and rich.
5. Roots products have won international favour because of their reasonable cost, fashionable designs, and high quality.
6. Intramural sports offer three important things to college students: a way to get involved in the school, an opportunity to meet friends, and a chance to stay fit.
7. Freud's psychoanalytic theories, developed in the early years of this century, not only have affected the course of psychology but also have had profound implications for education, art, and literature.
8. Many English words have similar meanings, but they come from very different root languages: for example, *spectre* comes from the Latin *spectrum* (appearance); *phantom* comes from the Greek *phantasm* (image); and *ghost* comes from the Anglo-Saxon *gast* (spirit).
9. Geologists are exploring several phenomena that may lead to an early-warning system for earthquakes: the variation of electrical resistance of rocks under pressure, the release of gas trapped in the crystal lattice of a rock, and the appearance of eerie lights, or luminous flares, in the sky before a quake.
10. It was the best of times; it was the worst of times; it was the age of wisdom; it was the age of foolishness; it was the epoch of belief; it was the age of incredulity; it was the season of Light; it was the season of Darkness; it was the spring of hope; it was the winter of despair.

Exercise 23.7
6. A politician should be well-liked by constituents, respected by colleagues, esteemed by the party, and trusted by the media. (Chronological order)
7. We have all been thinking of fitness, watching our diet, learning to exercise, and watching less television. (Logical order)

8. Excessive use of marijuana can increase appetite, induce lethargy, diminish ambition, and cause psychological dependence. (Climactic order)
10. To lower the crime rate, we must ensure that jobs and adequate housing are available, enough fair-minded police are visible, citizens are involved in their communities, and the courts work justly and speedily. (Random order)

Answers for Chapter 24: Writing the Outline (Pages 214 to 218)

Exercise 24.1
I. Antagonize your teacher
   A. Aim an occasional snort or snicker in the teacher's direction
   B. Wear your Walkman to class and turn up the volume when the teacher speaks
II. Disdain your studies
   A. Don't buy the text for the course
   B. Never take notes in class
   C. Stop going to class
III. Cheat on your work
   A. Copy research assignments out of an appropriate library book
   B. Sit at the back during exams and try to read your classmate's paper
   C. Tattoo your answers on your forearms

Exercise 24.3
"Flunking with Style"
Introduction
   Attention-getter: sentences 1–4
   Thesis statement: To fail your year in the grand style, antagonize your teachers, disdain your studies, and cheat on your work.
   I. Antagonizing your teachers
      A. Teachers like enthusiastic students
      B. Show you're bored
         1. slouch in the back
         2. wear your Walkman
         3. talk with classmates
         4. snicker at teacher
      C. Never answer questions in class
   II. Disdaining your studies
      A. Buy your books late or not at all
      B. Never take notes
      C. Stop going to class
   III. Cheating
      A. Copy out of a library book
      B. Adopt "appropriate" exam behaviour
         1. sit at back, read over classmate's shoulder
         2. write answers on your forearms
         3. stash cheat sheets in washroom
         4. send in a substitute to take test
Conclusion
   Summary: first sentence in paragraph 5
   Memorable statement: The challenge is yours! Become a legend—pick up the torch and fall with it!

Answers for Chapter 25: Writing the Paragraphs (Pages 219 to 233)

Exercise 25.1

Paragraph 2:
topic sentence
supporting sentences
conclusion

I have sought love, first, because it brings ecstasy—ecstasy so great that I would often have sacrificed all the rest of life for a few hours of this joy. I have sought it, next, because it relieves loneliness—that terrible loneliness in which one shivering consciousness looks over the rim of the world into the cold unfathomable lifeless abyss. I have sought it, finally, because in the union of love I have seen, in a mystic miniature, the prefiguring vision of the heaven that saints and poets have imagined. This is what I sought, and though it might seem too good for human life, this is what—at last—I have found.

Paragraph 3:
topic sentence
supporting sentences
conclusion

With equal passion I have sought knowledge. I have wished to understand the hearts of men. I have wished to know why the stars shine. And I have tried to apprehend the Pythagorean power by which number holds sway above the flux. A little of this, but not much, I have achieved.

Paragraph 4:
topic sentence
supporting sentences
conclusion

Love and knowledge, so far as they were possible, led upward toward the heavens. But always pity brought me back to earth. Echoes of cries of pain reverberate in my heart. Children in famine, victims tortured by oppressors, helpless old people a hated burden to their sons, and the whole world of loneliness, poverty, and pain make a mockery of what human life should be. I long to alleviate the evil, but I cannot, and I too suffer.

Exercise 25.7
1. definition
2. specific details
3. process (series of steps)
4. examples
5. descriptive detail
6. examples
7. descriptive detail (numeric facts)
8. specific details and examples
9. quotations
10. quotation and contrast

Exercise 25.10
   Though I'm new to college, I've discovered three ways of achieving the academic success that most of us desire. First, although going to class is not mandatory, regular attendance enables the student to master course content more readily. Second, the student must take personal responsibility for notes and assignments rather than relying on prodding by instructors. Third, the workload increases significantly by the middle of each term. Unless the student has made consistent efforts to stay on top of the material, he or she is in real danger of failing. Hence, the keys to academic success are self-discipline and responsibility for one's studies as a college student.

Answers for Chapter 26: Revising Your Paper (Pages 234 to 241)

Exercise 26.1 (suggested revision)

Ever since I came to Canada four years ago, I have been trying to adapt to the many differences between Canada and my former country. Social customs have caused me the most difficulty. The casual friendships and even sexual relationships that Canadians take for granted seem strange to me. The custom of dating is not known in my culture and, of course, my parents do not approve of it. The relationship between parents and children here is also very different from the formal relationship that exists between the generations in my former home. Similarly, the way Canadians criticize their country and its leaders still surprises me. Such talk would be considered unacceptable, possibly even criminal, in most nonwestern countries. While these customs and attitudes are hard for me to adjust to now, I realize that in a few years they will probably be as familiar to me as hamburgers and french fries are already.

Answers for Chapter 27: Choosing the Correct Tense (247 to 271)

Exercise 27.1
1. is snowing, rains, snows
2. works, is working
3. wants, needs
4. costs, doubt
5. believe, are trying
6. telephones, am still waiting, is doing
7. is crying, cries, leaves, stops, picks
8. is looking, is not listening, is explaining
9. am trying, votes, think
10. studies, is having, sits, is talking

Exercise 27.2
1. were smoking, walked
2. was hiding, saw, caught
3. was preparing, rushed, turned
4. was playing, saw, tried
5. was trying, hit, made
6. thought, realized, was
7. was telling, asked, heard
8. found, understood, took, was
9. was walking, began, waited, drove
10. was studying, discovered, was, tried, tempted, put, read

Exercise 27.3
1. made, has cut
2. was waiting, noticed, was
3. have been planning, decided
4. rang
5. has lived/has been living, has never visited
6. has been managing, has made
7. has always been, have been playing
8. has turned, has given
9. introduced, has increased/has been increasing
10. has been increasing, has changed

Exercise 27.4
1. closed/have closed, worked
2. met, have gone
3. has watched, was, has lost
4. have been waiting, has gone
5. has been planning, lived, has been telling

Exercise 27.5
1. realized, had already dropped
2. had promised, died
3. arrived, had left
4. had been planning, suggested
5. had worked, thought
6. had been looking, got, had
7. had known, was
8. retired, had been teaching
9. had decided, changed, told
10. realized, had heard

Exercise 27.6
1. is going to work, am going to help
2. will arrive, are going to meet
3. am going to buy, will help
4. is going to offer, will be
5. will not let, is going to look
6. are going to take, will enjoy
7. are going to go, will play
8. are going to build, will be
9. will be held, will move
10. will stand, will hold, will stand

Exercise 27.7
1. will do
2. will be working, will let
3. will be writing, will be praying
4. will marry, will be buying
5. will be working, will sell
6. will not answer, will be cooking
7. will be doing, will be
8. will be staying, are going to be (*Or:* will be). The statement predicts a future condition.
9. will go, will be living
10. am going to reorganize, will be working, will be able

Exercise 27.8
1. graduates, is leaving
2. has, plans *or* is planning
3. will answer, is
4. is, will hold *or* are going to hold
5. hear, will worry, know

Exercise 27.9

1. continues, will have given
2. gets, will have prepared
3. will have finished, figures
4. am going, will have earned
5. win, will have been
6. is, will have destroyed
7. will have been teaching, am considering
8. is, will have been drinking, is planning
9. will have been working, will have been
10. are going, get, will have arrived

Exercise 27.10

When we **are having** a bad day and it **seems** that we **are** unable to do anything right, we should pause and remember some of the mistakes that others have made in the past, mistakes so big that they **make** our small errors seem insignificant by comparison. Before long, you **will be laughing** when you **realize** how terribly wrong some otherwise brilliant people have been. For example, in 1962, executives at the Decca recording company **debated** (*or* **were debating**) whether or not to sign a contract with a new band. Their manager insisted, "This group **is going to be** (*or* **will be**) BIG!", but at the time they **were appearing** only in local clubs. The Decca executives **responded** by saying, "We don't like their sound; guitar music is on the way out," and they **rejected** the contract. Those gentlemen **are regretting** (*or* **regret**) their decision even now, because the group they **turned** down became known as The Beatles.

Exercise 27.11

Many of us **are studying** computers as part of our college programs. In fact, computer skills have become essential for success in almost all of the jobs we **will be doing** in the next decade. Most North Americans take the presence of a computer in the home, at work, and at school for granted. It is astonishing, therefore, to reflect that only a few years ago, many people **were treating** computers as a fad. During the forties, for example, *Popular Mechanics* magazine **was predicting** that computers in the future would weigh approximately one and a half tons. In the same decade, the chairman of IBM told his company, "We **aren't going to lose** sleep over these machines." He thought there would be a world market for "maybe five computers." A decade later, an editor at Prentice-Hall **was reassuring** his employees that data processing was a fad that would not last a year. In 1977, the founder, chairman, and president of Digital Equipment Corporation **was telling** the company's shareholders that there was no reason anyone would want a computer in the home.

Everyone who uses a computer today knows about Bill Gates, president of Microsoft. In the decades to come, his company **will be producing** many of the amazing programs and applications that will become the standard of the future, using hundreds of gigabytes of memory. It is interesting to note, therefore, that in 1981, Bill Gates **was telling** anyone who would listen, "640K ought to be enough for anybody."

Exercise 27.12

Many of us **study** (*or* **have studied**) computers as part of our college programs. In fact, computer skills have become essential for success in almost all of the jobs we **will do** in the next decade. Most North Americans take the presence of a computer in the home, at work, and at school for granted. It is astonishing, therefore, to reflect that only a few years ago, many people **treated** computers as a fad. During the forties, for example, *Popular Mechanics* magazine **predicted** that computers in the future would weigh no more than one and a half tons. In the same decade, the chairman of IBM told his company, "We **won't** lose sleep over these machines." He thought there would be a world market for "maybe five computers." A decade later, an editor at Prentice-Hall **reassured** his employees that data processing was a fad that would not last a year. In 1977, the founder, chairman, and president of Digital Equipment Corporation **told** shareholders that there was no reason anyone would want a computer in the home.

Everyone who uses a computer today knows about Bill Gates, president of Microsoft. In the decades to come, his company **will produce** many of the amazing programs and applications that will become the standard of the future, using hundreds of gigabytes of memory. It is interesting to note, therefore, that in 1981, Bill Gates **told** anyone who would listen, "640K ought to be enough for anybody."

Answers for Chapter 28: More About Verbs (For Those Who Need It) (Pages 272 to 280)

Exercise 28.1 (suggested answers)
1. may, should
2. should, could
3. might, would
4. can, must
5. may, might, must
6. should, can
7. might, should
8. should, could
9. might, would, could
10. should, might, would

Exercise 28.2
1. had, would choose (had had, would have chosen)
2. would improve, were (would have improved, had been)
3. realized, would give (had realized, would have given)
4. would (*or* could) have finished, had not begun
5. had spent, would (*or* could) have graduated
6. had not been, would not have eaten
7. saw, would lend (had seen, would have lent)
8. would not have run, had not given
9. would skip, were not (would have skipped, had not been)
10. would (*or* could) not have survived, had not left

Exercise 28.3 (suggested answers)
1. I would like a muffin.
2. Could you tell me what time it is?
3. May I use your phone?
4. Would you please close the window?
5. I would like to see the manager.
6. Would you please check the oil, too?
7. May I have a bowl of soup and a sandwich?
8. Would you send the applicant in, please?
9. Could you cash a cheque?
10. Would you please move your car so I can get past?

Exercise 28.4
   I **do not enjoy** the many crows that fly around my neighbourhood. Their loud cries **are not welcome** (*or* **are unwelcome**), especially in the spring when the

flocks grow in size and activity. I **do not think** they are very friendly birds; they call to one another in loud and argumentative tones. Crows **don't** seem to be popular with less noisy and aggressive species of birds. Seagulls and pigeons, for example, **are not** often found in the same vicinity as crows. You **may not** be aware that a flock of crows is technically called a "murder." This word, along with "clowder," which refers to cats, and "pride," which refers to lions, **is not** a widely known English noun. "A murder of crows" **calls** to mind a very **unpleasant** image: a group of crows getting together to assault the neighbourhood with their cries. **Could** they **not be plotting** to harm some innocent creature? Certainly, they **cannot be counted on** to leave my newly planted corn and beans in peace.

Exercise 28.5

Inventions are **not** always warmly welcomed by the general population. Innovation, however practical, **does not** normally **receive** immediate approval from the public. The early experimenters in aviation, for example, **did not** quickly **become** famous. They would **not** have been surprised to have been told, "If God wanted humans to fly, He would have given them wings." Orville and Wilbur, the Wright brothers, certainly **did not expect** large crowds to assemble and cheer them on as they took their first historic flight in 1903. They had **no** idea (*or* **did not have any idea**) that their flight at Kitty Hawk would result in fame and glory. Their desire for fame was **not** what drove them to experiment with the powered flight of a heavier-than-air, handbuilt aircraft. But the public **did not take** them seriously. Those who **did not think** the Wright brothers were fools thought they were **insane**. Today, thanks to the persistence of the Wright brothers, we **no longer** have (*or* **do not have**) to spend ten days crossing the Atlantic by boat.

Answers for Chapter 29: Solving Plural Problems (Pages 281 to 291)

Exercise 29.1
1. cigarettes, matches
2. mushrooms, berries
3. trees, leaves
4. quizzes, courses
5. activities, studies
6. libraries, wolves
7. cities, communities
8. inquiries, replies
9. knives, forks
10. nineties, attorneys

Exercise 29.2
1. children, men, women
2. vetoes, changes
3. analyses, statistics
4. echoes, hooves (*or* hoofs)
5. yourselves, *Mice, Men*
6. fish, anchovies, guppies, sardines
7. sheep, geese, oxen
8. goldfish, larvae
9. heroes, movies, tomatoes, onions, potatoes, groceries
10. criteria, teeth

Exercise 29.3
1. Where can we get **information** on how to work **this machinery**?
2. My **hair has** become thin from too **much stress**, but your stomach has become fat from too many sweets.
3. My children won't drink **milk** with their meals, but they drink several **glasses of milk** (*or:* **of it**) while doing their **homework**.

4. We arrived at the airport, collected our **luggage**, and passed through customs where we were required to pay duty on the **liquor** we had bought in Grand Cayman.
5. I would be able to get to work on time if it weren't for the rush-hour **traffic** that **causes** me **much anger** and **frustration** as well as many reprimands from my supervisor.
6. You can have a **lot of fun** in sports, but the **enjoyment disappears** if you play too **much hockey** or **football**.
7. This winter I caught **the flu three times**, but my family's **health was** good.
8. There is **much literature** on the subject of love, and other popular themes include quests for **justice**, the pursuit of **wealth**, and the search for happiness.
9. Young students often do not have the same **appreciation** of their **education** as mature students because many of them take **learning** for granted.
10. Many of Suniti's **poems** contain (*or:* **Much** of Suniti's **poetry contains**) sensitive descriptions of the **courage** her family showed on their long journey from India and expressions of the **happiness** they have found in Canada.

Exercise 29.4

The Internet is a technological **phenomenon** that has opened up a world of **learning** for today's students. On the Net, they can connect with **libraries** to look up **data, studies** and **analyses** written by **students** and **researchers** all over the world. They can communicate with people in other **countries** and discuss everything from **politics** to chess **matches** to the price of **potatoes**. Foreign **students** find the Internet especially appealing because they can keep in touch with their **families** without paying **postage** or long-distance **charges**. Some students are taking **courses** on the Internet, conducting **research**, getting **homework** from their teachers, and even taking **tests** on line. Before long, some clever student will probably figure out how to hold **parties** on the Net!

Exercise 29.5

Canadians who enjoy winter are strange **people**. With **their noses** red and **their** fingers frozen, **they** actually **seem** to take pleasure in shovelling the huge **mounds** of snow in **their driveways**. **They don't** mind when **their** cold water **pipes freeze** or **their cars don't** start. With **smiles** on **their faces, they bundle** up in thermal underwear, flannel **shirts, sweaters**, down **jackets, scarves**, boots, and woollen **toques**. Then **these** peculiar **creatures go** out into the bitter cold and howling **winds** to engage in **activities** that **leave** normal **people** completely baffled. **They look** for **rinks**, or **trails**, or **hills** on which to skate or ski. While sensible **people stay** indoors, huddle close to **their stoves**, and warm **themselves** with **hot drinks**, the winter-loving **Canadians are** outside behaving like **children** with **new toys** (*or* a new toy). I can't decide whether such **people are** to be admired or pitied.

Answers for Chapter 30: Using Articles Accurately (Pages 292 to 300)

Exercise 30.1
1. What is **the** name of **the** student you were talking to this morning?
2. I saw **a** young woman who looked very much like your daughter in **the** laundry room this morning.
3. **The** kind of vacation I enjoy most is **a** long train ride.
4. I don't need **a** special destination when I board **the** train; for me, **the** important thing is **the** journey.

5. Today it is not difficult for **a** woman to succeed as **a** lawyer; fifty years ago, however, women (*or* **the** women) who entered law school faced many obstacles.
6. Thinking it would enhance his image as **a** supersalesman, A. J. longed for **a** big, flashy car. **The** compact car his company provided was **a** big disappointment.
7. In North America, if not elsewhere, sports stars and journalists need each other to survive.
8. In Canada, college students begin school in September, and **the** school year ends in April.
9. It is generally believed that men enjoy playing violent, competitive sports more than women do; however, **the** women on my hockey team are even more aggressive than **the** men.
10. Oscar Wilde, **an** English writer known for his wry wit, wrote that Niagara Falls was every bride's second-biggest disappointment.

Exercise 30.2
1. Can you recommend **a** movie that is enjoyable without being full of violence and bloodshed? We'd like to see **a** good, old-fashioned comedy.
2. **The** students who will be graduating this year will pay **a** special fee if they choose to attend **the** convocation ceremony.
3. **The** movie industry agrees that 1995 was **the** hundredth anniversary of **the** birth of cinema, but there are conflicting claims about who is actually responsible for **the** first movie.
4. **The** fastest-growing segment of **the** Internet over **the** past few years has been **the** World Wide Web.
5. **A** recent public opinion poll conducted in **the** United Kingdom showed that **a** higher proportion of the general public want their police officers to be armed than **the** police officers themselves think is desirable.
6. Marisa, one of **the** few employees at our store who work part-time, claims that **the** fact she is working without **a** contract or benefits doesn't really bother her.
7. Earthquakes happen occasionally in B.C., but almost never in **the** prairie provinces, central Canada, or **the** Maritimes.
8. Many of **the** geographical names in Canada are derived from **the** languages of aboriginal peoples who lived here for thousands of years before **the** first European settlers arrived.
9. For example, in Lake Huron, there is **a** huge island called Manitoulin, whose name was given to it long ago by **the** native peoples.
10. Saskatchewan, Ontario, **the** Magnetawan River, Lake Huron, and even **the** name "Canada" itself are just **a** few examples of aboriginal influence on contemporary place names.

Exercise 30.3
You can tell all you need to know about **a** person from **the** shoes he or she wears. Our economics teacher, for example, wears worn-out, old brown leather loafers. From this, I know that he doesn't care about appearances, that he likes to save money, that he enjoys comfort, and that he does not have **a** wife who checks his appearance in **the** mornings when he leaves for work. On **the** other hand, our computer instructor is **a** fashionably-dressed woman who wears **a** different pair of shoes almost every day. My favourites are her black patent leather pumps with gold buckles on **the** toes. Such **a** stylish selection of shoes tells me that she is **a** clothes-conscious person who cares what others think of her appearance. She appreciates quality and is willing to spend **the** money necessary to buy it. If my theory about **the** relationship between character and footwear is valid, I would be interested in **an**

analysis of my English instructor, who wears black army boots one day, white running shoes **the** next day, **a** pair of cowboy boots one day and **a** pair of platform sandals another.

Exercise 30.4

While Josée was visiting her sister Marie, a cat walked into **the** room where they were sitting. It seemed like **a** friendly animal, but Josée was surprised because she knew Marie hated cats. So Josée asked her sister what **the** cat was doing there, and Marie explained that **the** cat had been lent to her by a neighbour to control the mice in her apartment. **The** cat had been with Marie for two weeks now, and there was not **a** mouse left in the apartment. In fact, Marie and **the** cat had become good friends. Josée quickly came to **the** conclusion that **the** neighbour may need to get **a** new cat.

Exercise 30.5

Ramon was searching **the** supermarket shelves for **a** box of detergent when he noticed sugar spilling from **a** broken bag in his shopping cart. He put **the** broken bag of sugar back on **the** shelf and put a new bag in **the** cart. Then, as he went up and down the aisles of **the** supermarket, he added coffee, orange juice, **a** jar of jam, and some fruit to his cart. After selecting **a** bunch of grapes and **a** basket of peaches, Ramon went to **the** vegetable counter where he chose broccoli, beans, grapes, and **a** kilo of field tomatoes. Finally, he added **a** package of cookies and made his way to the line-up at **the** cash register. Only after he had paid for his purchases and left **the** store did he realize that he had forgotten **the** detergent.

Exercise 30.6

I love travelling and have been to many interesting places around **the** world. My favourite places are China and Morocco because, of all **the** places I have been, they are **the** most different from Canada in culture, language, architecture, and cuisine. When I go to **the** United States or Great Britain or even Australia, I find **the** experience much like that of home, but in exotic countries, I am always conscious that I am far away from home. In Morocco, I sampled couscous, which is **a** very popular dish in North Africa. In **the** markets, people were dressed in long, flowing robes and **the** traditional turbans, or tasselled red caps, called fez. In **the** streets, the buildings were all made of pink clay, and many of **the** cities were surrounded by large walls. China, too, is fascinating to Canadians because it is so foreign, especially in **the** countryside. There, oxen are still used to plow **the** fields, and bicycles are more common than cars. **The** food is very spicy in some areas, and **the** visitor will be surprised by **the** variety of foods in **the** different regions. China is not **a** country like Canada, where, everywhere you go, **the** food, culture, dress, and architecture are pretty much **the** same. Travel is **a** wonderful way to learn about the world and discover other countries and other people.

Answers for Chapter 31: Practising with Prepositions (Pages 301 to 309)

Exercise 31.1
1. We all congratulated Harjinder **on** her speech.
2. After putting **away** my winter clothes too soon, I came down **with** a cold.
3. Ovie's girlfriend promised to hand **in** his assignment for him.
4. Sons often find it difficult to live **up** to their fathers' ambitions for them.
5. Most children in this world have to wear their clothes long after they have grown **out of** them.

6. Whenever my supervisor has to take care **of** her children, I have to fill **in** for her.
7. Our company decided to do away **with** DOS and settled **on** Windows 95 instead.
8. After a semester of trying to combine a full-time job **with** full-time study, Tung decided to give **up** his job.
9. I cannot agree **with** my supervisor's proposal to do away **with** overtime pay.
10. My boss asked me to put **aside** the inventory check and work **on** the department's sales figures.

Exercise 31.2
1. You can count **on** me; I never go back **on** my word.
2. The pipes have frozen, so we need to shut **off** the water supply.
3. When my uncle came **down with** pneumonia, we admitted him **to** the hospital for treatment.
4. Teenagers love checking **out** shopping malls to try **on** new clothes.
5. After arguing **with** my friends for more than an hour, I got fed **up** and left.
6. This book is not the one I was looking **for**, so I shall take it **back** to the store.
7. The concert was sold **out**, and the management had to turn **away** about 300 people.
8. It's time you faced **up** to your limitations; since you hate people, you will never succeed **in** the restaurant business.
9. As soon as Sati arrived **in** Canada, she applied **for** a job as a bank clerk.
10. I wonder how I should introduce my new friends **to** my wife. She will never approve **of** them.

Exercise 31.3
1. I am angry **with** my brothers when they make fun **of** me.
2. René applied **to** the Director of Human Resources **for** the technologist's position.
3. My boss's English is so poor that he often finds fault **with** me because I cannot figure **out** what he tells me to do.
4. The worst thing a teacher can do is talk down **to** his or her class.
5. After class, I went to the library to look **for** Aldo, who had promised to wait **for** me and drive me home.
6. Before she started college, Ruwaida arranged **with** her sister to take care **of** her two children.
7. I do not agree **with** the college's rule that students may not carry cellular phones **to** class.
8. The Appeals Committee is composed **of** five students and three faculty members.
9. When Sadik's restaurant went bankrupt, his employees agreed to stick **by** him.
10. Khai was so angry for being laughed **at** that he went away to make fun **of** his little brother just so he could take his anger out **on** someone.

Exercise 31.4
A good friend of mine recently introduced me **to** bowling. She said that she prefers bowling **to** any other game she has tried. Before long she had talked me **into** checking **out** this sport. Many cultures have games similar **to** bowling, such as boules in France and bocce in Italy, and I looked forward **to** learning how to play. When we arrived **at** the arena, which is called a bowling alley, my friend tried to explain **to** me the system of keeping score. But all I wanted to do was figure **out** how to knock down the clubs. My friend laughed and told me the clubs were called bowling pins, but I pointed **out** that they didn't look anything like pins. Eventually, she gave **up** trying to teach me how to keep score, and we just threw the balls down the alley, knocking over as many pins as we could. I admit

to you that I had a wonderful time, and that I can't wait for my friend to call me to set **up** another evening of bowling.

Exercise 31.5

I am working **on** a course in business writing that is offered by computer. I found **out** about the course from a friend who had looked **into** the possibility of taking it himself; however, since he does not own a computer, he had to settle **for** a classroom course. I attended class only once, to be introduced **to** the program that connects my computer to the "electronic classroom". It is quite a simple program, and, after I had looked **over** (*or* **through** *or* **at**) the manual, I succeeded **in** loading it on my computer without difficulty. Each evening, I call up the program, and it connects me to my course which comes from a college about 500 kilometres away. The program gets the messages, lessons, and assignments that are waiting for me and I read them **over** when I feel like it. When I get **around** to doing my homework assignments, I send them **off** to my professor by e-mail. I can put my work **aside** any time and return to it when I have time or am in the mood. I prefer this method of learning **to** regular classroom instruction because I don't have to show **up** at a certain place at a certain time, and I can work **on** my course for as long as I need to. This system will help me succeed **in** finishing my college diploma sooner than I would if I were attending classes in the regular way.

Answers for Chapter 32: Understanding Idioms (Pages 310 to 321)

Exercise 32.1
1. b
2. a
3. b
4. a
5. a

Exercise 32.2
1. Two days before Tony and Ramona's wedding day, Ramona **changed her mind**.
2. She knew she had to **break the news** to her fiancé **right away**.
3. Ramona felt bad about **breaking her word**, but she couldn't spend the rest of her life with someone who **made fun of her** to his friends.
4. Ramona decided it would be best to speak with Tony **face to face**.
5. She asked him to meet her in their favourite coffee shop at 6:00 **on the dot**.
6. As she waited for Tony, Ramona **got butterflies in her stomach**.
7. When Tony arrived, he was **on edge**.
8. When Ramona delivered the bad news, he **lost his temper**.
9. Tony's shouts and threats were **the last straw**.
10. His behaviour convinced Ramona that their relationship was **a lost cause** and that a reconciliation was **out of the question**.

Exercise 32.3
1. Instead of obeying the detective's order that he **give himself up**, the suspect made his escape through the **back streets**.
2. After **weighing the pros and cons** of continuing to chase the suspect, the police decided to **call it a night**.
3. **Under the circumstances**, it is hardly surprising that Brigitte believes she **has grounds for** suing her eleventh husband for divorce.
4. Anton seemed to be **ill at ease** when the boss told him it was his responsibility to **keep track of** the department's budget.

5. I could hardly believe that Tony would **make up** such a lie, and so I asked him to **explain himself.**
6. When you are **feeling blue**, it is not helpful to have your friends tell you to **make the best** of the situation.
7. Drivers who **tailgate** really **get on my nerves**.
8. To a driver fighting her way home in rush hour traffic, a car that is **double parked** can be the **last straw**.
9. Most gang leaders share two characteristics: they have **a chip on their shoulders** and they **know the ropes.**
10. When a gang's behaviour gets completely **out of hand**, the police must **draw the line**; otherwise, they will be unable to **save face** in the community.

Exercise 32.4

Soon after the term began, my roommate, Ganesh, and I got into the habit of **eating out** almost daily. Not surprisingly, we soon **went broke**. This problem forced us to **come to our senses**. We decided to begin cooking our own meals, sharing the responsibility **fifty-fifty**. Last night was Ganesh's turn; he cooked a delicious curry while I **hit the books**. Tonight, it was my turn in the kitchen. I decided to **play it safe** and make Kraft Dinner. But it soon became clear that even that simple dish was too difficult for someone so **out of practice** in the kitchen as I was. I cut my finger trying to open the package while the water in the pot reached the **boiling point** and spilled all over the stove. My screams of frustration caused Ganesh to **have second thoughts**. Taking pity on me, he suggested that we order a pizza. Only by paying for the pizza with my credit card was I able to **save face**. Now I am **in the red**. Tomorrow I will **make up** for tonight's disaster by cooking a masterpiece, even if it takes me all day.

Exercise 32.5

If I were **in shape**, I'd ride my bicycle to work every day. Many of my co-workers bike to work, and they claim they enjoy the **workout**. I, **on the other hand**, feel **ill at ease** at the idea of my colleagues **making fun of me** as I stagger, exhausted, through the front door and down the hall to the **men's room**. Driving my car to work is not the answer, either. There are no legal parking spaces near my work site, so I often have to **make do with** an illegal spot. This means that, **to be on the safe side**, I must leave my desk every few hours and move my car. I admit that I enjoy cycling and that I would benefit from the daily **workout**. However, after having had **second thoughts**, I've decided to **make time for** exercise on the weekends. For me, **finding time** during the week is a **lost cause**.

Exercise 32.6

1. c	6. a
2. e	7. g
3. h	8. f
4. i	9. b
5. d	10. j

Exercise 32.7

1. j	6. e
2. d	7. b
3. g	8. a
4. h	9. c
5. i	10. f

Exercise 32.8

1. d
2. a
3. h
4. j
5. i

6. g
7. f
8. e
9. c
10. b

Index

Getting straight "A"s doesn't have to be a mystery...

these practical, concise, and affordable study guides will tell you how!

The Harbrace Guides to
STUDENT SUCCESS
from Harcourt Brace Canada

Fit to Print: The Canadian Student's Guide to Essay Writing 3/e
Joanne Buckley

Learning for Success: Skills and Strategies for Canadian Students 2/e
Joan Fleet, Fiona Goodchild, Richard Zajchowski

Power over Time: Student Success with Time Management
Joan Fleet, Denise Reaume

Success in the Social Sciences: Writing and Research for Canadian Students
Richard Floyd

Getting into Law School: The Canadian Guide
Trevor Johnson

Speaking for Success: The Canadian Guide
Anthony Lieb

Transitions: Succeeding in College and University
Greta Hofmann Nemiroff

Graduate Student Success: The Canadian Guide
Manfred Szabo

Making your Mark: Learning to do Well on Exams
Catherine Taylor, Heather Avery, Lucille Strath

Career Success: The Canadian Guide
Shannon Whelan

Print Out: Using the Computer to Write
Wendy Wilson

...ook for copies of these best-selling books in your college or university bookstore.

Date Due

JAN 26 2001		
AUG 07 2001		
AUG 01 2001		
AUG 20 2001		

BRODART   Cat. No. 23 233   Printed in U.S.A.

OVERDUE FINES ARE $0.25 PER DAY

READER REPLY CARD

We are interested in your reaction to *The Bare Essentials Plus* by Sarah Norton and Brian Green. You can help us to improve this book in future editions by completing this questionnaire.

1. What was your reason for using this book?
   - university course
   - college course
   - continuing-education course
   - personal development
   - professional
   - other interests _____

2. If you are a student, please identify your school and the course in which you used this book.

3. Which chapters or parts of this book did you use? Which did you omit?

4. What did you like best about this book? What did you like least?

5. Please identify any topics you think should be added to future editions.

6. Please add any comments or suggestions.

7. May we contact you for further information?

Name: _____

Address: _____

_____

Phone: _____

(fold here and tape shut)

Heather McWhinney
Director of Product Development
HARCOURT BRACE & COMPANY, CANADA
55 HORNER AVENUE
TORONTO, ONTARIO
M8Z 9Z9